The Pioneer Route and Electric Railways of Northeast Ohio

SERIES ON OHIO HISTORY AND CULTURE

Series on Ohio History and Culture
    Kevin Kern, Editor

Timothy H. H. Thoresen, *River, Reaper, Rail: Agriculture and Identity in Ohio's Mad River Valley, 1795–1885*
Mark Auburn, *In the President's Home: Memories of the Akron Auburns*
Brian G. Redmond, Bret J. Ruby, and Jarrod Burks, eds., *Encountering Hopewell in the Twenty-first Century, Ohio and Beyond. Volume 1: Monuments and Ceremony*
Brian G. Redmond, Bret J. Ruby, and Jarrod Burks, eds., *Encountering Hopewell in the Twenty-first Century, Ohio and Beyond. Volume 2: Settlements, Foodways, and Interaction*
Jen Hirt, *Hear Me Ohio*
S. Victor Fleischer, *The Goodyear Tire & Rubber Company: A Photographic History, 1898–1951*
Ray Greene, *Coach of a Different Color: One Man's Story of Breaking Barriers in Football*
John Tully, *Labor in Akron, 1825–1945*
Deb Van Tassel Warner and Stuart Warner, eds., *Akron's Daily Miracle: Reporting the News in the Rubber City*
Mary O'Connor, *Free Rose Light*
Joyce Dyer, *Pursuing John Brown: On the Trail of a Radical Abolitionist*
Walter K. Delbridge and Kate Tucker, editor, *Comeback Evolution: Selected Works of Walter K. Delbridge*
Gary S. Williams, *"No Man Knows This Country Better": The Frontier Life of John Gibson*
Jeffrey A. John, *Progressives and Prison Labor: Rebuilding Ohio's National Road During World War I*
John W. Kropf, *Color Capital of the World: Growing Up with the Legacy of a Crayon Company*
Steve McClain, *The Music of My Life: Finding My Way After My Mother's MS Diagnosis*
Jade Dellinger and David Giffels, *The Beginning Was the End: Devo in Ohio*
Peg Bobel and Linda G. Whitman, eds., *Native Americans of the Cuyahoga Valley: From Early Peoples to Contemporary Issues*
Stephen D. Hambley, *The Pioneer Route and Electric Railways of Northeast Ohio: The Rise and Fall of the Cleveland, Southwestern & Columbus Railway System*

For a complete listing of titles published in the series,
    go to www.uakron.edu/uapress.

The Pioneer Route and Electric Railways of Northeast Ohio

The Rise and Fall of the Cleveland, Southwestern & Columbus Railway System

Stephen D. Hambley

The University of Akron Press
Akron, Ohio

All new material copyright © 2025 by the University of Akron Press
All rights reserved • First Edition 2025 • Manufactured in the United States of America.
All inquiries and permission requests should be addressed to the Publisher,
The University of Akron Press, Akron, Ohio 44325-1703.

ISBN: 978-1-62922-297-4 (paperback)
ISBN: 978-1-62922-298-1 (ePDF)
ISBN: 978-1-62922-299-8 (ePub)

A catalog record for this title is available from the Library of Congress.

∞ The paper used in this publication meets the minimum requirements of ANSI/NISO z39.48–1992 (Permanence of Paper).

Cover image: Adapted from "Official Electric Railway Map" issued by Electric Railways Freight Company, copyright © 1929 by the Central Electric Traffic Association. Cover design by Amy Freels.

Unless noted, all images come from the author's collection.

The Pioneer Route and Electric Railways of Northeast Ohio was typeset by Amy Freels in Minion Pro and printed on sixty-pound white.

Produced in conjunction with the University of Akron Affordable Learning Initiative. More information is available at www.uakron.edu/affordablelearning/

Contents

Acknowledgments — vii

Introduction — 1
1 Inventing Electric Traction — 9
2 Urban and Interurban Railways in Northeast Ohio — 64
3 The Cleveland, Southwestern & Columbus Railway — 77
4 Communities of the Southwestern — 132
5 Financing Northeast Ohio Electric Railways — 160
6 Reflecting on the Industry and the Southwestern — 204

Notes — 211
Index — 230

Cleveland, Southwestern & Columbus Railway postcard. (Courtesy of Northern Ohio Railway Museum)

Acknowledgments

I DEDICATE THIS book to the volunteers at the Northern Ohio Railway Museum and in remembrance of two people who were significant in the final development of this work.

First, to the memory of Northern Ohio Railway Museum member Ralph Pfingsten, who first contacted me in early 2020 to work with a team of railway historians in producing a definitive study on the Pioneer Route. His tragic death in 2021 taught me that time is not on our side and encouraged me to complete this comprehensive work on the Cleveland, Southwestern & Columbus Railway as soon as possible. Plans to eventually publish parts of my dissertation, "The Vanguard of a Regional Infrastructure: Electric Railways of Northeast Ohio, 1884–1932," were accelerated by the stark reality of his unfortunate demise.

Second, this work is a tribute to my University of Akron PhD adviser and famed railroad historian, Dr. H. Roger Grant, who passed away in late 2023. His renowned scholarship and love of transportation history were infectious and without equal. His patience with me as an atypical graduate student, as well as his approval of my predilection for political activism, was much appreciated. This work owes much to his insight and guidance. May he rest in peace and may his contributions to transportation history live on for generations of students and other historians.

Cleveland, Southwestern & Columbus conductor William Wallace Lynn, 1874–1954. (Courtesy of Northern Ohio Railway Museum)

Introduction

> Transportation is the key of civilization; in fact, it is civilization, for without it our existing social structure would collapse.
>
> —Frank J. Sprague, "The Father of Electric Traction," address at the Engineers' Auditorium, New York (July 25, 1932)

STARTING IN THE 1890s, a revolution in transportation emerged from Ohio's largest cities and within a single decade extended throughout the surrounding countryside, connecting those cities. This revolution came in the form of systems of interconnecting electric railways, called interurbans. Steel rails, wires, electrical power stations and substations, and railroad cars of varying purpose and design were being constructed, maintained, and used by people of similarly varying purposes and skills to transport travelers, products, and produce across miles of changing geography. The interurbans provided quick, reliable, and cheap alternatives to transportation via steam railroads, canals, dirt roads, and horses. These systems of electrified rails supporting streetcars and larger, heavier interurban cars would eventually link every major city of the state and were found in every city larger than ten thousand people. The technology predated the ascent of the internal combustion engine–powered automobile. The rise of the electric railway system in the United States would be meteoric, and its demise would be just as swift.

An explanation of how this transportation marvel of engineering and business acumen happened in Ohio and its effect on the Cleveland metropolitan region is found in the rise and fall of one of its largest systems. Known originally as the Pioneer Route, it was constructed by a group of investors, bankers, promoters, and industrialists, the so-called Pomeroy-Mandelbaum syndicate. But the story starts with the brilliance and tenacity of inventors, dedicated to advancing electromotive technology and fueled by the transportation needs of growing cities and of rural areas throughout the United States. It was the so-called Gilded Age of America, characterized by burgeoning industrialization, concurrent urbanization, and immigration. American life was increasingly influenced by big business, railroads, organized labor, and machine politics. The creation and development of faster, better, and cheaper transportation had an immense intrinsic, if not monetary, value to nearly all communities and people.

Inventing and improving traction technology across the nation took many forms, but fragmentation turned to consolidation and growth of investment opportunities predicated on optimistic expectations of a sizable financial return. The business culture of the steam railroad industry was easily applicable to the building of electric railway systems. Geography was to be conquered, dependable transportation service rendered, and good money made by the right investor at the right time. Driven by the growing population's desire for speedy transportation services, nascent business organizations acquired the cash, approval of local governments, and essential support of the incipient electrical goods manufacturing industry. In all of this, Ohio would be the leader. Ohio's people, businesses, and resources cultivated the emergence of the electric railway industry on a scale unsurpassed elsewhere in the United States.

Numerous experiments by ingenious individuals resulted in an explosion of electric traction systems in the 1890s. These inventors, assisted by business interests, had to eliminate three basic technical obstacles in the 1880s to prime the powder for this explosion. The first chapter provides an outline of the necessary, but rudimentary, work of these industry leaders and inventors that literally and figuratively laid the electrified rails necessary for the tremendous expansion of transportation services that would occur in the decades that followed.

The electrification of railways took several forms in the United States. The use of electric equipment on stretches of what would otherwise be steam railroad lines occurred infrequently in the United States. Generally, the electric railway industry was characterized by two types—city streetcars and interurban railcars. City streetcars in their infancy arose from horse-powered tramways as passenger traffic, geography, and the need for speed encouraged investors to take advantage of the emerging electromechanical technology. Interurban companies were either the direct offspring of these growing urban streetcar businesses or the consequence of investors seeing the opportunity to acquire long stretches of private right-of-way combined with some public rights-of-way between these urban centers on which to construct new electric railroad lines. While the term "interurban" took some time to solidify, generally it came to refer to an electric railway system that provided mainly passenger service instead of freight shipment from one city to another. The equipment was heavier and faster than city streetcars. Typically, most of the interurban trackage in Ohio was on private rights-of-way rather than on the streets as in city streetcar operations.

This book tells the story of the rise and fall of one of the interurban industry leaders in Northeast Ohio, initially called the Pioneer Route. It describes the technological and business setting that fostered the Pioneer Route's growth, as well as explaining its rapid decline. Recounting the rise and fall of the Pioneer Route is best done in the context of the other systems in the region. Often historical accounts of electric traction lines focus on a singular story of company names tied to specific geography, while underrating the connections to other transportation systems. This study provides a backdrop and recognition of how these other competing and corresponding systems—steam and other electric railroads—enhanced the region, served the varying needs of farmers, businesses, and other consumers, and contributed to the advancement of many communities.

Prosperity of the electric railway industry, while elusive in the long run, was heavily influenced by local governments. In their infancy, the Ohio interurbans multiplied in the twilight zone between private corporations and public utility. They operated under minimal state regulation but required local government permission for right-of-way access to cities and villages. Operating and building in this twilight zone brought out both the best attributes and the worst abuses of the industry. Their abuses of the system of financing through the region's banking infrastructure hastened and inflamed the fervor of public scrutiny. Eventually, as the public considered their services necessary for the common good, the oversight of their fares, fees, and scheduling challenged the industry's managerial decisions, as well as encouraging management to direct their corporate investments into other enterprises. The emergence of automobiles and trucks presented a powerful and fatal blow to the industry, as it hastened the abandonment of the comparatively young transportation systems. Within a single decade many of Ohio's systems peaked in ridership and profitability and then quickly started to cycle downward. Within another decade all but a few would be reduced in scale and then, during the fiscal strains of the Great Depression, abandoned.

Successive chapters describe the business history of the Cleveland, Southwestern & Columbus Railway (Southwestern), followed by portrayals of its effect on the communities it served. They illustrate the tangible economic and social linkages between the city and the countryside that the railway system provided. Much of its traffic originated in the rural towns and villages south and west of Cleveland. The Southwestern is an ideal example of how an interurban led the way to the development of a modern rural infrastructure in the region. It was a short history but an important step in northern Ohio's industrialization and modern patterns of urban, suburban, and exurban development.

These chapters also describe how Northeast Ohio farmers, the amusement park industry, community baseball teams, and changes in rural lifestyle relate to the system. The urbanization of Northeast Ohio that was underway in the 1900s and 1910s had social consequences by the 1920s. The farmers of the hinterlands became more like the middle class of the city. After a generation of close contact, socialization reduced the differences between the rural inhabitants of Ashland, Lorain, and Medina Counties and the citizens of Cleveland and its metropolitan communities. This was especially true as middle-class families moved into the outlying communities. In some respects, this also denoted the movement of urban attitudes and values out into previously rural environs. The metropolizing of the Cleveland region is unmistakable, and interurban lines like the Southwestern diverging out from its borders played a dynamic role in that process.

Lastly, explaining the demise of the interurban industry is the logical outcome of describing its creation. The reasons for its beginnings were transitory, as were the people who worked on the roads or benefited from their services. The weaknesses of the industry had more lasting effects. They resulted from the collective faults in its construction, financing, and operations. As the last chapters reveal, the Southwestern system did better than average for most of its life but could not escape the systemic trends of financing a capital-intensive industry and changing consumer preferences.

Ohio was the king of interurban railways in the United States. It could be argued that, unlike most others, the Buckeye State had the optimum combination of speedily expanding metropolitan areas, networks of wealthy capitalists experienced in building systems of steam railroads, and moneyed trust companies, as well as favorable geography. For most of Ohio, it all came together compellingly but briefly to result in the construction of more miles of electric railway than in any other state. At the peak of the interurban industry in 1916, Ohio led the nation with 2,798 miles of electric rails, while the nearest competing state, Ohio's westerly neighbor Indiana, had 1,825 track miles. The fellow midwestern state of Illinois followed behind with 1,422 miles, and the distant state of California reported 1,295.

Horse Trails to Regional Rails: The Story of Public Transit in Greater Cleveland by James A. Toman and Blaine S. Hays relates how the electric railways played a pivotal role in the development of the city of Cleveland and the surrounding metropolitan area in the functions of regional public transit services. As they point out, the story of public transportation helps explain how life changed for people living in the metropolitan region.

> It explains how neighborhoods developed and how residents got from their homes to their places of employment, to where they shopped, went to the doctor or dentist, or attended church. Public transit kept friends and relatives in contact and was even an influence on how they chose to spend their leisure hours. It constituted an integral part of the daily fabric of life. As transportation services and the people's attitudes toward them changed, so too did the values and folkways of the northeastern Ohio area.[1]

While Toman and Hays provide evidence of the effect of the electric railways on the urbanizing Cleveland area in a century of public transit development, prolific railway historian H. Roger Grant provides an additional viewpoint about the effects of the electric railways on farmers and small villages. In *Electric Interurbans and the American People*, Grant reminds us that the rise and most enthusiastic support of the industry came from the hinterlands, hamlets, towns, and out-of-the-way families engaged in agriculture. Farmers in particular appreciated the financial as well as the social and cultural benefits of this modern means of transportation, at least until another form took its place. As Grant succinctly stated, "When lines were available, these people of the soil relied on this transport form until the maturing Automobile Age and 'Good Roads' crusade pulled them away."[2]

Historians were not alone in recognizing the importance of these connections; a similar appreciation was also evident among those affected by their benefits. Mayor Josiah Quincy III of Boston, delivering the welcome address at the American Street Railway Association annual meeting in 1898, observed, "Electric railways tend to bind together the various cities and the various towns and the various communities into which mankind is divided into a great unit of communities, all of which understand each other better through the new and cheap facilities for moving about which have been brought to the world by this comparatively new agency of electricity."[3] As mayor of Boston, with a regional population of over one million at the time, he boasted of the benefits of highly developed systems of urban, suburban, and interurban street railway transportation. His expression of optimism that the physical connections would lead to a better understanding between communities was most likely more aspirational than observational.

All of these viewpoints relate to the Cleveland, Southwestern & Columbus Railway system. While the Cleveland neighborhoods affected by the Southwestern were on the west and far west side of the city, the Lake Shore Electric and the Southwestern interurbans did influence the neighborhoods of Lorain City, as well as the rural towns, villages, farming communities, and families that connected them all together. It was part of the larger industry that rose and fell so quickly that within a single generation individuals could recall its nonexistence and understand its obsolescence in their daily lives and in modern American society. There is a saying that our lives are made of two dates connected by a dash and that we all need to make the most out of the dash. The story of the Southwestern is one of understanding and appreciating that dash.

Introduction 7

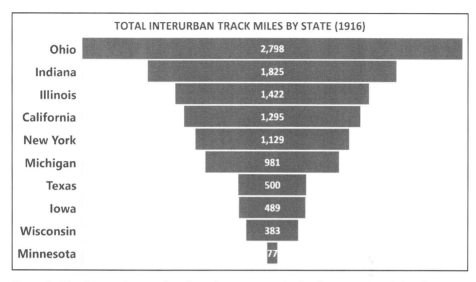

Figure I.1. Total interurban track mileage by state at peak of industry in 1916. (Chart by author)

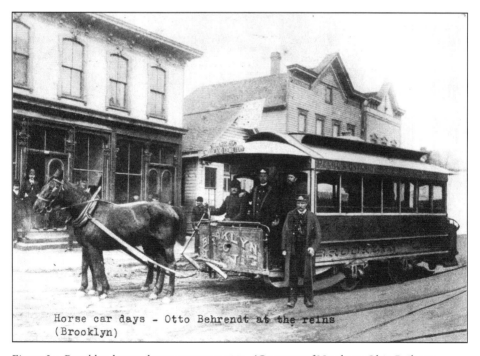

Figure I.2. Brooklyn horse-drawn streetcar, 1880. (Courtesy of Northern Ohio Railway Museum)

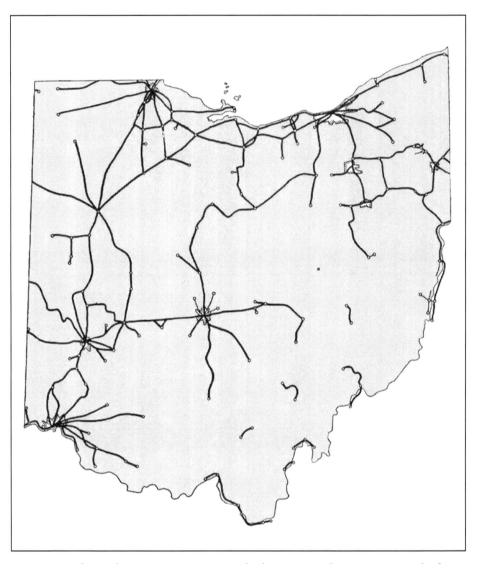

Map I.1. From horse-drawn streetcars to statewide electric interurban systems at peak of industry in 1916. (Courtesy of Northern Ohio Railway Museum)

1

Inventing Electric Traction

THE DEVELOPMENT OF an interurban railway infrastructure relied upon the commercial successes of urban railway lines and improved electrical technology. As steam railroads expanded across the American continent in the 1860s and 1870s, numerous inventors thought of replacing the steam engines with electric machines of equal traction power. To achieve these dreams required investing countless man-hours and dollars in overcoming technological challenges that appeared impractical if not insurmountable.

The technological problems that impeded the application of electricity to transit were solved incrementally and through trial and error. The accumulation of numerous experiments by ingenious individuals resulted in a rapid growth of electric traction systems in the 1890s. The elimination of three rudimentary technical obstacles in the 1880s cultivated their birth and development.

Electric railways had to surmount three basic problems in the 1880s to go beyond an experimental stage. First, railway designers needed to find an efficient and reliable method to supply a current to an electric motor attached to a vehicle. Second, electrical engineers had to improve the design of the motor to accommodate the varying speeds and intermittent stops required in transit operations. Third, the mechanical engineering of the electric motorcar had to be refined. The mechanical craftsman and engineer needed to develop a reliable and efficient means of conveying the physical power produced by the motor to the axles of the vehicle.[1]

The first basic problem, of supplying a steady current to a motor mounted to a vehicle, was attacked from several differing angles. There were two choices. The designer could either try to provide the necessary current from an installed storage battery or connect the vehicle to a network of conductors. Both methods were fully explored by the industry in cities throughout Europe and the United States. The system that eventually became the standard of the American streetcar industry—the overhead trolley—surpassed the alternatives only after much labor, ingenuity, and investment had been devoted to experimenting with all options.

In time, storage batteries proved incapable of providing the power required for the long durations needed in transit operations. However, the innovators of the 1880s had high hopes that the storage battery would eventually prove to be the "ideal" system. Powered by batteries, every car would operate independently, without the need for a central power station. Since they could stop, start, and change speeds as necessary, the battery-powered cars would nearly approximate the independence of motion typical of a horsecar operation.

Nevertheless, transit systems in the United States and England that used interchangeable storage batteries were only able to operate successfully on a commercial basis under very limited conditions. The New York City Fourth Avenue line, for example, successfully operated on a battery system from 1886 to 1888, but the track had to be straight and could not have grades of more than 5 percent. A fully loaded car could make a run of only forty miles before the batteries had to be replaced. Few American street railway firms operated lines under such ideal physical conditions. Neither could the transit owners justify the expense in comparison with other options available to them as competing systems developed by the late 1880s.

There was a strong and unfailing push by the public to develop a viable transit system powered by storage batteries. Out of a concern for public safety, cities nationwide objected to overhead wires strung along public streets. Lawmakers, such as city council members in Philadelphia, preferred abandoning failed storage battery car systems instead of granting the transit owners use of overhead wires. Philadelphia allowed the Lehigh Avenue Passenger Railway to revert to horsecars and to abandon the storage battery cars on January 1, 1891, only seven months after the new service started. Pleas of investors and promoters of the newfangled electric streetcars found it challenging to overcome the public's fears of electrified wires.[2]

Sometimes lawsuits were filed claiming that overhead trolley systems were inherently too dangerous to be used. Eventually the arguments in favor of the technology made by attorneys, engineers, and investors would prevail in court. For example, in early 1894, the Court of Appeals of Kentucky held in *Louisville Bagging Manufacturing Company v. Central Passenger R. R. Co.* that the operation of an electric street railway by the overhead wire system did not pose a disproportionate danger to residents or businesses.

> Practical application of electricity as a power to drive machinery or move carriages, as also for illuminating purposes, is of recent date, and it is shown the system best adapted for the purpose, if yet discovered, is by no means a perfect one. The evidence of experts and men having actual experience shows that three different systems for moving railway cars by electricity have been tried in this country, viz: The underground conduit system, the storage battery system, and that of the overhead wire; and it fully appears that the two first are as yet so defective or imperfect that, of several hundred electric railways in operation, there are not a dozen to which either system has been applied, all others being run by the overhead wire or trolley system, the same used by the Central Passenger Railway Company.[3]

The court expressed great confidence that the overhead trolley system would eventually provide speedier, more comfortable, and cheaper transportation than any competing mode of travel. As to safety, the ruling added, "The evidence in this case, which need not be considered in detail, shows that, although new and not fully perfected, the trolley system of operating street railway cars, when properly adjusted and supervised, is not much, if any, more dangerous than horse power, applied in the same way."[4]

Total abandonment of these ill-fated experiments with battery-powered cars occurred only in a few cases. Harold C. Passer, a historian of the electric equipment industry, suggests that the brief adoption of battery systems coincidentally produced some beneficial results. For one thing, battery-powered cars weakened the initial public opposition to overhead electrical conductors. The battery car gave the passengers a short period to witness the benefits of electric traction and thereby paved the way for a more amenable attitude on the part of the public and politicians regarding overhead trolley systems.[5]

The abandonment of storage battery transit systems did not result from a lack of desire on the part of their innovators to make them work. They were abandoned because the promoters could not surmount the technical limitations of the battery system. Aside from the technical problems, even modest operations with battery-powered streetcars proved too costly. The early experimenters thought that someday they would be able to replace the horsecar lines with battery operations. Even die-hard "trolley" men such as Cleveland's Henry A. Everett, a future partner in the Everett and Moore traction empire, believed that battery systems would eventually be perfected. He observed in 1892: "Almost all street railway men admit that the storage [battery] system, if successful, would be the ideal system, and all hope for its ultimate achievement; and in this age of progress it would be very short-sighted and bigoted to say that it will never come."[6]

Because of their technical and economic limitations, transit systems with storage battery–powered cars never had a wide following. Forty-five different lines operated only 280 cars in the United States by 1913. Even the best-equipped vehicle possessed a maximum range of 130 miles on level track and a maximum speed of 35 miles per hour. Industry experts suggested that storage battery cars were only appropriate under the following service requirements: crosstown lines with light traffic, lines with streets that were too narrow to allow conventional overhead systems, lines where legal requirements prohibited overhead construction, small roads, short steam roads with trains operating with frequent stops along their routes called "accommodations," and branch line service of large steam railway systems that had light traffic.[7]

It became evident in the 1880s that the best alternative for most street railway lines involved building a network of conductors for the moving vehicle to be in continuous contact. In the engineering of this approach, several complicating factors dramatically influenced the operating and capital investment costs of the railway. First, electric motors operate on circuits of electricity. That is, one conductor must carry the current from the generator to the motor while another returns it back to the generator or "grounds it" in order to complete the circuit. Various methods were devised and tested to accomplish this seemingly simple task, each with its own distinctive problems. A separate conduit with two wires could be placed below the vehicle, or the conductors could be suspended above the vehicles. Either approach required a supporting or protective structure to keep the conductors intact.

Comparable to the storage battery transit systems, conduit systems could address the objections city governments and the general public had to overhead wires. Conduits were tried in some of the first significant electric railway installations in the United States. Most notably, the first commercial electric railway in America appeared in Cleveland, Ohio, in 1884. The builders were Edward M. Bentley and Walter H. Knight, who had been doing research and development at the Brush Electric Company laboratories. The Bentley-Knight system employed a wood-encased conduit placed between the rails to transmit the electric current along the line. The two-mile-long road was the first electric system to operate actually in competition with horses on street railway lines. Starting on July 24, 1884, the line operated for about a year and ended when the Bentley-Knight Company moved its headquarters to Providence, Rhode Island.[8]

Like other dedicated inventors, Bentley and Knight did not abandon their first commercial efforts to use a conduit system. At the request of the city of Boston and West End Street Railway officials, the duo attempted a more elaborate conduit system in Boston (see fig. 1.1). The five-mile-long road using the new conduit design proved to be another failure. Less than a year after its installation, the company constructed an overhead Sprague system to replace the problem-prone conduit. Eventually Bentley and Knight sold their business to the Thomson-Houston Company, a major firm in the early years of the electric railway equipment industry.

The conduit system suffered from a number of technical obstacles that were only surmountable with much experimentation and capital expenditure. The conduits had to be constructed so that the conductors remained insulated from each other and from the ground at all times. Any material or object penetrating the outer protective housing and coming in contact with both poles of the electric conductors potentially shorted the circuit. The electrical conductors had to be encased in a structure that would endure the forces of heavy traffic and remain free of blockage for the car "plow" to maintain contact. These mechanical requirements proved to be persistent impediments to reliable street railway operation.

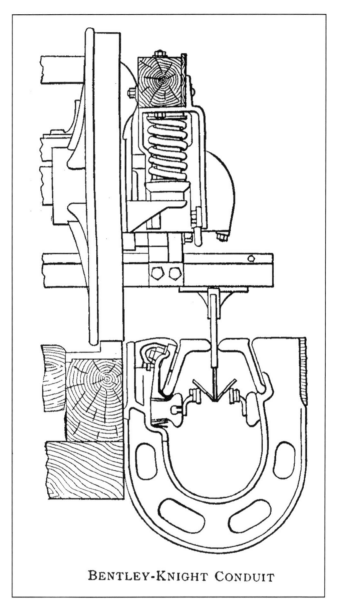

Figure 1.1. Bentley-Knight conduit. (Oscar T. Crosby and Louis Bell, *The Electric Railway in Theory and Practice* [New York, 1893], fig. 107.)

The chief problem of the conduit system was economic rather than technical, however. The substructure alone cost approximately $20,000 per mile in 1892, in comparison to $2,000 to $3,000 per mile of track for an overhead structure. It was the most expensive type of electric traction construction and was used almost exclusively in cities where municipal regulations prohibited overhead trolleys, such as New York City and Washington, DC. Without government mandates, there was no economic incentive for the electric street railway company to use the troublesome and expensive conduit technology.[9]

Another way for the railway innovator of the 1880s to distribute electric current involved a third-rail system. If the rails were used to transmit power, then the electric power would have to be low to prevent anyone crossing the circuit from being electrocuted or severely shocked. Several innovators, Leo Daft among them, attempted to use low voltages to solve this problem. However, the horsepower generated by motors operating at reduced voltages was insufficient for most transit requirements. As a consequence, the use of third-rail systems became primarily limited to elevated structures, subways, tunnels, and tracks on private rights-of-way. Even at the industry's peak mileage in 1922, third-rail track electrification amounted to only 1,893 miles in comparison to 41,418 miles of overhead trolley and 421 miles of conduit.[10]

After years of trial and error the single-wire overhead system of current distribution dominated the industry. Only a limited number of cities, like Cincinnati, Ohio, used double overhead trolley lines because of the added expense of doubling the amount of wire cable needed to complete the circuit. The double trolley system, however, had two advantages: it caused little interference with telephone circuits that used ground returns near the operating railways, and it more effectively insulated the motor windings from being destroyed by "grounding out." Yet, the most widely accepted system employed a single wire to transmit the current to the motorcar and used the rails as the return circuit to the substation or powerhouse. This practical system created a problem that persisted throughout the lifetime of the electrical railways—electrolysis.

A number of engineering details had to be in place to prevent electrically produced corrosion in a process referred to as electrolysis. If the return circuit rails were not properly bonded together or had too much electrical resistance, any nearby metal embedded in the soil—like water pipes, gas mains, or telephone cable sheathing—would corrode at an accelerated rate. Even after twenty-five years of study and engineering practice in which the electrolysis problem was understood and minimized, it was never completely eliminated. Electrical engineers C. Francis Harding and Dressel Ewing reported in 1916 that just mitigating the problem in Chicago to comply with a municipal ordinance would cost $3–4 million. Obviously, this was a task entailing considerable financial expense, as well as innovative engineering techniques.[11]

A smaller technical obstacle that was far easier to resolve than the electrolysis problem involved maintaining electrical contact between the vehicle and the overhead wire, especially over rough track conditions. The vehicle's electrical "running contact" was achieved by a trolley pole pushed against the underside of the conducting wire using spring tension. Charles J. Van Depoele is the first on record to adopt this kind of trolley pole system at the Toronto Exposition in the fall of 1885. As it became standardized in the 1890s, the trolley apparatus was a grooved wheel about five inches in diameter, mounted to a pole about twelve feet long and extending back from the top of the car roof at an angle of about thirty degrees from the vertical. Springs at the base keep the pole firmly in contact with the conducting wire overhead (see fig. 1.2).

The word "trolley" and its basic design trace back to a four-wheeled carriage that moved along the top of the overhead wire in a Kansas City street railway line designed and constructed by John C. Henry in 1884. The carriage or troller received its name because it trailed behind the car, drawn by a rope as it rode on the overhead wire. Employees of Henry's line used the word "trolley" as a contraction for describing the overhead system. Unfortunately, the carriage had a tendency to jump the wires and made construction of the supporting spans for the electric cable difficult, especially at intersections.[12]

The second fundamental technical problem resolved in the 1880s involved the design of the direct current (dc) motor. Motors prior to 1879 could be justifiably called mere toys. Often utilized for exhibition or study, they had no practical operating value. German electrician and inventor Ernst Werner von Siemens and his business partner J. G. Halske constructed a small electric locomotive for pulling three small passenger

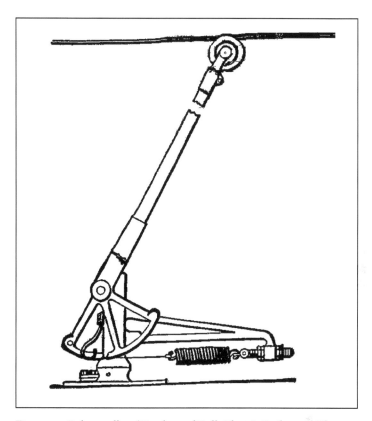

Figure 1.2. Baker trolley. (Crosby and Bell, *Electric Railway in Theory and Practice*, fig. 59, 110)

trailers around an oval track at the Berlin Industrial Exhibition of 1879. This event signaled the end of the electric motor as a scientific toy and the dawning of electric traction. Over the next several decades a number of American inventors and electrical equipment firms went to work on solving the major flaws of the Siemens-Halske electric motor.[13]

The electric streetcar motor had to be designed specifically to meet tough operating conditions—frequent stops and starts, varying speeds, and a wide range of temperatures and moisture conditions. The main source of the problem involved the electric motor's commutator and brushes. The commutator and the armature were mounted together on the shaft of the motor and revolved through the induced electromagnetic fields. The commutator converted the supplied direct current into an alternating current that produced the mechanical forces needed to rotate the shaft. The brushes provided the necessary physical contact between the conductors supplying the direct current to the rotating commutator. This contact between the two materials—commutator and brushes—posed the greatest challenge to inventors and engineers.

Solving the commutation problem meant making the brushes out of a material that could pass the heavy current at varying voltages through to the commutator rings and resist wear from the abrasive forces between the two surfaces in contact. Originally, copper and brass brushes were used because of their conductibility. Copper, however, was too malleable and lacking in abrasive resistance properties, while brass was more wear resistant but much more expensive to replace on a regular basis. To solve the problem, both Frank Julian Sprague's Richmond, Virginia, installation and Thomson-Houston's Lynn, Massachusetts, railway in 1888 employed carbon in the making of electric motor brushes. The carbon-brush solution meant that motors could run for over a month before needing maintenance, as opposed to replacement of the brass brushes several times daily.[14]

The third fundamental technical problem solved in the 1880s was the development of a means to transmit efficiently and reliably the mechanical forces generated by the motor to the axles of the vehicle. The earliest electric cars mounted the motor on the platform of the car, thereby requiring some method of driving the axle. In its earliest form, the direct current (dc) motor had to be placed in easy view and reach of the operator because of the poor performance of the motor. The metallic brushes required periodic adjustment to avoid harmful sparking and arcing. Various schemes of driving the axle were tried, including belts, sprocket chains, friction discs, worm gears, beveled gears, connecting rods, ropes and pulleys, and spur gears. They met with varying degrees of success.

Once the commutator-brush problem was resolved, motors could be installed near or on the axles, thereby reducing the complexity of the drive system required. By 1890 spur gears proved to be the most efficient, mechanically simple, and reliable method of driving the axle. Some early designs employed double reduction gears in order to give the car enough torque to overcome steep grades. Yet, as motor design improved and horsepower increased, a single reduction gear became the industry standard.[15]

Once the technological barriers had been hurdled by industrious and persistent inventors, electric traction firms quickly sprouted up throughout the country. From 1888 to 1907 both the number of street railway companies and track mileage grew dramatically. Innovators quickly solved the worst of the technical problems that affected the reliability and cost of electric railway equipment. They were able to successfully market these improved systems to railway companies nationwide.

Demand for new electric railway systems exploded overnight across the country in major cities, like Cleveland. On January 1, 1888, there were thirteen electric roads in operation in the United States and Canada. Six roads were constructed by Charles J. Van Depoele, three were using Leo Daft's designs, and the remaining innovators—Fisher, Sidney Short, John C. Henry, and Frank J. Sprague—each had one road operating. These roads together operated 95 motor cars over 48 miles of track. The largest road was the Daft system at Asbury Park, New Jersey, where 18 cars were in operation over 4.0 miles of line. Within less than two years, the number of roads grew to 176, operating over 1,260 miles of track, using 1,884 cars with overhead trolley systems. As the *Cleveland Plain Dealer* mentioned in late 1889 regarding delays in the construction of new electric rail lines in the city, "The demand is evidently beyond their immediate ability to meet."[16]

Several noteworthy inventors made significant contributions toward resolving the three basic technical problems that limited the development of electric transit. Table 1.1 contains a listing of some of these consequential electric traction projects that were undertaken during the 1880s. However unique and innovative each of these electric railway installations was, only one of them managed to resolve all of the technical problems that had hindered successful operation on a large scale. This one installation set the pattern for all electric street railway development that followed. That system was designed and constructed in Richmond, Virginia, by Frank J. Sprague, a former naval officer and one-time assistant to Thomas Edison.

The tinkering impulse that made Edison famous found little favor with his systematic problem-solving assistant, Sprague, whose inventions and refinements came as a result of engineering and mathematics and not from empirical experimentation. Sprague worked for Edison for less than a year before starting his own company in 1884. The relationship

Table 1.1. Early urban electric railways

Location	Power distribution, collection, and operating voltage	Date of opening	Duration of electrification	Track length / Number of cars at opening / Steepest grade	Inventor / Innovator
East Cleveland Horse Railway Company, Cleveland, OH	wood-encased conduit / truck-mounted plow	July 27, 1884	less than one year	2 miles / /	Edward M. Bentley and Walter H. Knight
Fort Scott & Gulf Railway, Kansas City, MO	2-wire overhead / grooved-wheel trollers / 1,000 volts dc	Fall 1884	less than one year	1 mile / 4 cars / 7% grade	John C. Henry
Denver Electric & Cable Company, Denver, CO	ground-level conduit	1885	two years		Sidney H. Short
Baltimore Union Passenger Railway, Hampden Line, Baltimore, MD	third rail / plow / 120 volts dc	August 10, 1885	two years	2 miles / 3 cars / 7% grade	Leo Daft (1843–1922)
Capital City Street Railway, Montgomery, AL	2-wire overhead / grooved-wheel trollers	1886	permanent*	15 miles / 18 cars / 7.5% grades	Charles J. Van Depoele (1846–1892)
Lima Street Railway and Motor Company, Lima, OH	2-wire overhead / grooved-wheel trollers	July 4, 1887	permanent*	4 miles / 8 cars	Charles J. Van Depoele

Inventing Electric Traction

Location	Power distribution, collection, and operating voltage	Date of opening	Duration of electrification	Track length / Number of cars at opening / Steepest grade	Inventor / Innovator
Mansfield Electric Street Railroad Company, Mansfield, OH	2-wire overhead / grooved-wheel trollers	August 8, 1887	permanent*	4.5 miles / 5 cars / 8% grade	Leo Daft
San Diego Street Railway Company, San Diego, CA	single-wire overhead / grooved-wheel trollers	Fall 1887	one month	3 miles / 9 cars	John C. Henry
Sea Shore Electric Railway, Asbury Park, NJ	2-wire overhead / grooved-wheel trollers	September 19, 1887	permanent*	4 miles / 18 cars	Leo Daft
Electric Rapid Transit Street Car Company, San Diego, CA	single-wire overhead / grooved-wheel trollers	January 1, 1888	eighteen months	4.25 miles / 8 cars	John C. Henry
Observatory Hill Passenger Railway, Alleghany City, PA	underground conduit for 1 mile / side-mounted troller for 3 miles	January 1, 1888	permanent*	4 miles / / 10% grades	Bentley & Knight
Union Passenger Railway, Richmond, VA	overhead wire / trolley pole / 450 volts dc	February 8, 1888	permanent*	12 miles / 40 cars / 12% grade	Frank Julian Sprague

* Permanent indicates electrification for life of railway, although newer technology used and systems updated over time.

between the two remained amiable, and Edison should be given credit for helping Sprague's motor manufacturing business become successful. Industrial engineers and craftsmen considered Sprague's motors to be quite good—designed as motors, not as dynamos used reversibly. Edison endorsed the motors for use in his lighting system, and orders poured into the company from cities throughout the United States and Europe. Tied to the growing fortunes of Edison's electric power systems, Sprague's profitable motor business supplied him with the cash needed to experiment and adapt the electric motor to railway traction.

In 1886 Sprague started experimenting on an electric railway car design, which included the spring-mounted motor elements that were later to be part of his noted "wheelbarrow" mounted design. In May 1887, the nominal success of his prototype car on a 200-foot stretch of track in a New York City alley led Sprague to boldly contract with Richmond, Virginia, officials for a completed electric railway system. Sprague estimated that he spent about $75,000 more than he was paid. But what he spent in setting up the system and engineering out the problems, his company made up in national reputation and technical experience.

Edward H. Johnson, president of the Boston Edison Company, joined with Sprague to form the Sprague Electric Railway and Motor Company in 1884. This company sold stationary motors to industrial firms that obtained electricity from an Edison-type central station or their own incandescent lighting generators. In the early years of the firm, Sprague and Johnson subcontracted the manufacturing of the motors to Edison. By October 1886, however, the company had sufficient demand and working capital to build its own factory in New York to manufacture larger motors. The firm developed a respectable reputation for specializing in large motors that proved to be reliable and efficient. By the end of 1889, Sprague sold direct current electric motors that ranged from fifteen to thirty horsepower. It was the profitability of this portion of the business that allowed Sprague to experiment with electric traction and enabled him to survive substantial losses in the Richmond electric railway installation.[17]

The Richmond experiment was the first successful large-scale electric railway in the United States. The local terrain and route posed significant technical problems that normally would have prohibited all but horsecar or steam railway technology. The twelve-mile-long road had twenty-nine curves, five of which had a radius of less than thirty feet, and faced grades of as much as 12 percent, something which most street railway men at the time thought insurmountable for an electric car.[18]

To tackle these difficult conditions, Sprague drew upon his technical education, knowledge of the failures of other experimenters, and his own expertise in stationary motor design. The Sprague approach used a trolley pole for conducting electricity to a spring-mounted electric motor. He employed the overhead single-wire method of transmission and bonded rails with continuous conductors and ground plates as the return circuit. Power from the central powerhouse supplied the system through feeder circuits. These were used to overcome voltage losses along long spans of wire due to electrical resistance of the wire and the rail-and-earth circuit. All of these technical features, although greatly improved upon, became a virtual standard for the electric railway industry which blossomed in the decades that followed.[19]

While Sprague lost money in the installation of the system, his client, the Richmond Union Passenger Railway, proved to be commercially successful. This was contrary to the predictions of electrical and traction experts. After opening up for fare traffic on February 8, 1888, the railway confounded detractors when it made a quantum leap in transportation by putting thirty cars into simultaneous operation on May 4 of the same year. In the face of further skepticism, the railway added ten more soon afterward.[20]

The triumph of this single installation, in spite of the adversity, inaugurated an extraordinary change in American transportation. Leaders of the industry at its height in the late 1910s claimed it to be the most significant urban transportation development to that time. "The success of this installation initiated the most extraordinary industrial revolution in transportation up to that time," Sprague later declared, "and is universally admitted to mark the date of the creation of the modern electric railway."[21] This claim was subsequently validated by the American Electric Railway Association when the group proclaimed May 4 as National Railway Day in recognition of Sprague's dramatic demonstration at Richmond.

Within eighteen months of opening the Richmond line, the Sprague Electric Railway and Motor Company emerged as one of the leading suppliers of railway equipment in the United States. At that time two firms,

Sprague's and the Thomson-Houston Company, dominated the national market. Of the 180 electric street railways operating in the fall of 1889, each company equipped 67 roads, while only 10 roads used Van Depoele's equipment, and the remaining smaller equipment manufacturers supplied 35 railway lines. By the end of that same year, Sprague's company received contracts to supply electric railway equipment for 113 systems. In that short time, Sprague claimed, 90 percent of all electric railway systems in the United States followed his design.[22]

Sprague's success meant that he needed capital to meet the demand for his systems. His firm's thirst for cash encouraged the newly formed Edison General Electric Company to acquire it in 1889. The Sprague Company's triumph at Richmond also marked the great rush of established American corporations to exploit these expanding opportunities in urban transit contracts.

By the beginning of 1888, the industry started to rapidly consolidate as the Thomson-Houston Company purchased Van Depoele. Within a year, Thomson-Houston also took over the Bentley-Knight interests. Thomson-Houston's profitable business in arc and incandescent lighting enabled it to strategically enter the electric traction market, purchase the patents and services of some of the most promising technological innovators in the industry, and secure the largest electrification contracts. Beginning in 1889, the firm secured a number of contracts with the Boston West End Company that amounted to over $3 million in revenues by 1892. The Thomson-Houston Company won the contracts because Sprague had been financially unable to make strong financial guarantees to the West End Company.[23] As the stakes of the traction game rose in the 1890s, so did the size of corporate players.

The lucrative business of electric railway equipment did not escape the attention of other corporations. Westinghouse Electric and Manufacturing Company, which had shown some interest in electric traction in 1886, entered the playing field as a serious contender in May 1890. The research and development activities of Westinghouse from 1886 to 1889 had been directed at using alternating current (ac) for electric traction. However, the technical limitations of the ac Tesla motor provided a stark contrast to the successes of the dc electric motor in the Sprague and Thomson-Houston installations.[24]

Westinghouse engineers quickly developed and introduced in May 1890 their own dc electric railway system. It generally mirrored the technology successfully used by Sprague. The Westinghouse system employed a 500 volts dc, single-wired overhead conductor to distribute the power to a single underrunning trolley. The fifteen-horsepower bipolar motors used double reduction gearing to transfer the mechanical energy to the axles. Within three years Westinghouse supplied 233 railways in the United States and made three major technological improvements in the design of their first motor. Westinghouse's subsequent improvement of electric railway motor design made it a leader in the field.[25]

Westinghouse's dramatic rise in the industry and added improvements in electric motor design forced competitors to respond. Westinghouse introduced the first railway motor of modern design, called No. 3, in February 1891. This single reduction gear motor outlasted and outperformed the early meager attempts of Thomson-Houston and Edison General Electric to replicate its design. These two major players in the industry sought to protect their respective market positions against Westinghouse. The directors of Edison General Electric proposed a combination to the Thomson-Houston Company, to end a costly patent war that raged between the two companies and try to remain competitive in the manufacturing of electrical equipment. In April 1892, the merger of Thomson-Houston and Edison General Electric created the General Electric Corporation with a total capitalization of $50 million. In the years that followed, Westinghouse and General Electric formed a virtual duopoly of the marketplace that actually resulted in a decade of pronounced competition in product development of electric railway and alternating current equipment.[26]

One of the greatest advances wrought out of this competition made long-distance transmission of electrical energy possible. Alternating current technology received much study during the 1890s because of two principal factors. First, in 1891 and 1892 General Electric and Westinghouse spent a great amount of talent and time competing for the lucrative electrical equipment contract with the Niagara Falls Power Company. A group of industrialists recognized that the city of Buffalo might be able to take advantage of the potential energy available from a hydroelectric plant at Niagara Falls. But the technology had not been developed yet for the long-distance transmission of electrical energy. General Electric and Westinghouse competed to develop the new technology and secure the contracts for the project. Westinghouse won the contest, but in competing both firms managed to accelerate the development of electrical engineering and technology.

The second stimulus to electrical engineering came from the entrance of a strong upstart in the alternating current equipment business, the Stanley Company. The founder of the electrical equipment firm, William Stanley, worked out a system of long-distance transmission of alternating current from an inductor type of generator. The company installed a plant using the new design in 1894 to supply electric power to textile mills in Massachusetts, which proved to be quite successful. The Stanley Company continued in the business until William sold the firm to the General Electric Company in 1905. Between 1894 and 1905, the electric power equipment company proved to be an unwavering competitor of the other two giants in the industry, Westinghouse and General Electric.[27]

The furious competition within the industry enabled the successful development of the ac induction motor and the invention of an inexpensive device for converting alternating to direct current. Electric railway systems benefited immensely from both of these developments. Street railways used direct current motors, which placed a limit on the distance that direct current could be economically transmitted. The actual distance depended upon a number of factors: peak amount and distribution of demand coming from railway cars, sizes of the rail and feeder wires, distance between feeder connections, electrical resistance of the rail-earth connection, and voltage tolerances of the dc motors. Individual feeders could be strung for considerable distances, but the size of the copper wire that was needed to keep the dc voltage drop to a minimum made it too costly. In practice, the Akron, Bedford & Cleveland Railway stretched the technical limits of the dc system in 1895, when it built a powerhouse at Silver Lake Junction, Ohio. At the time of construction, this powerhouse reportedly supplied current as far north as Northfield Township, a distance of about twelve miles.

The introduction of substations and high-voltage alternating current transmission systems in the late 1890s solved this problem. Alternating current systems have a distinct advantage over those using direct current. Under ac systems, the electric current could be more economically transmitted long distances from the central power stations. The high copper costs of the dc system made it simply unaffordable in areas of low population density. The electrical substations received the high-voltage alternating current, ranging from 24,000 to 33,000 volts, and transformed it into 500 to 600 volts direct current for transmission on the trolley line. Therefore, prior to the invention of the rotary converter by C. S. Bradley in the early 1890s and its refinement by Benjamin C. Lamme with Westinghouse in 1897, dc power stations had to be built at frequent intervals in order to supply current along street railway lines. Substations allowed the central power stations to expand the effective territory to which they could supply the necessary current. By 1900 a single power station could serve over 200 miles of track and use the substations to distribute the current to the line. The power transmission costs of expanding electric railways between cities were therefore lowered with the use of alternating current for transmission to substations.[28]

By the late 1890s advances in technology enabled urban streetcar lines to extend their track outward into surrounding towns and countryside. This fundamentally altered the character of the industry. As shown in figure 1.3, the industry track mileage rose steadily throughout the nineties. Improvements in electric railway equipment and transmission technology furthered the total amount of track mileage and the number of operating companies in the nation. The average mileage per company also grew quickly as the transmission technology enabled electric railway companies to extend their lines further away from their central power plants. The improved technology enabled the construction of an interurban infrastructure throughout the region. The expansion of the rail system throughout Northeast Ohio increased gross operating revenues for transportation services as well as for electric power sales. Reducing electric generation and transmission costs gave traction companies the capacity to sell their excess power to customers over their lines, a development that helped offset losses from declining transportation sales for many electric railway lines in the 1920s.

The improved engineering technology and competitive electrical equipment industry of the 1890s enabled the growth of the traction industry on a national scale. But the technology by itself did not accomplish this feat. The infrastructure of electric railways was expressly the product of entrepreneurs, bankers, industrialists, land speculators, and enthusiastic promoters. Under their collective ventures, the city and suburban routes expanded into interurban routes. The electric railway promoters tied together neighboring cities using a twentieth-century network of electric wires and steel rails.[29]

COMMON GROUND WITH THE STEAM RAILROAD INDUSTRY

The successful electrification of street railways in the United States from 1890 to 1900 came about as the result of several factors, all of which were readily evident in the centers of industry that peppered Ohio. Few factors were more important than the men of finance and industry who decided to invest, build, and oversee street railway operations. Many of these men had prior involvement in steam railroad properties and envisioned similar investment opportunities as well as utilizing related operating methods in the street railroads. Building miles and miles of track funded by the sales of securities, promises, and speculation was nothing new to these men. Afterward, they were followed by consolidation and organization of transit lines in order to conquer urban and a nascent suburban America in the new web of electric-powered transportation. In sum, the electrified enterprise of urban, suburban, and exurban Ohio transit was akin to conquering the continent with steam railroads.

Electric traction encouraged a pattern of consolidation and centralized administration of urban transit that would resemble, in a limited way, the steam railroad industry. Every level of street railway manager, as well as the financiers, tended to borrow from lessons learned in financing, building, organizing, and administering a large network of steam railroads. Some scholars have argued that the professionalization of middle management, which started within the railroad industry, permeated industrial America by the end of the nineteenth century as businesses grew to unparalleled size and complexity. Along with other American industries, street railways became almost exclusively the domain of big business.[30]

The rise of nineteenth-century big business followed the construction of the steam railroads across the nation and the rapid industrialization of the domestic economy. The "trustification" of America's industries followed suit. By 1890 the size of firms engaged in manufacturing or processing was increasing briskly, and trusts had been formed around important commodities. Even as electric traction was born, the production of

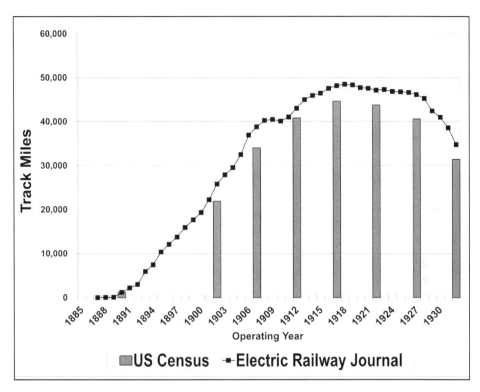

Figure 1.3. Total mileage of electric railways in the United States, 1886–1932. *Note:* Numbers for US Census and *Electric Railway Journal* are not fully comparable for same years because there were fewer restrictions regarding classifications of companies, according to the US Bureau of the Census. (Chart by author)

refined petroleum, sugar, cotton, linseed oil, matches, tobacco, whisky, and the like was dominated in each case by a single large corporation. It would not take long for the nation's largest businesses to take notice of opportunities in urban transit. Steam railroad magnates, still "bullish" on investments dealing with rail transportation, could easily understand and identify with the new urban transit technology.

America's railroad systems after 1880 replaced iron rails with more durable steel ones and expanded their lines into new areas of the country to transport the raw materials needed by a burgeoning industrialization. Starting with 52,922 route miles of road in 1870, American steam railroad companies expanded to 93,922 miles in 1880 and 163,697 miles by 1890, as shown in table 1.2. In a matter of twenty years the route mileage tripled.

The railroad lines grew faster in the 1880s than in any prior or subsequent decade, with an added 69,775 miles gained from 1880 to 1890. At the end of the century, most states, including Ohio, could claim that every county enjoyed steam railway service. In fact, Ohio could boast that it had more miles of railroad to the square mile than any other state in the Midwest.[31] The railroaders, who made fortunes building steam railroads, could easily imagine similar opportunities within and between America's cities if they enjoyed the right conditions. As transit system investors emulated railroad magnates, urban operators of the 1890s could exploit a decade of innovation in railroad building, promotion, and management techniques.

Table 1.2. Steam railroads, total route miles of railway in United States and Ohio

	Year	Miles	Change in miles	% Change	Average annual growth rate
UNITED STATES	1850	9,021			
	1860	30,626	21,605	239.50%	23.90%
	1870	52,922	22,296	72.80%	7.30%
	1880	93,922	41,000	77.50%	7.70%
	1890	163,697	69,775	74.30%	7.40%
	1900	193,346	29,649	18.10%	1.80%
	1910	240,439	47,093	24.40%	2.40%
	1920	252,845	12,406	5.20%	0.50%
STATE OF OHIO	1850	300			
	1860	2,946	2,640	882.00%	88.20%
	1870	3,538	592	20.10%	2.00%
	1880	5,792	2,254	63.70%	6.40%
	1890	7,912	2,120	36.60%	3.70%
	1900	8,807	896	11.30%	1.10%
	1910	9,134	327	3.70%	0.40%
	1920	9,002	-133	-1.50%	-0.10%

Source: Department of Commerce and Labor, Bureau of the Census, *Statistical Abstract of the United States* (Washington, DC: Government Printing Office, 1922), table no. 235.

Railway equipment and business procedures made tremendous strides beginning in the 1870s. By 1880 about 80 percent of all steam rail mileage had adopted "standard gauge" rails (4 feet 8½ inches). Railroad equipment became standardized to aid the interchange of traffic. The business organizations that grew within the railroad companies also became much more sophisticated as they developed systems for coordinating passengers and freight schedules. A class of managerial capitalists, as Alfred D. Chandler Jr. labels them, emerged within the railroad enterprise and pushed for rationalization and standardization of the industry to seek long-term integration and corporate stability. Interfirm cooperation was needed to facilitate through traffic, and in its expected form, to control destructive competition. But their own preferences for consolidation and combination found a ready fellowship among other actors who more fully influenced corporate behavior: the financiers.[32]

The expansion and technological improvements of steam railroads required massive financing. What resulted in the long term was a marked trend toward consolidation. The high costs of construction and equipment could be covered either by selling stock to shareholders or by selling bonds to investment bankers. With the expansion of lines, particularly in regions already being served by other steam railroads, competition and duplication of services resulted in most communities. Those dealing with railroad equity and debt tended to see competition as a perilous development to their interests. These concerns provided added impetus for centralization and consolidation of operations.

The consolidating trend of business interests likewise found its way into the banking and finance industry. Investment banking houses had formed syndicates in the post–Civil War era in order to handle railroad securities issues that totaled millions of dollars. Big corporations like railroads and public utilities generally raised their capital by public sale of securities. The investment bank was an intermediary in the sale of these new securities. Investment syndicates received commissions that ranged from 1 to 5 percent on the sales of the securities. For an additional fee, the investment banker could underwrite a new security issue, that is, agree to purchase at a fixed price any securities that the issuer was unable to sell after a certain date. Or the investment bank could initially purchase the security issue and resell the securities to the ultimate purchasers or to other intermediaries. This need of railroads and other large corporations for a close working relationship with large sources of capital eventually led to a period in which investment banking interests were actively setting corporate policies for their "clients."[33]

From 1880 to 1888, almost two-thirds of American railroad companies were absorbed by the remaining third. Leading investment banks had already gained influential positions on railroad boards of directors by the end of the decade. The financial Panic of 1893, however, highlighted the inadequacies of the American commercial banking system, as well as the problems with national monetary policies. The poor financial conditions surrounding the Panic forced steam railroad companies into receivership in record numbers. Twenty-six companies amounting to 2,963 miles of road fell into receivers' hands in 1890. In the next three years, those numbers grew dramatically to seventy-four firms, which represented 29,340 miles of railway, as shown in table 1.3.

The bankruptcy laws furthered an alliance between steam railroad management and the investment banking industry. Indeed, the latter became an increasingly assertive force in the affairs of the former. A company went under receivership when it failed to meet financial obligations as they matured. Typically, these bankrupt carriers were operated by an agent of the court and under the direction of the court.

Under bankruptcy laws in the late nineteenth century, management might remain in control in order to meet its financial obligations, provided it could successfully refinance the debt. Investment bankers, like J. Pierpont Morgan, could practically dictate the terms of refinancing and assert de facto control through seats on the road's board of directors. So widespread were these developments that the financial reorganizations became known as "Morganizations." The unprecedented number and extent of the receiverships in the railroad industry from 1891 to 1897 reinvigorated the control of the nation's banking syndicates over the industry. Arguably, it would give many of them a taste for other transportation ventures, like electric railways.[34]

Opportunities for investment banks to expand their influence over a number of railroads furthered the concerted efforts to stifle "destructive" competition among them. Immediately following the depression of 1893, financiers and investors realized increased opportunities to reorganize

Table 1.3. Number and mileage of railroads under receivership, 1876–1905

Operating year	Miles of road	Number of roads	Operating year	Miles of road	Number of roads
1876	6,662	42	1891	2,159	26
1877	3,637	38	1892	10,508	36
1878	2,320	27	1893	29,340	74
1879	1,102	12	1894	7,025	38
1880	885	13	1895	4,089	31
1881	110	5	1896	5,441	34
1882	912	12	1897	1,537	18
1883	1,990	11	1898	2,069	18
1884	11,038	37	1899	1,019	10
1885	8,386	44	1900	1,165	16
1886	1,799	13	1901	73	4
1887	1,046	9	1902	278	5
1888	3,270	22	1903	229	9
1889	3,803	22	1904	744	8
1890	2,963	26	1905	3,593	10

Source: US Department of Commerce and Labor, Bureau of the Census, *Statistical Abstract of the United States* (Washington, DC: Government Printing Office, 1906), table no. 184, p. 590.

the industry. They protected their properties by establishing "communities of interest" among competitive lines that virtually substituted rivalry with cooperation. System building was the answer to controlling competition, and the financial cooperation between the banking houses of J. P. Morgan and Kuhn, Loeb provided funds that enabled the transcontinental system of corporate alliances.[35]

The business historian David Kotz suggests that even though there was some rivalry between the various banking houses, competition was minimized by informal agreement. Kotz contends that the investment bankers tended to respect one another's established banking relationships. Hence, perilous competition even among the investment houses might be avoided. Everyone gained so long as all the key people in the financial world played in the game. In return for hefty commissions, investment banks overseeing Morganizations forced companies to issue additional blocks of stock to stockholders in return for lower dividend payments. In the long run the banks forced the firms to float even more bonds to raise capital and thereby increased the funded debt. However, in the short term the fixed charges drawn against income were dramatically reduced. So successful were the terms of these financial arrangements for the investment bankers, and so poorly had the financial affairs of most railroads in the 1880s been handled, that control by Eastern financial powers was seen by most business historians as necessary to rationalize the industry.

Investment bankers' control over American firms was not reserved solely for the steam railroads. The growing investment opportunities in the electric railway systems of the 1890s at first fell outside the boundaries of these arrangements between the banks. In the early years, local sources of capital financed most of the lines. Many of the eastern bankers considered the electric railway securities to be too speculative for their conservative clients. But as the industry matured and the electrical power–generating properties showed some promise of profitable growth, investor confidence in their securities improved. The nation's largest banking houses extended their influences into selected companies in that industry as well. For example, by 1912, the House of Morgan controlled over ten large railroad systems, three street railway corporations, U.S. Steel, General Electric, AT&T, International Harvester, and Western Union.[36]

The corporate victories realized by J. Pierpont Morgan and others made them heroes in the eyes of many, including some notable historians. The respected historian James Ford Rhodes called Morgan the "Hero of 1899" because of his singular achievement of forcing the industry to replace speculation and cut-throat competition with "excellent business management and the proper payment of interest and dividends." And business historian Albro Martin suggested years later that these bankers were commonly skilled financial analysts and operators, qualities which were much underappreciated by Progressive Era reformers. Even after twenty years, when the politicization of these "communities of interest" had passed, Rhodes properly characterized the philosophical underpinnings of Morgan's behavior, as well as of the other successful bankers. Morgan apparently heeded the sage advice of his father, Junius S. Morgan, to always be a "bull" on America and never a bear. "Bullish" rightfully describes the attitudes of typical nineteenth-century capitalists and the prevalent expectations which businessmen were supposed to espouse, if not demonstrate, in their business transactions.[37]

The professionalization of railroad management and the rationalization of the industry by the largest investment houses in the country, as aptly described by Alfred Chandler, do not explain entirely the business fervor of the entrepreneurs who were creating the urban transit systems of the late nineteenth century. Economic conditions pushed American businessmen to either invest or lose their fortunes. The railroad boom of the 1880s accompanied a soaring output of goods and services and a deflationary trend as wages dropped more slowly than prices. Businessmen retired old debts with dollars that were more valuable. One way to get out from under the debt was to get better returns on investments. Once considered a terrifying proposition by some traditional businessmen, bullish investments became the operative philosophy of the 1880s. Investments produced especially lucrative results in industries that were capital intensive, energy intensive, and manager intensive. As Martin explains:

> Thus, the businessman who tried to stand still by paying all his profits out in dividends, or who sank them in emotional or egotistical expansion projects, or who dissipated them in sterile price or rate wars, eventually lost out to the man who consistently sought ways to invest profits and new money in order to produce more cheaply than his competitor.[38]

Electric traction in the decades that followed would be that cheaper way to provide short-distance transportation services. Bullish investors only had to look around them to see the prospects of urban transit and imagine the eventual profits that would come from their investments in cheaper, faster ways of urban and suburban travel in all weather conditions.

THE NEED FOR SPEED

Charles W. Cheape concluded in *Moving the Masses: Urban Public Transit in New York, Boston, and Philadelphia, 1880–1912* that, setting aside topography, the private sector's response to demands for urban transit depended upon the technological choices available at that time, the character of local politics, and the pervasiveness of business leaders in local decision-making. Demand for urban transit was stimulated by growing populations and geographic dispersal of residential and com-

Figure 1.4. Early Cleveland & Berea Line streetcar at the Lake Shore & Michigan Railroad station in Berea, mid-1890s. (Courtesy of Northern Ohio Railway Museum)

mercial operations from an expanding central business district. Businessmen of the late nineteenth century saw profitable opportunities in meeting those changing market conditions. Cheape's point, which is replicated in studies of other American cities, reveals that the technology each city applied to exploit those market demands varied with time.[39]

As Cheape pointed out, "Transit development reflected the changing nature of American enterprise: the rapid application of new technology, expansion of output, and the coming of new men, the so-called robber barons or industrial statesmen, who directed the creation of large enterprises which replaced many small units with a few, dominant firms."[40]

Cheape's comparative study of transit systems and public policy in New York, Boston, and Philadelphia indicated that each city's size, timing and rate of growth, geographic location, topography, and local politics affected the developmental phases of its mass transit. New York, for example, differed from Philadelphia and Boston in that its urban transit system was mechanized first because of its early urban growth. When the first elevated steam rapid transit opened in Gotham in 1878, it predated the first electric streetcar by a decade. This was unlike the pattern in Boston, Philadelphia, and Cincinnati, where streetcar mechanization came before construction of a rapid transit line over exclusive rights-of-way. Investors in the Cleveland-Akron-Lorain metropolitan area likewise developed public transit systems in ways unique to Northeast Ohio.[41]

Two powerful developments, namely urban growth and technological innovation, characterized American cities of the 1880s and enticed transit entrepreneurs into new ventures. Much like the steam railroads, transit operations followed a familiar pattern of development: competition followed by cooperation and then consolidation. The explosive growth of electric streetcar lines in the 1890s increased competitive pressure on transit firms that had not already established interfirm cooperation or consolidation. Community enthusiasm pressured local governments to grant lucrative franchises and encourage added investors to competing lines. Franchise monopoly privileges were interpreted by even the most skeptical transit operators as a guarantee of certain earnings, even though parallel routes by competing firms commonly occurred in the fastest-growing cities. This resulted in the construction of a network of rails that were denser than could have been normally justified by the revenue potential alone. The electric trolley intensified urban congestion, rather than lessening it, thereby heightening the expectations for even more profits from expansion. Electric transit attracted more people into the central city from the suburbs and hinterlands, utilizing public streets that were already crowded with animal and pedestrian traffic.[42]

Overinvestment and overstated financial expectations of some electric railways in the United States eventually damaged investor confidence and the public image of the industry. Some early syndicates managed to make tremendous profits, but on average most transit operations became only marginally profitable. According to contemporary observers and transit historians, the rapid overexpansion of and overinvestment in electric railway transit in the 1890s resulted in a dismal pattern of industry profitability. Only a handful of railway firms made large profits; a small number of lines had marginal profitability, while most roads proved incapable of paying a competitive return on their common stock. The high expectations and rare successes in the electric railway industry meant that the public perceptions did not match the financial austerity of reality.[43]

The mixed financial performance of the electric traction industry did little to deter its expansion geographically. Completion of street railway electrification in the United States came by 1902, when electric power operated about 97 percent of all track mileage. Capital stock (preferred and common) amounted to about 56.9 percent of the $2.3 billion total capitalization of all street and electric railways in 1902. Funded debt (bonds or mortgages), therefore, made up the remaining 43.1 percent of capitalization. In comparison, the $12.1 billion capitalized in American steam railroads in 1902 was composed of 50.4 percent funded debt and 49.6 percent capital stock.[44] This meant that in general the stocks of electric railway companies were more attractive to investors than those of steam railroads. As a rule, when stocks become unattractive to investors, a company turns to the bond market, thereby paying more in fixed payments. Those fixed payments must be made regardless of business conditions or fluctuating interest rates. Operators, however, prefer to issue capital stocks, which require only dividend payments. In bad times, when the company has greatest need of cash, dividends simply would not be declared. But management must balance the need for cash from stock sales with maintaining control of the corporation.

Capitalization represents the sum total of all securities issued by a corporation and should not be confused with the total cost of equipment and construction. It represents the speculative worth of the corporation as well as its real net asset value. Stocks whose real net asset values were considerably less than their par or stated value were commonly referred to as "watered stock." The advantage to the promoters or underwriters was to overstate the par value of the stock in their sale to investors. However, this meant that the buyer had to be convinced that the stock was worth the asking price. It was commonly charged that railway companies issued substantial amounts of watered stock, although these charges are difficult to validate for many individual lines. Such financial behavior came with a price, as fixed charges would eventually be increased. As one industry observer said at the time, "Much of the capitalization was, of course, water, having been freely thrown in during various consolidations and reorganizations, and making still heavier the burden of fixed charges and dividends."[45]

The actual amount of watered stock at the inception of a new street railway line, unfortunately, remained a secret closely guarded by early investors. Observed one contemporary participant, the intricacy of the financial linkages between syndicate members, the underwriting syndicate, and subcontractors were like "wheels within wheels.... The members of the general syndicate may be very far from being on the real inside. There are often many cellars below the ground floor, and but few know their contents."[46]

Stock was distributed not only to the syndicate members that had made an initial investment, but also to an underwriting syndicate and to important subcontractors such as construction companies, materials suppliers, and engineering firms. Investors who functioned through trust companies that carried the loans could also receive some of the common stock and thereby exercise some control of the transit line through the trust company. The actual mechanisms of influence and control over corporate behavior are significantly blurred by the complexity of the relationships and the confidentiality that was an inherent part of American business and finance. Over time the individuals actually in control of street railway systems revealed themselves and are thus within the grasp of historical analysis. But for the better part of the industry, the actual relationships can only be broadly outlined and partially reconstructed.

At least three major stages of urban transit organizations between 1880 and 1910 can be discerned. Each successive stage represents an increasing scale of business organization and financial linkage in response to local market conditions and technological developments. As Cheape reveals, the timing of the technological improvements did influence the scale of finance and business organization required to adequately exploit the actual and latent demand for urban transit. Table 1.4 summarizes the successive changes that occurred in transit operating companies, according to Cheape's description.

The changes in corporate ownership and organization from the first to the second stage were not wholly attributable to the rising cost of new technology and increasing influence of bankers and industrialists. In fact, this transition from entrepreneurs to professional managers in the electric railway industry came much more quickly than for a similar period in the steam railroad industry. Pioneer entrepreneurs in urban traction found themselves replaced more quickly by salaried managers that created systematized organizations for operating the enterprises. This changing of the guard quickened because the public were able to scrutinize the street railroads more closely than contemporary steam railroads and other industrial concerns. The need to acquire franchises and rights-of-way from local governments and the constant pressure by urban passengers on the transit operators to provide better scheduling of runs and keep fares low accelerated the push for salaried management to take over street transit operations.[47]

Table 1.4. Cheape's three basic stages of urban transit, 1880–1910

First Stage ⇩	Considerable numbers of small horsecar transit firms exist. Each is competing for a share of an urban market that is relatively fixed by geography.
Second Stage ⇩	Entrepreneurs in established industries develop alliances with investment bankers to take over the small, competing firms and merge them into large combinations.
Third Stage	A new class of professional managers take over these operations and rationalize them through creation of bureaucratic organizations that can effectively administer the large firms. Interests in exploiting related businesses, such as real estate development or electric power production, are accomplished through an arm's-length relationship.

Source: Charles W. Cheape, *Moving the Masses: Urban Public Transit in New York, Boston, and Philadelphia, 1880–1912*, ed. Alfred D. Chandler Jr. (Cambridge, MA: Harvard University Press, 1980).

Generally speaking, these stages can be broadly described and applied across the urban areas of the United States within this thirty-year period. Examples of Cheape's three-stage evolution of urban transit can be found in cities other than Boston, New York, and Philadelphia. This staged transition provides a striking model for the urban railway development in Cleveland. However, it does not fit with as much precision in describing the history of railways in other large cities of Northeast Ohio, such as Akron, Canton, or Youngstown. When electrification emerged as a viable technology in Cleveland, eight street railroad lines served the public. Electrification spurred on consolidation in Cleveland—the Little Con and Big Con syndicates were as much about financing electrification as about the fights for market and territory. But in the nearby Akron and Youngstown regions, electrification encouraged an initial round of street railroad competition. The needs and the benefits of street railroad unification had already been recognized in Cleveland by the early 1890s, while in Akron, Canton, and Youngstown a period of struggle between competing street railway and interurban companies occurred years later. The sequence of electrification, consolidation, and exploitation of related business ventures describes aptly the behavior of these investors and local business interests that adapted quickly and decisively.

In 1891, J. S. Badger, of the Edison Company, performed a comparative analysis of twenty-two electric, forty-five horse, and ten cable transit systems, highlighting the stark advantages that electric railway systems had over horsecars and cable cars (see table 1.5).[48] Most of the horsecars' expenses were daily operating costs and not capital invested. Operating expenses per car mile for horse roads were 24.32 cents, in comparison with 11.02 cents for the electric roads and 14.12 cents for cable roads. Stated simply, electric railways meant that the capital costs per mile of street length would be about 15 percent higher than for horsecars. Yet it also meant substantially lower operating and interest costs per car mile or about 48 percent of the horsecar's cost of operation.

For the investor, an electric road would pay off in areas of lower traffic density where a horsecar or cable car operation simply could not. In other words, electric car systems needed only about 85 percent of the traffic that horsecar operations required to make a street line investment worthwhile. In comparison, cable roads required about 5.1 times the traffic density of horsecar systems. This gave the investor a greater incentive to choose an electric railway system when lines were extended away from the certain traffic of a city's central business district, rather than taking a greater risk with extending a horsecar line. Seemingly, electric streetcars generated their own traffic in a way that horsecars could not. As John Beckley and others reported, people preferred the cleaner, faster, and more frequent running travel of streetcars.

Eugene Griffin, head of the Electric Railway Equipment Department of the Thomson-Houston Company, became a strong advocate of the advantages the electric railway systems bestowed upon the common laborer. In 1888, he conducted a detailed analysis of the various methods

Table 1.5. Comparison of operating expenses and investment by type of public transit

Comparison by transit type	Electric roads	Horse roads	Cable roads
Average total investment (real estate, road, and equipment) per mile of street length	$38,500	$33,406	$350,325
Operating costs			
Operating expenses per car mile run	11.02¢	24.32¢	14.12¢
Interest charge per car mile (6% on total investments)	3.03¢	4.62¢	6.97¢
Total of operating expenses and interest per car mile	14.05¢	28.94¢	20.91¢
Cost per passenger carried, interest excluded	3.55¢	4.18¢	3.22¢
Cost per passenger carried, interest included	4.53¢	4.98¢	4.77¢
Ratio comparison with horse road			
Ratio of investment, per mile of street length	1.152	1.00	10.486
Ratio of car miles run annually per mile of street length	1.757	1.00	7.138
Ratio of cost of operation per car mile, interest included	0.485	1.00	0.722
Proportional traffic that must be done, per mile of street occupied, to pay operating expenses and 6% on the investment	0.852	1.00	5.154

Source: J. S. Badger, quoted in Carl Hering, *Recent Progress in Electric Railways* (New York: W. J. Johnston, 1892), 106–9.
Note: Data for horse roads are a six-year average for all roads in Massachusetts operated exclusively by horses from 1885 to 1890.

of urban transportation throughout the United States for the Washington, DC, Board of Commissioners. This extensive work positioned him as a leading expert in the formative years of the industry. A gifted salesman as well as an able administrator and engineer, Griffin claimed that for the same amount of money and time, laborers tended to live as far as they could away from their places of work, using electric traction. As he suggested, "An increase of only three miles per hour in rapidity of transit doubles the available residence area without increasing the time or expenses of the laborer in going to and from his work." Griffin's argument assumed a radial pattern of railways, which happens to also be a general description of the layout of rail development in Cleveland, as well as in other major cities in Ohio, such as Columbus, Dayton, Lima, and Cincinnati. A radial pattern of electric railways for Akron and Canton could also be seen but to a lesser degree.[49]

Although Griffin did not fully explain all the dynamic factors that actually influenced residential patterns, his assertion was obviously beneficial to street railway investors, land developers, and speculators. First, urban growth could be accelerated by building electric streetcar lines; and second, land that was accessible to these railways would increase in value. The electric railways could stimulate demand for the otherwise less-marketable land on the outreaches of the city. Griffin concluded that such transit systems would increase land values both within and outside a city.[50]

Such arguments found widespread recognition and approval among bankers, street and steam railroad investors, land speculators, and industrialists. These early entrepreneurs recognized the constant pressure for outward development that was created by increasing industrialization, commercialization, and urban population growth. They used transit technology to fill those needs and make a return on their investments. In the years following the invention of the streetcar, "Population follows transportation" became as much a dictum of land developers and street railroad entrepreneurs as it was a historical account of urban development in Northeast Ohio.

As the historian Sam Bass Warner Jr. viewed the situation, traditional investors became accustomed to a slow generation of profits from real estate deals. The street railway industry changed those expectations. Not only could a streetcar railway line increase the potential value of out-of-town property, it also could generate substantial profits on its own. Real estate developments in various Northeast Ohio communities, like East Cleveland, Lakewood, Brooklyn, Shaker Heights, and Cleveland Heights in the Cleveland area or Akron's Kenmore neighborhood, were noteworthy examples that involved the expansion of electric railway lines from the central city to the benefit of commuters. The spatial pattern of residential and commercial development in the 1890s followed the lines of the streetcars to produce eventually the twentieth-century shape of the central cities, their neighborhoods, and the outlying suburbs—typically radiating outward from the center as geography and terrain permitted. As prosperity continued, so did the migration of people and land development outward from the central city. The street railway entrepreneur and the real estate developer fully exploited the demand of the middle class and affluent to escape the city, while also providing industry within the reach of a sizable workforce. But to build an urban network of rails also required men of finance.[51]

STEAM RAILROAD EXPANSION DECLINES AS ELECTRIC RAILROADS GROW

The men of finance and industry who decided to invest, build, and oversee electric street railway construction and operations were confident, but not naive. Many of these men had prior involvement in steam railroad properties and envisioned similar investment opportunities and operating methods in the street railroads. Some industry observers, like Edward E. Higgins, editor of the *Street Railway Journal,* questioned whether they were seeing in the electrification of street railways the repetition on a smaller scale of the steam railway boom of 1869-73. His analysis of the street railways concluded in 1895 that, "Its future is bright, and, in spite of the many instances of unrealized hopes which time will surely bring, its intrinsic earning power is certain to compare most favorably with that in other fields of industrial enterprise."[52] The year before publishing his detailed analysis of the industry, he boldly declared that the municipal transportation industry in the United States was intrinsically profitable.[53] Those investors and promoters who had profited from the prior steam railroad building booms could hardly be convinced that they weren't seeing similar opportunities in the quickly expanding street trailway industry.

Just as Ohio's steam railroad track construction declined in the 1880s, new street railway track mileage seemingly took up the slack (see fig. 1.5 and table 1.6). As steam railroad track construction dipped permanently in the 1890s, contracts for electric railway lines appeared to more than make up the difference. To an investor with a yearning to build railroads, promises of profitable electric traction could not have appeared at a better time. Perhaps it may have been only a coincidence that one industry grew as the other slowed, but that is unlikely. Evidence suggests that dozens of Northeast Ohio industrialists who had heavily invested in new railroad lines and associated heavy industry in the 1870s and 1880s broadened their financial interests to include another type of railway investment, and this meant electric traction.

In Northeast Ohio the conditions were right for industrialization. The economic development of Northeast Ohio required a complex infrastructure that developed after the Civil War and was refined further in the 1870s and 1880s. Cheap sources of energy and a ready supply of skilled and unskilled labor helped prepare the region for industrialization. Systems of finance, transportation, insurance, marketing, and entrepreneurs made up the infrastructure supporting a manufacturing base economy. Of these infrastructure components, finance and transportation played the most critical roles in raising the economic base of the region beyond primarily mercantile interests to those of manufacturing.[54]

After passage of 1883 and 1894 laws relaxing state banking regulations, additional sources of capital became available in Ohio through an innovative financial institution called a trust company. Bankers and industrialists argued that this innovation was needed to overcome the financial distress caused by antiquated banking regulations of the 1860s. Under this statute, state-regulated trust companies received greater flexibility in making investment decisions than banks. The trust companies had lower reserve requirements than banks and thus enjoyed the advantage of being able to lend out a larger percentage of their assets than the older form of financial institutions could. Increasing the available money supply to finance new businesses therefore stimulated the economy. Promoters argued that unlike banking practices of the time, these trust companies could pay interest on deposits, thereby reducing the likelihood of a run by depositors.

In numerous ways, trust companies operated much like investment banks but with far fewer restrictions and a more active role in securities. Explained a Cleveland banker in 1908: "Banks take on the risk of the business success of mercantile enterprises, while trust companies incur only

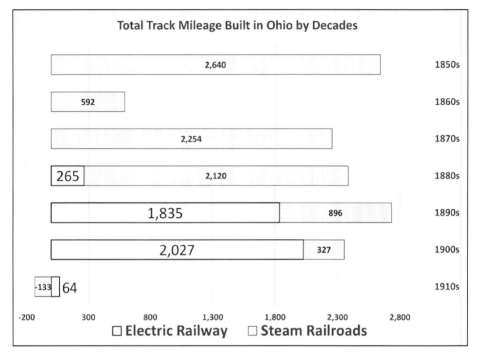

Figure 1.5. Construction of track mileage by Ohio electric and steam railroads by decade. (Chart by author as cited in Stephen D. Hambley, "The Vanguard of a Regional Infrastructure: Electric Railways of Northeast Ohio, 1884–1932" [PhD diss., University of Akron, 1993], 81)

the risk of a decline in investment values. Banks actively promote commerce, while trust companies manage investments." Taking advantage of this flexibility, Cleveland investment banking trusts attracted a considerable share of the regional currency and played a substantial role in directing the capital investments of the regional economy. For the Cleveland, Southwestern & Columbus Railway Company, the capital funding portfolio included bonds issued by notable regional companies, such as the Citizens Saving and Trust Company, Cleveland Trust Company, and Guardian Savings and Trust Company.[55]

Nationally, the trust company emerged as a key player in industrial investment and securities in the last quarter of the nineteenth century. Ohio was just one of several industrialized states to allow such innovations in finance capitalism to occur. National economic statistics and contem-

Table 1.6. Ohio electric and steam railroads, construction of track mileage by decade

Decade	Electric railway			Steam railroads			Total mileage built
	Miles built	% Change	Average annual growth rate	Miles built	% Change	Average annual growth rate	
1850s	0			2,640	882.0%	88.2%	2,640
1860s	0			592	20.1%	2.0%	592
1870s	0			2,254	63.7%	6.4%	2,254
1880s	265			2,120	36.6%	3.7%	2,385
1890s	1,835	692.5%	69.2%	896	11.3%	1.1%	2,731
1900s	2,027	96.5%	9.7%	327	3.7%	0.4%	2,354
1910s	64	1.6%	0.2%	-133	-1.5%	-0.1%	-69

Source: As cited in Hambley, "Vanguard of a Regional Infrastructure," 81.

porary accounts indicate that trust companies increased the buoyancy in the market for industrial securities. That is, their financial activities and innovative management enabled capital investments in enterprises, such as street railways, which more conservative banking interests would not have even considered. The trust companies bought the securities directly, changed the composition of their investment portfolio more rapidly than other financial institutions, and indirectly increased the regional money supply. While their innovative financial role did not become manifest nationally until 1897, trust companies played an important part in influencing the direction of regional economies like Northeast Ohio.[56]

At the same time, the transportation components of the region's manufacturing infrastructure were also being improved. From the 1860s to the 1890s, steam railroad lines took advantage of Ohio's strategic proximity to raw materials. Steam railways shipped coal from northeastern and southern Ohio, Pennsylvania, and West Virginia. Lake boats and steam railways brought iron ore from the upper Great Lakes. Understandably, Northeast Ohio's urban centers swiftly grew in population. Migrants from the farmlands and immigrants from Europe poured in to meet the labor demands in the expanding industrial sector. The railroads brought the raw materials long distances to the factories and hauled out the finished goods to other markets throughout the country, while the street railways conveyed a growing portion of their labor force to the plants. Between 1870 and 1888 Ohio's population soared from 2,665,260 to nearly 4,500,000. Simultaneously, the number of route miles of steam railroad in Ohio advanced from 3,538 to 7,636, and railroad earnings increased from $42,331,733 to $83,723,736.[57]

As an industry, the tremendous growth in the miles of track came primarily because of the attractiveness of their success. Henry V. Poor's *Manual of Railroads* for 1889 described the prevailing conditions: "Great success in the form of dividends was certain to lead to the construction of rival railroads to share in the profits of the first comer. There was no monopoly in their right of construction. There could be no monopoly in their operations, as all were competitors for each others [sic] business."[58]

Cleveland, thanks in particular to geographical factors, became a focal point for steam railroad transportation between the American Northeast and the Midwest. Located on the southern shore of Lake Erie, the Interior Lowland following the shores of the lake abruptly ends at the edge of the Appalachian Upland. Northeast Ohio's geography was ideal for building railroad lines affordably, and they provided linkages between eastern and midwestern manufacturers and merchants, transporting raw materials and finished goods. This physiography helped make Cleveland a transshipment center as well as a final destination of raw materials—like coal and iron—for manufacturers sensitive to transportation costs.[59]

According to the historians Ronald Weiner and Carol Beal, the dominant variable in the structural growth of Cleveland from 1870 to 1900 was the change in long-distance and short-distance transportation technology, that is, railroads and streetcars. Transportation technology and the physical features of the land jointly shaped the patterns of land use for residential and commercial purposes. Factories frequently located near long-distance transportation connections—either rail or water. Their locations tended to disperse over time southward along the Cuyahoga River Valley, east and west along the railroad inner belt, and east along the lakeshore.[60]

By 1920, Ohio had more miles of railroad per square mile than any other state in the Midwest. For the region's farmers and merchants, the railroads added value to the Ohio commodities that they shipped. Because of the incidental advantages they gave to other industries and the entire region, railroads were a highly valued enterprise. Street railways, especially as they became electrified after 1889, could seemingly provide the same benefits to the urban neighborhoods and suburban communities.[61]

Contemporary observers also suggested that interurban lines reaching into the farming hinterlands surrounding Cleveland provided a valuable connection to the urban marketplace for milk, butter, eggs, and other produce. The exurban territory of Northeast Ohio provided a ready clientele for less-than-carload freight shipments, as well. Therefore, experienced railroad magnates found willing business associates in equally seasoned street railway operators, bankers, industrialists, and railroad contractors. Together, they built the new electric railways of Ohio in the 1890s and early 1900s. They commonly transplanted the same business methods learned in other industries for use in financing, building, and operating electric railways.[62]

George Hilton and John Due's work on interurban railways argues that leaders of the midwestern traction syndicates had little firsthand experience with the transportation business. The historical record for Northeast Ohio, however, refutes this characterization. The leadership of Cleveland's street railway and interurban lines had a demonstrative wealth of talent and experience in all forms of transportation business, including urban transit. Most of the elite who invested heavily in rail transportation came from Cleveland's old merchant families that had made fortunes from the emerging iron and petroleum industries. From these families came men of talent, experience, and most importantly, entrepreneurial energy and insight.[63]

Because of the latent demand for transportation that was better than the horse and wagon, the venture of electrified railways into Ohio's rural regions was only a matter of time. The transit needs of Northeast Ohio's urban middle and upper classes and its rural communities stimulated the electric railway expansions. Their patronage and encouragement provided the mainstay of the interurban industry. On the rural demand side, from the late 1890s to World War I, Ohio's farmers enjoyed a wave of previously unequaled prosperity. Dairy farmers, particularly in the Western Reserve, increased in number, and their herds also increased as whole milk production for urban consumption continually expanded. Hundreds of orchards, vineyards, and vegetable patches sprang up to supply the city markets with fresh produce. With rising affluence, Northeast Ohio's farmers soon craved access to the modern conveniences, services, and entertainment that electric railways enabled.[64]

The interurbans also facilitated affluent urbanites' propensity to escape the pollution and perceived corruption and ills of the cities. Urban population dispersion, which the metropolitan street railways enabled, was only magnified by the extension of the lines outward into suburban and exurban communities. Those reformers concerned about urban ills brought on by immigration and industrialization of the central cities believed that this dispersion produced moral, social, and economic benefits, rather than furthering urban distress, as might be argued in hindsight. Remarked a Canton newspaper editor in 1905:

> The greatest boon these interurban trolley roads confer on Americans, particularly those resident in the central west, is in keeping the population scattered and preventing congestion in cities, which has been a most marked trend in America the last three or four decades. Public health, individual health, prosperity and morals are all affected by the massing of people in cities, but the electric trolleys, affording easy access to the country, will tend to keeping the population spread out.[65]

With demand for extension of the electric railway lines originating from affluent urban and rural sources, promoters could hardly contain themselves. Using financial practices adopted from railroad construction, the traction investors stood to make considerable profits when their projects completed laying track to rural destinations. The attractively high profits made in the expansion and building of new lines in Northeast Ohio catapulted the investment fervor of capitalists in other parts of the country.

On the other hand, urban transit catered to the urban working classes. They provided the bulk of revenues to the city's street railways. In places like Cleveland, where expansion had already occurred in the 1880s and early 1890s, there were no large profits for successful system building. Business success, measured by a sizable return on investment, came from careful management of operations and avoiding costly government encroachment on the lines' scheduling, fares, or improvements. Government influence, when successfully applied, pushed for low fares in the interests of the working-class riding public. In Cleveland, political pressure to reduce and keep fares to three cents throughout the 1890s and first decade of the 1900s kept charges within reach of the urban working classes. The opportunities for profits declined in comparison with operations that could fetch more sizable gains without government interference.

It would appear that the two systems of electric railway transportation, urban and interurban, facilitated the dispersion of people by socioeconomic class. The segregation of the riding public by class in urban mass transit was common in many American cities. Decisions about city streetcar routings and extensions frequently took class into account. The rate structures and routings of interurban service likewise continued the separation of urban working classes from the more affluent suburban and exurban riders. There is little doubt that the interurbans also helped perpetuate social division and political fragmentation in Northeast Ohio, as well.[66]

The story of the region's electric railway industry extends from the first commercial operation in 1884 to the present-day rapid transit system of the Regional Transit Authority of metropolitan Cleveland. But the methods of financing, operations, and construction that the industry subsequently followed took shape in the decades before its birth on Cleveland streets. The syndicates of promoters that had the most influence over the region's traction industry originated in Cleveland. The men who financed, built, and operated the largest interurbans of Northeast Ohio learned valuable lessons in street railway operations in Cleveland.

Finally, it was in meeting the transit needs of Cleveland that the initial affiliations of men from multiple industries took place. Men from various business enterprises combined to solve the urban transit problems of a growing city before the birth of electric traction. Their business combinations altered the character of the local industry and set it on a path that would eventually lead to the existence of only one street railway company: a monopoly. Gains made from profitable urban electric street railways elevated investor faith in the developing technology and the certain increase of traffic once the lines were built. They also found that substantial profits could be made in extending the electric railway technology beyond the urban frontier and into the suburbs and beyond. The region's largest city, in effect, hosted the growth of a business culture that encouraged interurban building and financing. The syndicate that gave birth to the Cleveland, Southwestern & Columbus Railway system was deeply embedded and invested in the Cleveland region.

PROSPERING IN THE TWILIGHT ZONE

The electric railways of Northeast Ohio offered a versatile assortment of transportation services to businesses and residents located throughout the state. Their services were competitive with, if not better than, those offered by horse-drawn wagons and steam railroads. The electric railways provided the region's farmers with direct and speedy transportation to the dairy and produce markets in nearby cities. Countless rural communities unaccustomed to the technical benefits of a modern industrialized America obtained electrical power. With it came the advantages of new electrical devices to light their barns and houses and pump their water.

Given better access to urban centers, Northeast Ohio's town and village residents became accustomed to "store-bought" bread, current daily newspapers, and more frequent excursions to amusement parks, department stores, and regional sporting events. The people's standards of living improved, as did their expectations of the services provided by the interurbans for flat cash fare rates. The rural communities became dependent upon the conveniences offered by the electric railways. Likewise, factory workers in the city depended upon the urban street railway system for daily transportation to and from the workplace. The services became essential to the public, and thus the railway companies passed from being private concerns driven by market demands and pricing to public utilities regulated by government.

In examining the political economy that regulated the economic activities of public utilities in the 1920s, the economist Martin G. Glaeser differentiated between business concerns that dealt with private functions and those that dealt with public functions. His observations came at a time of great flux in the field of public utility regulation. Academics and urban progressives carefully studied the extent of government's role in regulation, while state and local politicians hotly debated issues regarding ownership, pricing, and management control. Urban rail transportation as a public utility still prevailed in most of America's cities when these comments occurred. As Glaeser understood the situation in 1927,

> It sometimes happens that the community over the course of time becomes so dependent upon certain services, first rendered as private functions, that the state in obedience to this awakened public interest takes a hand in controlling them. They never were public functions, for

they owe their origin to the initiative of private persons.... These are sometimes spoken as "public utilities in the twilight zone" because they are "affected with a public interest"; but they have not become true public utilities.[67]

The "twilight zone" described by Glaeser became a transitory phase which certain industries passed through to become public utilities. Some businesses, however, continued to exist in this limbo for some time because they did not meet the two essential criteria which brought on public oversight. According to Glaeser, two concepts made up the notion of a public utility: the ideas of monopoly and necessity. Both had to be present for the industry to become a public utility. It was within this intermediary step between private and public functions that much of electric railway industry in Ohio managed to operate throughout its formative years.[68]

Once an interurban line emerged from this twilight zone, its relationship to the public was no longer subject to conjecture, at least morally. Many in the affected rural communities saw the connection between the patron and the traction line as a sacred trust between the public and the company. A local paper in a suburban Cleveland village reported in 1914 that the council challenged an interurban fare increase based "on the broad moral principle that a commuter rate of fare once established and in effect for years, is at least morally binding and that a substitution of higher rate necessarily works a hardship on settlers in the territory affected by the change."[69]

This statement highlights an important point in the development of the public infrastructure in Northeast Ohio. The electric railways of the region, although built without public financing, became part of the public's infrastructure because they provided essential functions to the citizens and businesses. The provision of transportation services to the outlying communities became as much a morally binding contract as any other solemn promise. It was a moral covenant because of the social and economic ties it enabled. When politicians challenged the rights of interurban railways to use public streets, their indispensable effect on Ohio's communities became immediately revealed. As one judge declared at the turn of the century, "the interurban car, which tends more than almost any other material influence to make the residents of country and city a homogeneous people, is a proper vehicle on the city street."[70]

As part of the local public infrastructure, the electric railways could not avoid entirely the scrutiny of local government by jumping to the next level of regulatory framework that existed to deal with the steam railroad industry. By the time the electric interurbans emerged from the cities, the steam railroads operated within a dense regulatory framework of legislation, commission oversight, and court review. Local governments had little if any control or influence over the operations of steam railroads operating within their domain. In comparison, the interurban railways operated during their formative years legally between the laws governing city street railways and those governing steam railroads. In Ohio they remained inextricably tied to the local governments that granted their franchises of operation. State oversight in the later years by the Public Utilities Commission of Ohio placed another level of regulations upon them, even though it was comparatively minimal.[71]

Unlike other components of the regional infrastructure, such as electric power and the telephone, the essential functions of the electric railway systems had a limited duration. The "good roads movement" of the 1910s focused local and state governments' investment goals on publicly owned roads and bridges, not on a publicly regulated and privately owned transportation infrastructure like the interurban lines. Consequently, what was deemed a necessity from the 1890s to the late 1910s became an amenity in the late 1920s and could be abandoned as unnecessary by the 1930s.

Street railway industry problems became the focus of discussions in national media and associations starting in the late 1910s. The debate over the public oversight of urban railways came down to one of two choices: public ownership or public regulation. Delos F. Wilcox, a renowned expert in street railways and public utility regulation, observed in 1919 that public ownership and operation provided the only possible solution to the nation's street railway problems. He argued that public regulation proved inadequate in securing efficient operation of urban transit. He admitted, however, that America's cities were generally not ready for the transformation from private capital to public ownership. As Wilcox wrote in *The American City*, "The cities are unready. Generally they lack authority, most of them are in financial straits, all but a very few are lacking in the technical knowledge and initiative demanded by so great an enterprise." Instead, he suggested that local governments look closely at "service-at-cost" agreements as the first step toward public operation and ownership. Some of Ohio's cities not only heeded his advice but had already come to the same conclusions before him and provided Wilcox with evidence to support his claims.[72]

In Cleveland, Youngstown, and Ashtabula, where the electorate saw electric streetcars as a necessity, the local governments moved toward public ownership and financial support. Before the approval of municipal home rule in Ohio's constitution of 1912, the state's cities were primarily limited to using their police powers to regulate street railways through franchise agreements. Municipal ownership of the street railways, although becoming a legal possibility in 1912, did not become a political reality until 1921 in Ashtabula. But this was not the route chosen at first by Ohio's major cities.

Led by Cleveland in 1910, Youngstown, Cincinnati, Toledo, Westerville, and Findlay, between 1917 and 1921, chose "service-at-cost" franchises, instead of ownership. Under these agreements, although the street railways were technically still owned by the traction company, service and improvements were controlled by local officials. The service-at-cost method allowed the municipalities to increase public control of a corporation beyond that normally permitted under Ohio's public utility regulations. It granted the local government control without making the sizable financial commitment of public ownership.[73]

If service-at-cost franchises proved to be a moderately successful solution for urban electric railway problems, Ohio's interurban railways did not have that option. The interurbans fell within the "no-man's-land" of intergovernmental relations. Northeast Ohio's interurban lines operated mostly on private rights-of-way and as systems outside the police powers of their connecting municipalities and villages. It was typically in the renewal of franchise agreements after a decade or two of operation that the interurban lines heard reminders of their moral duty to the connecting cities. In their earliest years, once the street railways broke out from the urban boundaries, state government proved ill prepared to oversee their operation or financing. Steam railroads, on the other hand, were already regulated by state and federal statutes, and in Glaeser's frame of reference, were fully recognized public utilities.

State government oversight of interurban financing and expansion through its formative years had negligible influence on traction promoters and investors. A regulatory structure of legislation, commission oversight, and court review that had covered the steam railroads since the 1870s extended to Ohio's interurban lines starting in the late 1890s. The state, however, did not significantly debate legislation regulating interurban railroads until 1904, with the Lefever Franchise Bill. Reportedly, Cleveland's traction syndicates drew up the draft of the bill that affected all public service corporations and placed them under a state franchise commission. This move limited the control of local governments over the conditions of franchises while providing some restraints over interurban operations. Although it failed to be fully enacted by both houses of the General Assembly, it was a strong introduction demonstrated by winning Ohio Senate support of limiting the powers of local government over street and interurban railway operations.

In 1906 the state legislature created the Railroad Commission of Ohio (RCO) to replace the commissioner of railroads and telegraphs and granted the three-member commission new powers to regulate the railroads. In the same year, lawmakers also passed an act providing for a passenger fare rate of two cents per mile that applied only to steam railroads. The state legislature did not give the RCO effective authority to enforce its decisions and provided little legislative direction on public policies regarding interurbans. Stronger regulatory oversight of the steam and electric railways did not occur until the creation of the Public Services Commission of Ohio in 1911. Two years later the Public Utilities Commission of Ohio (PUCO) replaced it.[74]

Ohio's interurban railroads did not face keen public scrutiny or regulation in their earliest years because most calls for action came from municipal reformers battling with established monopolistic urban railways. The people had only just begun to recognize that the electric railway system being extended into their villages and towns would become a necessity. To cities and villages lucky enough to have steam railroad connections and an interurban line, the new electric railways provided competition for passenger and express services. So long as the public perceived the interurban as a competitive force against the steam railroads, they remained in the twilight zone of public scrutiny. The interurbans did not become a public utility until the people recognized them as a necessity and as a local monopoly for short-haul transportation.

Pluralism best describes the pattern of early twentieth-century public policymaking and reveals the other contributing factor that limited regulation of Ohio's interurban railways. Various interested parties had to come to grips with the issue before a political consensus could be reached and embodied in the law. The appropriate role of the public sector in regulating the economy was a matter of political debate in the 1900s, just as it is now. The development of policies regarding public utilities took shape after years of political contests and deliberation that characterized the Progressive Era. Its slow and turbulent progression reflected the changes in American society as it adjusted to a new economic structure and demography. Morton Keller, in *Regulating a New Economy: Public Policy and Economic Change in America, 1900–1933*, suggests that American pluralism shaped how new technologies would be overseen by the public. "The coming of a new economy did not produce a concentration of authority in ever-fewer, more powerful corporate or public hands," argues Keller. "Instead, modern American economic regulation emerged from an expanding, boiling aggregate of interests, issues, institutions, ideas: in sum, an increasingly pluralistic American polity."[75]

As a result of their own actions, Northeast Ohio electric railways by the 1920s faced regulations and public oversight shaped by this pluralism. From the start, profits and market demand drove the interurban business, not public policy. Progressive Era reforms shaped how the businesses might survive and thrive in the twilight zone of regulations, while their abuses of the system of financing hastened and inflamed the fervor of public scrutiny. The business leaders promoting these enterprises, however, followed the norms of their time. The statuses and roles of syndicate members, the norms and sanctions which governed their actions, and the operative rules defining social and business exchanges provided a cultural context for the human side of the industry. Organized around syndicates, the members collectively mirrored the dominant business culture of the region. They were interwoven in the very social fabric of its values and energy. Therein is the story of the industry's ultimate achievements and eventual demise.

EXPLAINING THE RISE AND DECLINE

One of the more important aspects of electric railway system development in Ohio, rarely mentioned, is how the local transit industry went through three stages of development: from a phase characterized by small family-owned enterprises, to an entrepreneurial phase allied with the forces behind steam railroad system builders, and finally into networks dominated by investment bankers and holding companies. The consequences of this transitory development had some undesirable repercussions for the individual lines, especially involving their financial structures and relationships with the public.

Amid competition from more populous states, Ohio led the nation in route mileage. By 1914 Ohio ranked in first place nationally with 2,798 route miles of track, and the Midwest contained one-third of the total interurban mileage in the country. The earliest developments of the industry in Ohio set the pattern of ownership that followed throughout the Midwest.

Over the years, contemporary observers offered various suggestions explaining why Ohio led the nation in interurban mileage. Hilton and Due, the US Census, and Middleton invariably pointed out that Ohio was particularly well suited for the construction of electric railway lines. It had numerous medium-sized towns close to one another, the rural population was relatively dense and prosperous, and the terrain was comparatively flat, with the exception of the southeast portion.[76] Others thought it was because of higher average earnings per electric line. Reported the US Census in 1907:

> It was at one time assumed in many quarters that, owing to the favorable conditions, interurban roads in Ohio could earn from 20 to 25 percent more per mile than roads in the adjacent states of Indiana or Pennsylvania. The reason given was that there was more manufacturing in Ohio than in the other states, which would tend to create a large amount of travel not to be found in rural or agricultural districts.[77]

Statistics that followed in that same report showed that these presumably favorable conditions were not exclusive to Ohio, nor could they explain the early differences in track mileage. Other historians indicated that several large Northeast Ohio urban centers developed industrially and commercially at a rapid pace. These cities required specialized transportation services that were not being met by the conventional transport.

Industry and commerce in Cleveland, Lorain, Akron, Canton, and Youngstown expanded quickly over the same period and drew hundreds of thousands of people to the region. Electric railways not only transported those people to places of work and play, but also carried mail, express freight, milk, and produce. The accelerated growth in population and industry provided favorable conditions that furthered the development of the electric railways and interurbans in the region. Importantly, it was also the men who financed and built the roads who made the difference and utilized the surrounding demographic and geographical features to meet consumer demands. A supportive business culture played as significant a role in promoting electric railway construction in the region as did the conditions listed by Hilton and Due or the US Census report.

Northeast Ohio provided a habitat for the largest, most profitable, and enduring electric railway lines in the state. Leaders in the industry, like the Northern Ohio Traction and Light Company (NOT&L), Lake Shore Electric Railway Company (LSE), Cleveland Railway Company (CRC), and Cleveland, Southwestern Railway and Light Company (CS&C), served Northeast Ohio. By the mid-1920s these four companies alone accounted for around 40 percent of the total number of revenue passengers carried by all interurban, city, and suburban railways in the entire state. The Cleveland Railway Company operated more miles of track than any other city line in Ohio. At the same time, the NOT&L, LSE, and CS&C were the three largest interurban railway companies in the state in terms of total track mileage operated and in total revenues from transportation.[78]

However, the companies' individual successes were fleeting. Only the Cleveland Railway Company and the Lake Shore Electric survived most of the Great Depression, and the latter was abandoned in 1938 after a receivership auction. The Cleveland Railway Company operated until 1942, when it was purchased by the city of Cleveland and began operation as the Cleveland Transit System (CTS). The CTS kept streetcars running until 1954, when they replaced them with buses and trackless trolleys. In 1952 the CTS started construction of an electric rail rapid transit system that eventually connected the Cleveland Union Terminal with Cleveland's airport on the far west side and with the suburban community of Windermere to the east. At the start of 1975 the newly formed Greater Cleveland Regional Transit Authority took over the CTS and within ten months bought the municipally owned Shaker Heights Rapid Transit system. Thus, electric railway transportation in the Cleveland area still exists to this day, although the streets have been abandoned in favor of traffic-free rights-of-way and the systems upgraded to modern light rail standards.[79]

Explanations for the decline of the electric traction industry in the nation have been published over the last century. Even at its peak, a great number of threats to the long-term health of the industry were recognized and studied. Appointed by President Woodrow Wilson, the Federal Electric Railways Commission (FERC) conducted four months of hearings in 1919 to examine the problems reported by the traction industry. In its final report, the FERC provided a fully detailed listing of traction company complaints about what was threatening their future viability. The list that follows summarizes the purported causes of decline discussed in the FERC's examination of the traction industry:

Inflexible fares
Increased cost of labor
Increased costs of materials and supplies
Increased taxes
Inflation or deflated value of fares
Use of private automobiles
Jitney competition
Longer average haul because of population dispersion
Increased use of free transfers
More stringent service requirements
Cost of increased traffic at "rush" hours
Street congestion
Unprofitable track extensions
Public opinion which opposed "cost of living" fare increases
Widespread belief that electric railway will survive anyway
Overcapitalization
Payment of excessive rentals for franchise rights
Overconsolidation
Failure to provide adequate replacement reserves[80]

Not all of these industry complaints are germane to Northeast Ohio's electric railways and need to be consolidated into broader categories.

However, factors identified in the FERC report do appear to have some influence on Northeast Ohio's railways, including the Cleveland, Southwestern & Columbus Railway system.

Instead of repeating the FERC's laundry list of problems, Hilton and Due's seminal work provides a more reasonable grouping for identifying the causes of decline. These scholars asserted that the interurban industry suffered from at least five distinct weaknesses that became apparent even in the good years and contributed greatly to their collective demise. First, numerous lines never reached planned destinations and lacked any period of continuing prosperity. Second, the limited rate of return, even in their best years, never permitted them to weather the financial storms of the bad years. Third, large amounts of capitalization came from debt, and interest payments on those obligations accounted for much of the operating expenses. Fourth, physical limitations, such as lack of high-speed entrances into downtowns of central cities, poor track construction, extreme curves and grades, and inadequate signal systems and ballast made the interurbans particularly vulnerable to other emerging forms of short-distance travel. Fifth, their adversarial relationship to local governments concerning street running, paving costs, and public opinion, which was openly hostile to public utilities after 1900, restricted their ability to raise fares enough to offset increased costs.[81]

In Hilton and Due's study of how the interurban industry faced decline, they observed that "the most significant lesson that can be learned from the story of mistaken expectations in the interurban field is how difficult it is for an industry which is declining to realize it is actually experiencing a secular decline that will eventually destroy it."[82] Although Hilton and Due can attribute this description to the traction industry, there is little evidence to suggest that it could apply to many of the interurban systems in northern Ohio.

In fact, it could be argued that the behavior of the Commonwealth & Southern Corporation, owner of the Northern Ohio Traction & Light Company (NOT&L) based in Akron, demonstrated that its stockholders saw the end of the traction industry coming and made the best of a bad situation. The NOT&L's A. C. Blinn did not share the optimism of F. W. Coen with the Lake Shore Electric or the renowned enthusiasm of Thomas Conway with the Cincinnati & Lake Erie Railroad that electric railways could survive. In 1930, he chose to go with the electric power part of the business instead of the traction properties. Blinn continued with Ohio Edison until his death in 1960. In hindsight, who could reasonably argue that he made the wrong choice in 1930?[83]

The robust freight traffic of the Northern Ohio Traction & Light Company, Lake Shore Electric, and Cleveland, Southwestern & Columbus Railway in the 1920s suggests that these companies provided a needed transportation service. The goods shipped over these networks and the connecting interurban and steam railroad lines consisted of manufactured products from high value–added industries such as finished and fabricated metals and rubber products. Speed and just-in-time delivery, whether planned or by accident, were qualities that the shippers were willing to pay the interurbans a premium price to obtain in the twenties. Most of the commodities shipped over the interurbans emanating from the Ohio River Valley consisted of low-value bulk materials, including coal, aggregates, clay tiles, and some agricultural products. Speed of delivery was not an important factor to the shippers or the receivers. Therefore, as the cheapest method of conveyance, steam railroads became the preferred choice over interurbans for those kinds of commodities.

Without a network of interconnecting lines to route freight and passenger traffic long distances, interurbans could not normally compete with steam railroads. As the network of Northeast Ohio interurbans became dismembered in the late 1920s, they competed for the short-haul passenger and freight traffic along their own lines. However, they could not effectively compete even in this arena. As depicted in figure 1.6, the widespread adoption of the automobile for private transportation, fierce competitiveness of truck lines, and improving economics of bus transportation ultimately spelled doom for the interurbans because their foundation-level business—revenue passenger traffic—was in a nosedive.

The urban railways that still existed in the 1930s operated in isolation from one another and remained precariously dependent upon the wishes of the traveling public and city governments. In Northeast Ohio, the only mass transit rail system to survive two world wars, the Great Depression, and rise of the interstate highway network descended from the Cleveland Electric Railway system and Van Sweringen's Cleveland Interurban Railroad, later the Shaker Heights Rapid. These operations survived because they abandoned the streets in favor of dedicated rights-of-way and even-

Inventing Electric Traction

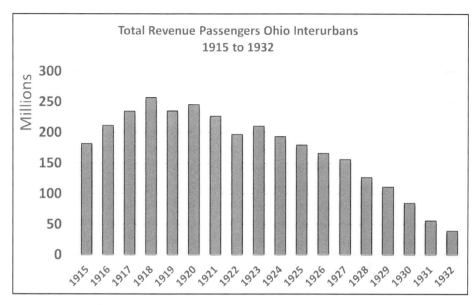

Figure 1.6. State of Ohio total interurban revenue passengers, 1915–32. (Chart by author. *Sources:* Public Utilities Commission of Ohio Reports, various years; Hambley, "Vanguard of a Regional Infrastructure.")

tually became the property of local government. Private enterprise of Northeast Ohio abandoned mass transportation by railway because it became unprofitable. Only the government could afford to support a concern in which private enterprise saw no economic value or the possibility of a return for risking the investment. Wise investors placed their money elsewhere. Certainly, the demise of so many electric railways in the 1930s, even those industry giants that represented the best in system building, unequivocally proved the unprofitable nature of the enterprise.

2

Urban and Interurban Railways in Northeast Ohio

WHAT IS THE difference between an interurban and a street railway line? Given the varied nature of railway lines throughout the United States at the start of the twentieth century, a rigid definition is difficult. For the most part, interurban cars, and consequently their steel rails, were heavier than those used on electric streetcar lines and carried more passengers. Transportation economists George Hilton and John Due contended that interurbans, by definition, met three or four criteria. Besides the heavier equipment, an interurban railway's main source of power was electricity, its primary emphasis was on passenger service, and it operated in streets while in the cities but on private rights-of-way in rural areas. Hilton and Due's criteria, however, do not successfully differentiate between interurban and urban streetcar systems in Northeast Ohio. Almost all interurbans and streetcar lines in the Buckeye State used electricity, generated most of their revenues from passenger service, and operated in streets in the cities. Of course, one significant difference was that the streetcar lines usually did not venture far beyond corporation limits.[1]

In Northeast Ohio most interurban lines augmented their operating revenues by carrying freight, offering express services, and selling electric power. These auxiliary services played a significant role in the development of the urban and regional economies in which they operated. In contrast, the city streetcar lines in Cleveland and Youngstown did not offer such a comprehensive list of services. As passenger revenues declined in the early 1920s, streetcar firms commonly created autobus line subsidiaries to maintain their share of the urban ridership market. In contrast, the interurban lines typically responded with strategies to increase electric railway ridership and boost revenues from their auxiliary operations, namely electric power sales, freight, and express services. However, eventually even they capitulated to creating and using motorbus subsidiaries as they abandoned various unprofitable routes, but not without attempting to boost revenues from other services first. Operationally, differences existed between interurbans and streetcar lines in the services provided and the strategies used to offset declining passenger revenues.

On another level there were substantial legal differences between interurbans and street railways. According to an opinion rendered by State Attorney General Frank S. Monnett in 1897, Ohio statutes recognized three classes of railroad. Interstate and intrastate steam railroads were the first class and city street railroads were the second class. Both were recognized as distinct and different from each other. The third class, interurbans, developed in the 1890s, were without any statutory recognition and differed from the other two classes in their functions and powers.[2]

According to Monnett, the steam railroad acted as a common carrier of passengers, freight, mail, express, and other goods. Its operations were regulated by both state and federal statutes, but not by municipalities. The city street railroad was

> designed for and used in the streets of cities and towns, and their suburbs, and intended as a supplement or a substitute for the ordinary traffic of the streets; it was not a common carrier, did not acquire its title by right of eminent domain, was limited in its powers, and was subjected closely to the police regulations of each municipal corporation, and doing only a passenger business. It had no power to carry livestock, express, mail, or in fact, freight of any kind.[3]

The interurban emulated the nature of the other two classes. Starting first as a means of urban transportation, its operations allowed it to carry passengers through territory that was outside of the police regulations of the municipality. This legally permitted the interurbans to carry property, express, and mail between communities. Legal recognition of the right came in May 17, 1894, along with the power of eminent domain (ability to expropriate private property for public purposes) and the authority to draw up contracts of agreement regarding traffic arrangements with street railroads.

Once interurban lines entered Ohio municipalities, they were subject to the same statutory regulations and municipal control as the street railroads. But they also had equal protection and could not have more adverse conditions placed upon them than those imposed upon other street railroads. Interurbans had no power to build lines in a city or village. They could only do so under the same conditions as other street railroads or by making leasing arrangements for use of their lines.

The early street railway lines dependent on horsecar technology operated on a few selected main thoroughfares. Prior to the era of electrification, street railway operators managed to persuade the state legislature to pass the "Ohio Consent Law," which effectively limited competition. This act stipulated that street railway tracks could not be laid until a majority of the abutting property owners approved construction. In effect, a city franchise would not be granted to a traction company until it provided evidence that a majority of property owners approved of the project. Once the company secured their consent, it did not need to renew that consent even when the franchise expired and the company sought a renewal from the city. A new firm which wished to bid for the expiring franchise, however, had to secure the majority consent of the property owners in order to qualify to bid. Therefore, a traction company hoping to compete had to find another route along streets that were not already occupied. This law benefited existing firms and limited opportunities for a new street railway company to take over a franchise beyond outright purchase of an existing line.[4]

Because of Ohio's Consent Law, interurbans were frequently precluded from constructing their own entrances into Ohio's urban centers on public streets. Only those interurban promoters that had congenial relations with existing urban lines or steam railroads could hope to have access to the cities. The Ohio Consent Law stayed in effect until the Schmidt Bill replaced it in 1908, well after the construction of Northeast Ohio's major interurbans.[5]

As C. B. Fairchild explained in the *Electrical Engineer* in 1898, "This class of railways is distinct from all others: it is true, they have wheels and rails in common, but in function, equipment, speed and management there is a glaring contrast, and they require for their inception, construction and control an otherness of intellect from that found in ordinary street railway practice." In other words, they were less like street railways in financing, design, construction, and operation and more like steam railroad enterprises. For example, interurban roads followed steam railroad standards in their roadbed construction and track work, where practical. A decade later, an industry textbook remarked, "The same care and exactness that are observed in steam-road construction should be observed in electric railroading, where the train speeds are often almost as high and other conditions just as severe."[6]

The criteria offered by Hilton and Due also ignore another critical way of distinguishing between urban/suburban and interurban electric railways. Their definition fails to recognize that human behavior defined the operations of the line as much as did the geography. George W. Knox, vice president and general manager of the Oklahoma Railway Company of Oklahoma City, Oklahoma, rendered this definition in 1914:

> A suburban railway as opposed to an interurban railway is a road running to a community serving people closely allied to and quite completely dependent upon a large business center—as an example—those people situated not far from, but beyond the corporate limits of a large business center or community, the majority of whom have positions, business, or do a large part of their trading at or in the large business center, or travel to and from there regularly, may be called 'suburbanites.'
>
> A railway is regarded as Interurban which goes into a community where the remote separation of such community—from a large business center—is more pronounced by reason of considerable distance intervening, a portion of which will, perhaps be rural. The people living in that Interurban Community have their places of permanent business and residence and do their regular every-day trading in such communities and travel only occasionally to the largest surrounding business center.[7]

This definition describes the role of the electric railway in a community's economic and social life and its economic relationship to a larger urban center. This is an important distinction to make between the two types of electric railways, as it helps explain why some of Northeast Ohio's lines prospered in the early 1900s. It also provides some understanding of how some lines were especially vulnerable to competition from the automobile in the 1920s, while others were able to last another decade or more.

A definition that distinguishes between an interurban and an urban/suburban railway must consider how people used the railway services and how access to speedy transportation services influenced where they lived. Some researchers have used conceptual models like "Journey-to-Work" (JTW) to examine the influences of transportation on the spatial differentiation of urban areas. Sam Bass Warner Jr. examined the JTW tendencies of Boston's suburban population in the last three decades of the nineteenth century. He noted how middle-class residential homogeneity in the suburbs could be largely explained by the arrival of the streetcars.[8]

Theodore Hershberg, Dale Light Jr., Harold E. Cox, and Richard R. Greenfield studied a multitude of reasons for increasing average JTW from 1850 to 1880 for Philadelphia area residents. These researchers found that the improved transportation technologies of the horsecar and steam railway lines allowed some professionals, lawyers and bankers for example, to reside at considerable distances from their work. For most workers, however, the Philadelphia transportation system did not serve their JTW needs even after a reduction in average fares and electrification of the lines from 1894 to 1897. Instead, it is their contention that until reorganization of the system in 1910, most of the passenger traffic was for non-JTW purposes, such as recreation, shopping, and long-distance travel.[9]

Using the concepts and the findings of the studies of Boston and Philadelphia, it could be argued that a great amount of Northeast Ohio's interurban passenger traffic was for non-JTW purposes. As can be seen in map 2.1, the interurban network of Northeast Ohio was quite extensive, but it served a decidedly different type of traffic than the urban/suburban lines. The urban/suburban railways of Akron, Cleveland, Lorain-Elyria, and Youngstown became increasingly used for JTW purposes. The major employment centers in each of these cities were located beyond the primary residential neighborhoods of the workers. These urban roads provided a service that was essential to the working classes on a daily basis, and subsequently they became a critical component in municipal politics. In some cases, these urban lines were able to acquire the protection of the municipal governments to survive the first onslaughts of competition from privately owned automobiles and bus companies. This assistance was not afforded

Urban and Interurban Railways in Northeast Ohio 69

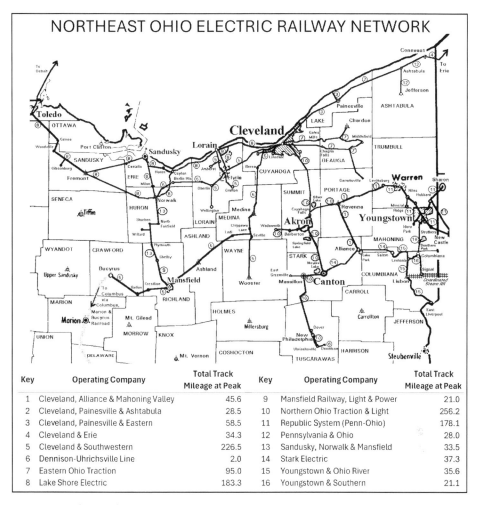

Map 2.1. Northeast Ohio electric railway systems at their peak in the 1920s. (Map by author)

to those non-JTW dominant systems because they did not actually serve a significant portion of the municipal constituency. The Cleveland, Southwestern & Columbus Railway would be one of those vulnerable systems.

SERVICES AND INTERCONNECTIONS

As mentioned, Northeast Ohio interurban lines also offered freight and express services; urban/suburban railways typically did not. There were three types of freight traffic in the interurban industry: carload

Figure 2.1. Southwestern Electric Package Express Car No. 407. (Courtesy of Northern Ohio Railway Museum)

freight, package express, and light package freight of either merchandise or agricultural products. The greatest percentage of freight handled by interurbans in Northeast Ohio was the less-than-carload package traffic.

Carload freight typically involved traffic interchanges with connecting steam railroads or interurban lines. Package express was handled by an express department or contract with an independent express company and transported not only on the passenger coaches but in special freight cars and trailers that were operated for that purpose. Some roads had arrangements with the old-line steam railroad express companies. In Ohio, the four largest express companies in order of total mileage covered were the Adams Express Company, American Express Company, United States Express Company, and Wells Fargo & Company. These four express companies in 1918 consolidated into the American Railway Express Company and secured an exclusive contract with the United States Railroad Administration, which excluded interurban participation.[10]

The third class of freight involved either merchandise from the cities distributed to retailers and customers in the outlying rural areas, or the

Urban and Interurban Railways in Northeast Ohio

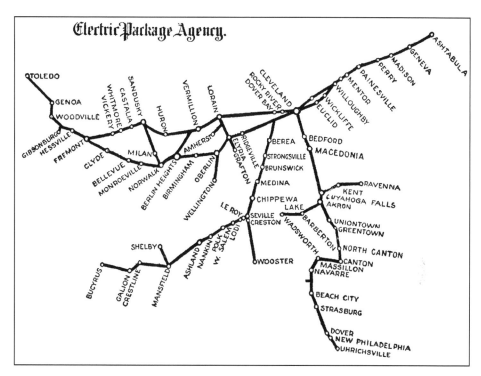

Map 2.2. Electric Package Agency stations, 1918. (Map reproduced from "Electric Package Agency, 1918," Ohio Edison Collection, The University of Akron Archives, box 151.)

incoming agricultural products from the farms like milk, produce, and fruit. Hilton and Due correctly observed that express operations and less-than-carload (LCL) freight services were mixed together by many lines so that no clear distinction across all interurban lines was possible.[11]

Interurban express traffic consisted of shipments of any merchandise or commodity that was typically a higher class than handled in freight and for which a faster transport time was needed. Local express then was normally conducted by a department of the railway or by a subsidiary owned company. "The principal distinction to be drawn between the locally operated express service of these lines [electric railways] and their freight service is the preference given to the former traffic in movement and the additional pick-up and delivery service where it is maintained."[12]

To that end, several interurbans in Northeast Ohio banded together to form their own regional express company to specialize in the express services, while allowing them to develop individually their own LCL or carload freight services. The predecessors of the Cleveland & Southwestern Traction Company combined in 1898 with Lake Shore Electric (LSE), Northern Ohio Traction & Light Company (NOT&L), and Cleveland, Painesville and Eastern Railways (CP&E) to form a joint corporation called the Electric Package Agency (EPA). The EPA could ship to and from stations ranging from Toledo to Ashtabula, as shown in map 2.2, to Bucyrus in the southwest and to Uhrichsville in the southeast. Interchange agreements with steam railroad express companies and a Lake Erie steamship line allowed through service to Detroit, Columbus, and Pittsburgh.[13]

The participating interurban lines of the Electric Package Agency retained control of their own milk traffic, but most used and owned the same cars that carried the EPA express. The company operated a large freight depot in Cleveland, and it was active twenty-four hours a day. The creation of the EPA suggests that the interurban railways recognized something the steam railroads had known for some time. They concluded that combined services would benefit their own separate interests while they competed against the steam railroad lines and stimulated new growth in express traffic. Their successful operations further show how the interurban infrastructure provided a competitive service to the regional economy.

Within a few short years, business over the EPA grew with the regional economy. The EPA had forty wagons picking up and delivering freight in Cleveland at rates equal to the steam railroad express, fifty-three agents, and fourteen express messengers throughout the system by 1906. The principal shippers were city wholesalers who saw great advantages in the radial pattern of the interurban line for shipments to local retailers at tremendous speed. For farmers the service was fast enough that perishables could be shipped without refrigeration, something the steam railroads were usually incapable of providing. These advantages enabled the interurban to siphon off the less-than-carload freight of competing steam railroads.[14]

As the *Electric Railway Journal* stated in 1913, "The development of a freight business on electric lines depends largely on the same fundamentals which control freight traffic on steam roads, namely, adequate station and track facilities located as advantageously as those of competing carriers. In this commercial era shippers deal entirely on an economical basis, and only in a few instances will sentiment divert a shipment from a road offering the quickest delivery, particularly after reliability of service has been established."[15] Interconnectivity for freight shipments between interurban and steam railroad lines was an effort worth pursuing, the electric railway industry argued for years, especially during World War I. The difficulties of the steam railroad systems in providing thorough and efficient freight services across the nation were recognized by many, including the Wilson administration.[16]

> Fortunately, enough instances exist to prove not only that electric railways can do great things to relieve freight congestion, but also that they can do it in the fullest cooperation with their older steam brother. Where there is a duplication of facilities, as between a steam railroad and an electric line, the facilities of the electric line should be used to their maximum capacity to relieve the steam line of the short-haul traffic. The general equipment, the motive power and cars of the steam railroad which are used in this short-haul service could then be released for long-haul through freight and passenger service. Thus the present unprecedented congested condition of the steam railroads could be very materially relieved.[17]

Map 2.3 provides a visual demonstration of that duplication of routes and facilities within Northeast Ohio. The article further argued that in order to accomplish this logistical cooperation a number of changes would need to be made at various strategic locations nationally. The author suggested such actions as removing local franchise restrictions, the extension of steam railroad interchange arrangements, federal aid in financing the purchase of new rolling stock, the carrying out of some specific track alignments and the improvement of some terminal facilities.[18]

At the time, the only entity with the authority or ability to make any of that happen was the United States Railroad Administration. It was an independent agency created by Presidential Proclamation on December 26, 1917, under authority of the Army Appropriation Act and later in March 1918 by congressional action, the Railroad Control Act. The US Railroad Administration operated such railroads, coastwise steamship lines, inland waterways, and telephone and telegraph companies that were seized by the government in the interest of national defense. Railroads and other seized carriers were returned to private control on March 1, 1920, under terms of the Transportation Act, on February 28, 1920. Electric interurbans were excluded from the order.[19]

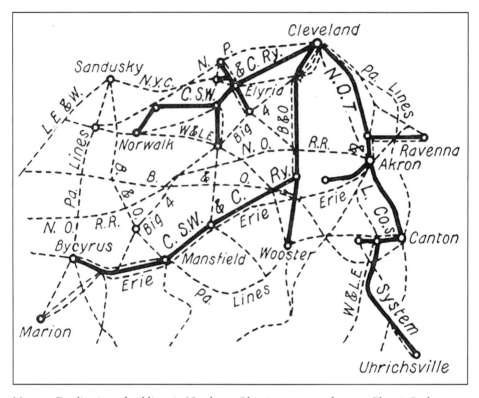

Map 2.3. Duplication of rail lines in Northeast Ohio in 1918, map from an *Electric Railway Journal* article arguing that duplication of steam and electric rail lines and facilities could be helpful in reducing the congestion of freight traffic that was frustrating the war effort. (Reproduced from A. B. Cole, "Electric Railways Are in a Position to Haul More Freight," *Electric Railway Journal* 51, no. 19 (May 11, 1918): 894, fig. 6.)

Furtherance of that industry conversation in search of a coordinated and comprehensive national system of freight services involving the steam and electric railroads working together met with great skepticism. In an analysis of electric versus steam railroad routes in Northeast Ohio, Charles J. Laney, traffic manager of the Northern Ohio Traction & Light Company, demonstrated in the *Electric Railway Journal* that the Big Four Railroads in the region had shorter routes and faster run times than the collection of interconnected electric railroads. He concluded, "We cannot compete with steam road operation on long-haul express service."[20] However, he touted the great success of the Electric Package Agency in

Figure 2.2. Joint ticket station for Lake Shore Electric Railway (LSE car on right) and Cleveland, Southwestern & Columbus Railway (Southwestern car on left) in Lorain, Ohio. (Courtesy of Northern Ohio Railway Museum)

the same article. He explained, "It is a success because its business is a part of each road, its executive committee being the general manager of each road represented. The electric package revenue of each road is the earnings of each road after operating expenses have been deducted. So you can see that it is a department, so to speak, of each road represented."[21]

As passenger revenues declined on Northeast Ohio interurbans in the 1920s, companies became increasingly dependent upon freight, mail, and express-generated revenues. As a result, it made them as vulnerable to motor carriers as they were to the automobile. Roadways were improved during the twenties, and truck lines took a significant share of the freight hauling business that had belonged to the interurbans. Competing truck lines offered door-to-door services that were inexpensive and faster. Although Northeast Ohio's electric railways responded with similar services, the cost and practicality of transferring bulk items made it difficult for the interurbans to compete. Interurbans, however, had exploited the short-haul freight traffic for over two decades and car-load freight since World War I. Their losses in the 1920s to the truck lines were much akin to those they had inflicted earlier upon the steam railways.[22]

The EPA operated the baggage and express services of the member railways until November 1, 1928. A new combination of lines formed a successor firm called the Electric Railways Freight Company (ERF), and it consisted of the Lake Shore Electric, Northern Ohio Power & Light Company (renamed in 1926 from the Northern Ohio Traction & Light Company), Penn-Ohio Transportation Company, Ohio Public Service Company, and the Toledo & Indiana Railway. Motor truck lines seriously ate away at the ERF's express traffic during the Great Depression. The backbone of the ERF was broken when the Northern Ohio Power & Light Company abandoned its freight operations in June 1931. This action isolated the Penn-Ohio-Youngstown area interurbans from the other midwestern lines and effectively signaled the closing days of coordinated electric railway freight services in Northeast Ohio.[23]

3

The Cleveland, Southwestern & Columbus Railway

A Pioneer System

THE PIONEER YEARS

THE STORY OF the Cleveland, Southwestern & Columbus Railway (Southwestern) is short, but important. It illustrates the tangible economic and social linkages between the city and the countryside that the railway system provided. Much of its traffic originated in the rural towns and villages of north-central Ohio. The Southwestern is an ideal example of how an interurban system provided an important step in the development of a modern rural infrastructure in the region.

In addition to its significant role in connecting Cleveland with rural communities to the west and south, the Southwestern provided a vital transportation link between regions of the state. It was the sole electric railway in Northeast Ohio to have a through route to the interurban network surrounding Columbus. By the end of the 1910s, it became an integral part of the region's freight and express traffic system to central Ohio. By the late 1920s, it carried parcel posts and provided less-than-carload (LCL) freight services throughout Ohio and into Indiana and Kentucky. Even near the end of its existence, management expanded services to provide direct rail to airline ticket sales at ten cities along the route with connection to Cleveland Airport. As the Southwestern manager E. L. Hukill boasted in 1928, "It brings the Southwestern in direct

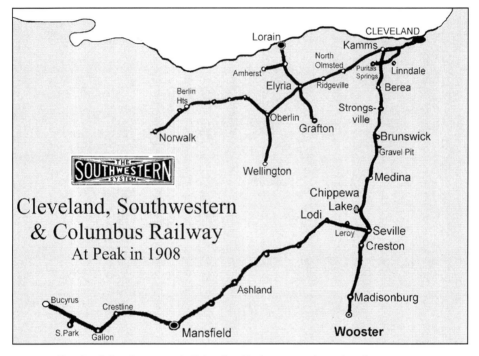

Map 3.1. Cleveland, Southwestern & Columbus Railway at peak track mileage in 1908.

contact with four modes of travel, rail, water, air and highway, and marks the greatest achievement in its history."[1]

The Southwestern was the only major interurban line in the area to parallel another major interurban line. The Western Division of the Southwestern competed against the Lake Shore Electric Railway (LSE) for traffic from Cleveland to Elyria, Lorain, and Norwalk. Here was an instance where two major syndicates provided ongoing transportation services to the same urban destinations. There was enough passenger, express, and freight traffic to support both systems for a good number of years. How it came to be that two of the region's largest interurbans paralleled each other can best be explained by looking at the business interests behind the Southwestern: the Pomeroy and Mandelbaum syndicate.

The Southwestern, owned by the Pomeroy-Mandelbaum syndicate until 1924, was one of Ohio's great interurbans. In the earliest years it was referred to as "The Pioneer Route." However, its more commonly used name after 1907 was the "Green Line," because of the dark green color and gold lettering that for years distinguished its cars and even its public timetables. At its peak, the Southwestern was the second-largest interurban system to radiate from Cleveland, surpassed only by the Northern Ohio Traction and Light Company (NOT&L). A part of the Everett-Moore syndicate, the NOT&L operated 338 miles of track at its apex, as compared to 226 miles for the Southwestern.[2]

Surprisingly, the electric railway companies that later became part of the Southwestern and the "building stone" of Northeast Ohio's second-largest interurban syndicate had humble beginnings in the Cuyahoga County community of Berea, not the big city of Cleveland. The Berea sandstone mined near this small town was famous for its excellent quality and was used to manufacture grindstones and building stones. At one time, Berea sandstone was mined and shipped to destinations around the world at a rate of 400 tons per day. The town was also the site of German Wallace College and Baldwin University, which merged to form Baldwin-Wallace College in 1910.[3]

The Berea Street Railroad Company opened in April 1876 with $15,000 in capital stock to haul passengers from the village center and local colleges to the nearby Lake Shore & Michigan Southern Railroad depot north of downtown. The firm started with two $800 horse-drawn streetcars equipped with fare boxes, bells, platform, and dashboard. The 1.25 miles of track had a gauge of three feet six inches, which was not the standard gauge of most other horsecar street railways in the Cleveland area.[4]

The company was originally financed by a group of local businessmen consisting of Joseph Nichols, a local hotel owner; A. W. Bishop, a poke (small bag) manufacturer; and Ed Richards, a merchant. Within a year, ownership of the horsecar line expanded to include Alson H. (A. H.) Pomeroy. A. H. Pomeroy operated a dry goods store in Elyria for ten years before buying an interest in the First National Bank of Berea (later called the Bank of Berea Company) in 1875. He first served as secretary and treasurer of the street railway company, but as the line prospered his investment and control over the corporate holdings increased. His eldest son, Fred T. Pomeroy, who served as assistant Cuyahoga County treasurer from 1884 to 1893, joined the company's board of directors in 1884.[5]

With a mind toward expansion and conversion to electric streetcars over standard gauge track, the company was reorganized and renamed

Figure 3.1. Cleveland & Berea Line on Front Street, Berea, Ohio, ca. 1892. (Author's collection)

as the Cleveland & Berea Street Railroad Company (C&BS) in September 1891. A year later it began purchasing property northward to extend the line into Cleveland. Within a year the firm finished building standard-gauged tracks to Cleveland's corporate limits at West Ninety-Eighth Street. There it joined the Lorain Street and Woodland Avenue Railway.

The company did not immediately convert to the conventional trolley system of railway electrification. Instead, it chose to experiment with storage battery–powered streetcars for several reasons. The Cleveland electric power plants said it was uneconomical to supply current over the long-distance lines needed to electrify a railway line in Berea. In addition, Cleveland industry required all of the power that the plants were capable of producing at the time. Building their own power station at that time required more capital and expertise than the Pomeroys had available. An added reason for the company to explore the storage-battery streetcars was the resistance by village council to string overhead power lines through town.[6]

The battery streetcars, utilizing the Ford & Washburn system, were used during the winter of 1893 and 1894 but proved inadequate. However, the few months of traffic totaled over twelve thousand passengers, demonstrating the public demand in the marketplace to investors and local officials. The Pomeroys convinced the village council to allow the line to abandon the battery cars in favor of the Westinghouse trolley system the following year. Faced with cash shortages following the Panic of 1893, the Pomeroys, Miller, and Bishop invited other prominent businessmen and another Pomeroy son to join the venture. They needed additional investors to raise the capital to electrify the property. The new participants included Orlando D. Pomeroy, also involved in his father's Bank of Berea Company, and Albert E. Akins, the Cuyahoga County auditor from 1890 to 1893 and 1896 to 1899 and director of the Union Savings and Loan Company.[7]

The first overhead power streetcar ran over the line on May 10, 1894. The expansion of the Pomeroy's traction investments brought them in close association with other equally active electric railway promoters and builders. The electrical trolley system was constructed by the Cleveland Construction Company, the most active builder in Northeast Ohio and headed by Will Christy who was backed by the Everett-Moore syndicate. Albert Akins insisted that the Pomeroy interests award the construction contract to Christy's firm and offer Christy the option to invest in other anticipated electric railway ventures. Christy was an investor and board member in Pomeroy's subsequent electric traction ventures from 1894 to 1902 and later closely associated with Everett-Moore's Northern Ohio Traction and Light Company. In 1902 he became president of the newly formed Firestone Tire and Rubber Company[8]

Christy and Akins also joined with the Pomeroy interests and another three electric railway builders from the Cleveland area, Leon M. Coe, Frank D. Carpenter, and Milton A. Sprague in 1894 to form the Cleveland & Elyria Electric Railway (C&EE). A year later Coe, Sprague, and Carpenter started to promote an interurban not affiliated with the Pomeroy interests, the Cleveland and Chagrin Falls Electric Railroad east of Cleveland. This line eventually merged with another to form the Eastern Ohio Traction Company.

The C&EE immediately started construction to extend the C&BS line from Kamm's Corners on Lorain Avenue to Elyria. Will Christy personally directed the construction of the twenty-two miles of line. The C&EE reached Elyria in September 1895 and completed construction of a bridge over the Rocky River in December. At the end of the year the two Pomeroy companies merged to form the Cleveland, Berea & Elyria Street Railroad. Forming a new and separate company in order to construct new lines and then merge them to form a single corporation fit the typical pattern of financing the construction of interurbans. This archetype of corporate lineage was fostered by the sale of securities to finance the mergers. This is also how the original promoters made their fortunes.[9]

As depicted in figure 3.2, in the years that followed, the Pomeroy syndicate grew using the same general pattern of incorporation, promotion, and merger. At the creation of new companies, additional investors joined with the Pomeroy ventures, and then the lines merged once they had acquired franchises and finished construction. The power to draw investors into the ventures depended upon the intangible value of the railway property. This is where the promoters were able to make the sizable profits on their initial investments, and where the seeds of feverish speculation throughout the industry were sown.[10]

Each successive interurban company built upon the speculative value of the preceding lines. What arose out of this financial arrangement were syndicates of electric railway owners that gained more out of building and financing new lines than in running actually established routes. The earlier an investor joined the syndicate the greater the rewards as each new line was built and consolidated.

In early 1897 the Pomeroy interests joined with a prominent Cleveland banker and railway promoter, Maurice J. Mandelbaum, to build several traction lines in northeast and southwest Ohio. Mandelbaum, the son of a wealthy retail clothier in Cleveland, made his first fortunes as founder of the Fisher Book Typewriter Company, which later became the Underwood Elliot Fisher Company. His banking affiliations included him on the list of founders of the Western Reserve Trust Company and later on the board of directors of the Cleveland Trust Company following the merger of the two institutions in 1903. The year before his enlistment in the Pomeroy interests, Mandelbaum formed the Western Ohio Railway along with his brother-in-law Leopold Wolf.[11]

Boosted by new financial connections, the Pomeroy and Mandelbaum syndicate created and merged with other electric railway compa-

The Cleveland, Southwestern & Columbus Railway

Operating Company	1887	88	89	90	91	92	93	94	95	96	97	98	99	1900	01	02	03	04	05	06	07
Berea Street Railroad (1876)							O	m													
Cleveland & Berea Street Railroad							M	E		m											
Cleveland & Elyria Electric Railway										m											
Cleveland, Berea & Elyria Street Railroad										M	m										
Elyria and Oberlin Electric Railway Co.											m										
Cleveland, Berea, Elyria & Oberlin Railway										M			m								
Lorain County Street Railway Co.													m								
Oberlin & Wellington Railway													m								
Ohio Central Traction Co.											C										m
Cleveland, Elyria & Western Railway Co.											M				M	m					
Elyria, Grafton and Southern Electric Railway															m						
Cleveland, Medina and Southern Railway														m							
Cleveland and Southern Railway														M	C	m					
Norwalk Gas & Electric																m					
Cleveland & Southwestern Traction Co.																	M				m
Cleveland, Ashland & Mansfield Traction Co.																					m
Cleveland, Southwestern & Columbus Railway																					M
Mansfield Railway, Light & Power Co.																	M				C
Citizens' Electric Railway, Light & Power Co.							N									m					
Mansfield Electric Street Railway								N													

POMEROY-MANDELBAUM SYNDICATE INTERESTS
Significant Corporate Events

LEGEND OF CORPORATE EVENTS
m = MERGER (Constituent Company)   A = Abandoned Operations
M = MERGER (Parent Company)   C = Controlled (Subsidiary of Parent Firm)
N = Name Change, no reorganization   E = Electrified
O = Reorganized

- Year of Panic or Financial Crisis"
Panic of 1893   Rich Man's Panic (1903)
Silver Campaign Depression 1896   Panic of 1907

Figure 3.2. Cleveland, Southwestern & Columbus system corporate timeline, the Pioneer Route phase, 1887–1907. (Chart by author)

nies, eventually to become the second-largest interurban builder in Ohio. By 1905 it owned or controlled other lines such as the Western Ohio Railway; Cincinnati, Dayton and Toledo Traction Company; and for a short period, the Mansfield Railway Light and Power Company, besides several other smaller properties. Its interurban system building took it over the longest stretches of countryside in the state. For a brief time the syndicate also operated an electric railway over the towpath of the old Miami and Erie Canal used for towing barges from Cincinnati to Dayton. Since the project proved to be unprofitable, it was scrapped in 1905.[12]

In Northeast Ohio, the newly formed Pomeroy-Mandelbaum syndicate financed an extension of the Cleveland, Berea & Elyria Street Railroad (CB&ES) into Oberlin. The Cleveland Trust Company, in which

Mandelbaum was a board member, underwrote the $100,000 in bonds used to finance the extension. The Elyria and Oberlin Electric Railway merged with the CB&ES to form the Cleveland, Berea, Elyria & Oberlin Railway on December 2, 1897. Thirteen days later, the Pomeroy-Mandelbaum syndicate ran its first passenger car into Oberlin.[13]

On several occasions, the Pomeroy-Mandelbaum syndicate purchased other independently promoted electric railway lines, like the Lorain County Street Railway Company in 1900, the Elyria, Grafton and Southern Electric Railway and the Norwalk Gas & Electric Company in 1903. It also acquired competing companies with active franchises and private rights-of-way, such as the Cleveland, Medina and Southern Electric Company (CM&SE). In this case, however, the CM&SE was only a "paper" interurban. What the Pomeroy-Mandelbaum syndicate purchased in 1901 through a subsidiary company, Cleveland and Southern Railway Company, were exclusive franchises and property rights. Organized in 1895, the CM&SE planned to build an electric railway line from Berea through Medina to Chippewa Lake Park, a growing amusement and recreation park, and eventually to Wooster. By December 1900, the CM&SE owned franchises and private rights-of-way stretching from Berea to Wooster.[14]

THE TWO DIVISIONS OF THE SOUTHWESTERN SYSTEM

As depicted in figure 3.2, the Pomeroy-Mandelbaum properties consolidated on January 21, 1903, to form the Cleveland and Southwestern Traction Company (C&SW). The new company created two divisions, Western and Southern, and operated a total of 120 miles of completed track, with twenty-six miles under construction at the time of consolidation. It operated two power stations and thirty-three motor cars between Cleveland and Medina to the south and Oberlin, Elyria, and Wellington to the west. By September 1903 the Southern Division line through Medina reached Wooster.[15]

Amid the first burst of intense interurban building that George Hilton and John Due place between 1901 and 1904, syndicates often promoted grandiose schemes that would dramatically expand their networks. The Pomeroy-Mandelbaum syndicate was more in touch with reality than most, but nevertheless all of their plans did not come to pass. In fall 1901 the Pomeroy-Mandelbaum syndicate bought controlling interests in the

Figure 3.3. Western terminus for the Cleveland, Southwestern & Columbus Railway and connection to the Columbus, Delaware and Marion Railway, or CD&M, which provided interurban service connecting Columbus, Delaware, Marion, Worthington, and Bucyrus, Ohio, totaling eighty miles of track. (Author's collection)

Ohio Central Traction Company (OCT), an electric railway between Bucyrus and Galion. The syndicate hoped to construct a line between their C&SW Western Division terminus at Wellington to Mansfield through Ashland. As shown in map 3.2, the syndicate also envisioned a route between Mansfield and Columbus, via the Columbus, Delaware and Marion Railway.[16]

In 1904, another syndicate from New York proposed connecting the Southern and the Western Divisions of the CS&C through a line from Wooster to Mansfield. The New York syndicate members never revealed their identity, but operated through a Mansfield attorney, David Collier. They also suggested building a line from Wooster to Columbus through Loudonville and Mount Vernon. Unfortunately, both projects were ill conceived and ill timed for two reasons. The traffic needs of the businesses and people between Wooster and Mansfield were already well served by the Pennsylvania Railroad, according to Wooster businessmen

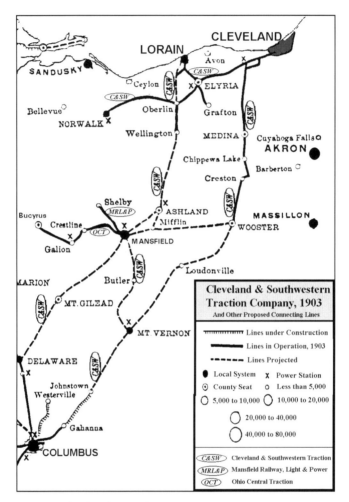

Map 3.2. Cleveland & Southwestern Traction Company in 1903 and other proposed connecting lines of the Pomeroy-Mandelbaum syndicate. (Map by author as cited in Stephen D. Hambley, "The Vanguard of a Regional Infrastructure: Electric Railways of Northeast Ohio, 1884–1932" [PhD diss., University of Akron, 1993].)

at the time. Secondly, the population in the intervening areas between Columbus and Wooster were too sparsely populated to make construction over the inhospitable geography worthwhile. Contrary to the public declarations of the promoters in December 1904 that the lines were a certainty, neither project was built or successfully financed.[17]

While the New York syndicate promoted the Wooster to Mansfield line, the Pomeroy-Mandelbaum syndicate engaged in activities aimed at improving the profitability of their properties rather than expanding them. As Wallace McCook Cunningham, professor in commerce at the University of Pennsylvania, stated in 1910, "The syndicate managers often operate the road for a while, trying to work the earnings up so that it can 'bear the bond interest,' as they say." This is exactly what the Pomeroy-Mandelbaum managers were doing from 1903 to 1905.[18]

Several factors encouraged the Pomeroy-Mandelbaum syndicate to slow the pace of construction. First, A. H. Pomeroy, the old street railway builder and promoter who had energized the syndicate, retired as president on August 28, 1903, and was quickly replaced by his son, Fred T. Pomeroy. In addition, Will Christy and Frank D. Carpenter, both enthusiastic electric railway builders and promoters, left the syndicate when it consolidated its Cleveland area interests into the C&SW. Christy took on added responsibilities with the Everett and Moore properties and the presidency of the Firestone Tire and Rubber Company. Carpenter only departed from active involvement in the syndicate's properties in Northeast Ohio. He retained a role in the promotion and management of the syndicate's Western Ohio Railway Company, which operated 107 miles of track between Lima and Piqua and from Wapakoneta to Celina.

Another factor that stunted expansion of the C&SW line involved a major downturn in the national economy. The tremendous growth in passenger traffic after 1900 enjoyed by the Pomeroy-Mandelbaum line declined sharply starting in 1903 and did not pick up again until 1906, as shown in Figure 3.4. The small business recession that followed the Panic of 1903 lasted until the beginning of 1905 and temporarily slowed the Southwestern's passenger traffic and cooled the Pomeroy-Mandelbaum syndicate's feverish expansions. Although the road continued to see some growth in operating revenues, primarily from gains in freight revenues, the stagnant passenger traffic induced the syndicate to wait out the recession.

Feeders to Steam Railroads Not Foes

A *Street Railway Journal* article reported in 1904 an analysis that showed the significant impact the first major expansion of the Western Division of the C&SW line had on a competing steam railroad, the Lake Shore & Michigan Southern (LS&MS). As demonstrated in table 3.1,

LS&MS serving Oberlin to Cleveland in 1895 had an average monthly traffic of 16,918 passengers. A mere seven years later, that number had dwindled to 7,647. The article also highlighted a similar impact of competing electric and steam railroad lines between Cleveland and Painesville and between Cleveland and Lorain. While the author of the article further claimed that electric railways also generate new traffic, because of their frequency of services and other qualities, the dramatic reduction of passenger traffic for the competing steam railroads was indisputable.[19]

Table 3.1. Lake Shore & Michigan Southern Railroad, change in passenger traffic between Cleveland and Oberlin

Year	Westbound	Eastbound	Total	Average per month
1895	104,426	98,588	203,014	16,918
1902	46,328	45,433	91,761	7,647

Source: "Trolley Versus Steam," *Street Railway Journal* 23, no. 26 (June 25, 1904): 978.

As dire as the data might seem for steam railroad trunklines, apparently a high official with the LS&MS was reported in 1901 to be underplaying its negative impact on their bottom line. According to the *Street Railway Journal* article, the LS&MS spokesperson cautioned, "If truck lines could abolish short hauls and frequent stops, it would mean money in the pocket of the stockholders. The short haul is a drain, and if electric roads will take care of this class of business, it will prove a boon to us. I believe the ideal arrangement would be to have electric roads act as feeders to the steam roads. Travelers could be brought from the towns into the larger cities on the electric cars, and take through fast trains for distant points."[20] Thus, with this kind of success, once the effects of the financial panic cleared up, the syndicate was assured that their efforts would be similarly rewarded in the next phases of its expansion further outward from Cleveland. They felt destined to see growing passenger traffic as feeders to the major steam railroad lines, as well as express freight and other related services for the newly connected communities of the Southwestern system.

GROWTH AFTER THE 1903 PANIC

Although the Southwestern and Pomeroy-Mandelbaum syndicate had announced plans to extend the line from Wellington to Ashland and

Mansfield, they were additionally frustrated by a factor that had nothing to do with the economy or the syndicate members. The line from Wellington to Ashland was blocked by an obstinate farmer who refused to sell a right-of-way strip through his property. The farmer owned the property on both sides of the road, and the CS&C owners were unable to change his mind. Although the CS&C lawfully could have pursued the right of eminent domain, the legal proceedings would have delayed the project and probably cost considerably more than the syndicate wished to pay for a narrow strip of land. The uncooperative farmer forced the CS&C to redirect the route instead through the Southern Division from Seville to Ashland and Mansfield. This rerouting delayed completion. Fortunately for the Pomeroy-Mandelbaum syndicate, it was able to buy a recently abandoned section of Baltimore & Ohio Railroad right-of-way between West Salem and Leroy (Westfield Center).[21]

On January 15, 1905, Francis E. Myers, a prosperous pump manufacturer from Ashland, joined the Cleveland & Southwestern Traction Company (C&SW) board of directors. Myers's personality was one befitting a railway promoter. He was known as an aggressive businessman, with a head for finances, marketing, and administration. Myers was willing to take chances and to borrow heavily and finance an idea or invention that he believed would bring a profit. In sum, he was a model entrepreneur during what has been called the Birth of the American Century. In addition to his continued affiliation with the CS&C and the F. E. Myers & Brother Company, he served on the board of directors of the Nickel Plate Railroad, the Union Trust Company and Guarantee Title & Trust Company of Cleveland, Faultless Rubber Company and the First National Bank of Ashland.[22]

Myers wanted the Southwestern to build into Ashland so that his factory could draw from a wider labor market. He financed much of the forty-four-mile extension of the line through the Cleveland, Ashland and Mansfield Traction Company, a part of the Pomeroy-Mandelbaum syndicate. In June 1906 the company started construction of the line between Mansfield and Seville, but completion of the system required the acquisition of some additional properties and reorganization to leverage the syndicate's capital structure.[23]

On March 4, 1907, the syndicate consolidated the Cleveland & Southwestern Traction Company; the Central Ohio Traction Company; and

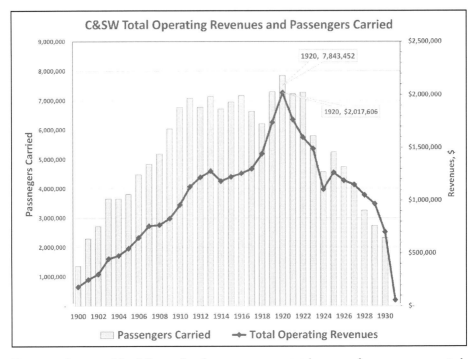

Figure 3.4. Pomeroy-Mandelbaum Southwestern system, total revenue for passengers carried and railway operating revenues, 1900–1931. Companies included Cleveland, Elyria & Western Railway Company (1900–1902); Cleveland & Southwestern Traction Company (1903–6); Cleveland, Southwestern & Columbus Railway (1907–23); and Cleveland, Southwestern Railway & Light Company (1924–31). (Chart by author)

the Cleveland, Ashland and Mansfield Traction Company to form the Cleveland, Southwestern & Columbus Railway Company (Southwestern or CS&C). The new company authorized $10 million in additional consolidated mortgage bonds, of which $3.5 million were held in escrow to retire all the underlying bonds of the company and $6.3 million held in the treasury to cover the costs of building the line between Mansfield and Seville and other extensions or improvements. The Cleveland Trust Company served as the trustee of the mortgage bonds.[24]

Infused with new cash, the Southwestern purchased 78 percent or $500,000 of the common stock of the Mansfield, Railway, Light and Power Company (MRL&P) in late 1907. The Southwestern needed the MRL&P to enter the city of Mansfield and join its incoming line from

The Cleveland, Southwestern & Columbus Railway 91

Figure 3.5. Cleveland Wooster car at Seville Depot track split-off between Wooster and Mansfield termini. (Courtesy of Northern Ohio Railway Museum)

Ashland with the Ohio Central Traction line from Crestline. In the bargain, the syndicate also gained control of the twelve-mile-long interurban line to Shelby, the nine miles of track and equipment of the Mansfield city street railway, and the city's only electric power generating system. In addition, the MRL&P was a reasonably profitable public service company. Strategically, through control of the MRL&P, the syndicate was able to divert the previous stockholder dividends to pay for power plant expansions needed for the Southwestern operations and line extensions. Being the dominant electrical power supplier to the region in combination with a franchise in Mansfield City that extended to 1925, the MRL&P showed promise of bringing in revenues sufficient to pay for the expansions. Much to the chagrin and despite the lawsuit of prior MRL&P investors, the Southwestern owners prevailed in this typical means of system building.[25]

With completion of the line to Mansfield in 1908, this was the Southwestern at the greatest extent of its electric rail empire. F. E. Myers became president of the Southwestern and served in that capacity until 1922, while F. T. Pomeroy served as vice president. The Western Division of the

Figure 3.6. Ashland, Ohio, residence of F. E. Myers, industrialist, progressive employer, and CEO of the Cleveland, Southwestern & Columbus Railway and financier for expansion of Southern Division from Seville Junction to Mansfield through Ashland. (Courtesy of Dennis Lamont Collection)

Southwestern connected the communities of Norwalk, Oberlin, Lorain, Wellington, and Elyria to Cleveland. Concurrently, its Southern Division extended to Medina, Wooster, Mansfield, and Bucyrus. Of the system's 209 route miles, 177 miles or 84.7 percent of the trackage ran over private right-of-way. In comparison, only 45 percent of the interurban trackage of the Northern Ohio Traction and Light Company operated over private right-of-way. The relatively large proportion of trackage over private right-of-way kept the Southwestern's street running time down to a competitive level and limited the number of costly village and municipal franchises. It also enabled the line to develop intensive freight and express services with only a modest amount of local government harassment or restrictions.[26]

Later in 1908, a subsidiary of the Columbus, Delaware and Marion Railway (CD&M) extended its line eighteen miles to Bucyrus. Meeting at the recently constructed Union Station, the two lines in Bucyrus

Figure 3.7. CS&C Railway "Y" in downtown Bucyrus. (Courtesy of Northern Ohio Railway Museum)

enabled direct electric railway transportation between Columbus and Cleveland. The through passenger service from Cleveland to Columbus was never heavily promoted by the Southwestern because the New York Central's "Big Four" route was forty-five miles shorter and much faster. However, both the Southwestern and the CD&M transported overnight carload freight with great frequency starting in 1916.[27]

After the so-called Bankers' Panic of 1907, as shown in Figure 3.4, both the urban and rural territories served by the Southwestern experienced a resurgence of business activity. This was the time for Southwestern management to work down the proportion of the revenues needed to make bond interest payments. The capitalization of the system building up to that point had to be whittled down to a manageable size if the company were to have a bright future. As illustrated in figure 3.9, from 1907 to 1914, total operating revenues from Southwestern operations steadily grew because of revenues from increased ridership, mail contracts, transportation of milk and dairy products, and package express

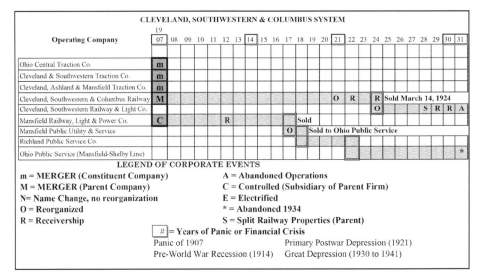

Figure 3.8. Cleveland, Southwestern & Columbus system corporate timeline, 1907–31. (Chart by author)

services. If the pace had continued for a few more years, the extension of the Southwestern southward to Mansfield might have paid off.

What also hurt the line during this period was fierce competition from the Lake Shore Electric in the traffic from Elyria to Norwalk and between Elyria and Lorain. Contemporary observers stated that during the best of years there was enough traffic for both lines. However, during recessions these routes lost money. The recession of 1914 and 1915 caused a decline in total revenues for the Southwestern, and that depressed condition continued until 1917. As noted in figure 3.9, the revenues did sharply increase again starting in 1917, but total expenses grew at an even faster rate.

The management of the Southwestern concentrated on a number of strategies to boost transportation net income over the years. Collectively, these tactics adhered to principles espoused by J. N. Shannahan, president of the American Electric Railway Transportation and Traffic Association, in a 1912 article in the industry's trade publication, *AERA*. Shannahan identified four principles that electric railways needed to follow in order to create new trolley business. First and foremost, Shannahan said, was to infect more people with the "trolley habit": namely, to get the people to use traction at least once and make certain the train crews treated them with politeness and attentiveness. Shannahan, like most railway managers, believed that the natural benefits and ease of traveling by electric car would ultimately encourage the passenger to venture to even more destinations than ever before. The underlying belief was that given relatively easy traveling conditions, new destinations or reasons for journeying would be, in effect, created for and by the passenger.[28]

Shannahan's first principle dealt with the demand side of the equation, while his last three guidelines focused on the supply side of transit operations. Shannahan's second principle suggested that the goal of railway managers should be to increase the gross revenues of the property in order to spread out the costs from fixed charges. His third principle directed that railway operators use surplus equipment in everyday traffic as much as possible so that some return could be made on the investment. Shannahan indicated lastly to railway managers, "It is of the utmost importance to bear in mind, in seeking to promote passenger traffic, that any increase in your 'peak' means ultimate increase in investment and fixed charges and that the object of this increase of business is to level your 'peak' and not to increase it."[29] Regardless of whether various managers of the Southwestern system actually knew of Shannahan's sage advice, it represented a good summation of the conventional wisdom that guided the business decisions of most electric railways during the 1910s.

Getting new passengers to ride the railway system could be achieved by hosting special events, offering excursions, or promoting amusement parks. As will be discussed later, the promotion of the excursion business boosted gross revenues of the Southwestern and helped to create a demand for passenger service when there would not have normally been one. A Sunday school excursion or company picnic did not come at peak rush hours when the Journey-To-Work (JTW) needs were the highest. Instead, they occurred on Sundays and holidays when the demand for recreation and entertainment could be cultivated and when normal traffic would be at its lowest point.

By 1912, the Southwestern's management realized that the interurban was overextended. Fred T. Pomeroy, representing the company at a Berea Village Council hearing in 1914, admitted as much: "We have some parts of the road that never should have been built. If this company had con-

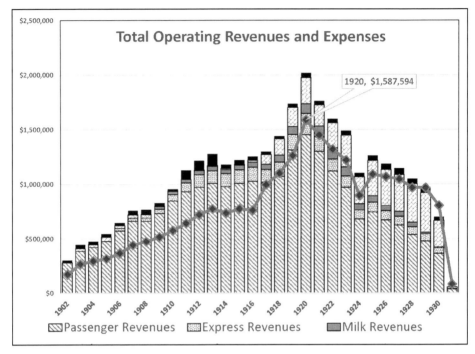

Figure 3.9. Pomeroy-Mandelbaum Southwestern system, total operating revenues and expenses, 1902–31. Companies include Cleveland, Elyria & Western Railway Company (1902); Cleveland & Southwestern Traction Company (1903–6); Cleveland, Southwestern & Columbus Railway (1907–23); and Cleveland, Southwestern Railway & Light Company (1924–31). "Other revenues" are the combined total of income from power sales (1902–14 only), switching revenues, property rental, and net amusement park earnings. (Chart by author)

fined its efforts to Cuyahoga and Lorain counties it would have been a paying proposition."[30]

The year 1912 was a critical one for the company. Starting in that year the firm took dramatic steps that marked an important shift in business strategy. The Southwestern abandoned its previous business philosophy of building up the suburban territories by offering special fare inducements. Instead, the road expanded its freight and power services while increasing passenger fares. Officials believed that the line would operate more profitably by carrying fewer passengers at higher fares and diversifying its services while encouraging electrical power sales along the sparsely populated segments of the network.[31]

The Southwestern used a financial restructuring in December 1912 to initiate an extensive campaign aimed at expanding power and light services, as well as to start a program of rebuilding its cars for limited passenger service. The syndicate used the proceeds from new bond sales to eliminate the road's floating debt, retire some outstanding bonds, and provide working capital to promote the power and light business, with only a modest reinvestment in passenger services. Harris, Forbes and Company of New York handled the bond sales for the Southwestern, and the Cleveland Trust Company again acted as the mortgage trustee.[32]

According to a November 1913 article in *Electric Traction*, all of the limited service cars were rebuilt into single, front-entrance cars with a smoking compartment at the rear and eliminating the baggage compartment. Since the city of Cleveland limited freight traffic, the Southwestern was increasing the space available for up to seventy-eight passengers in the 62-foot-long cars. Space was too valuable to be wasted for an unused baggage area, and the Southwestern wanted to increase the operating revenues of the limited passenger service while maintaining the same running schedule.[33] Regardless, starting in 1913 the company was largely focused on expanding its power sales to residen-

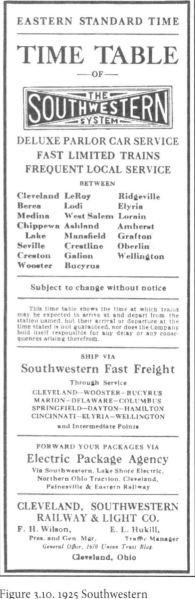

Figure 3.10. 1925 Southwestern timetable. (Courtesy of Northern Ohio Railway Museum)

Figure 3.11. Morning lineup of Southwestern cars at Rockport Barn. (Courtesy of Northern Ohio Railway Museum)

tial and commercial customers, as well as to local community power companies. While the company expanded electrical production and distribution capabilities in order to increase the number of customers along its power lines in the 1910s, the system was benefiting from power investments dating a decade prior in its earliest system-building years.

POWERING UP IN THE EARLY YEARS

In 1903 and 1904, two 1000 kW Westinghouse turbine units, some of the first manufactured in the United States, were installed in the Southwestern's main power station located at Carlisle near Elyria. While the early commitment by the Pomeroy & Mandelbaum syndicate to a more reliable and powerful electric generation system would have made them pioneers in the interurban industry, they were not entitled to that national distinction. A three-year delay in the design, purchase, and construction made their power plant one of the first steam turbine installations in the country, but not the first. Noticed by the trade publications, the *Street Railway Journal* offered, "The long delay in completing the Cleveland &

The Cleveland, Southwestern & Columbus Railway

Figure 3.12. Southwestern Carbarn and Station on North Grant Street, Wooster. (Courtesy of Northern Ohio Railway Museum)

Figure 3.13 Elyria Powerhouse at Carlisle featuring Westinghouse turbine generators. (Courtesy of Northern Ohio Railway Museum)

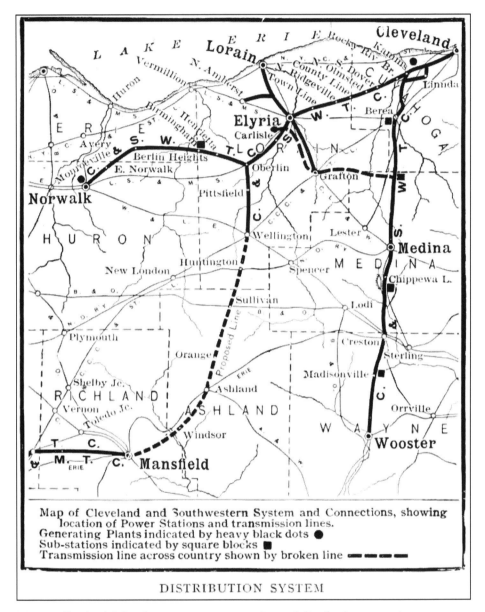

Map 3.3. Cleveland & Southwestern power generation and distribution system in 1904. The Madisonburg Sub-station is misidentified as Madisonville, while the Brunswick Sub-station was actually constructed about two miles south, as indicated on the map. (From "Improvements in the Power Equipment of the Cleveland & Southwestern System," *Street Railway Journal* 23, no. 5 [January 30, 1904]: 162.)

Southwestern turbines has robbed this plant of its true position, namely, that of being the first large plant in which turbines were definitely in operation in America, but there is little doubt that this was the first electric railway in this country to place contracts for large turbines."[34]

The Elyria power plant turbines, the first constructed in the Midwest, used reciprocating steam engines and hand-fired boilers to supply 25 cycle three-phase alternating current power for lines from Cleveland to Elyria and Oberlin and from Cleveland to Berea. As the railway lines were extended in the Western and Southern Divisions, substations were constructed in Birmingham, Brunswick, Chippewa Lake, and Madisonburg as depicted in map 3.3. A high-voltage transmission line was constructed between the Elyria power plant and the Brunswick Substation, also shown on the map. While a major investment and technological advancement for the time, in twenty years it became outmoded and prohibitively expensive to operate. By 1924, reports on behalf of F. H. Wilson for the Southwestern to District Court Judge D. C. Westenhaver, from consulting engineer W. E. Davis, Westinghouse Electric & Manufacturing, General Electric Company, and Superintendent G. H. Kelsey, all argued either that the plant be abandoned, and power be purchased elsewhere, or that at least $500,000 be spent to repair the plant to supply the 25 cycle power to the system. As engineers contended at the time, modern conditions demanded 60 cycle distribution for electric railways and lighting and power purposes, and that such investments in the obsolete plant were unwarranted, if not far more expensive than the alternative. As W. E. Davis explained, "Electrical power is being sold to railroad and other companies in this vicinity by the said large utilities (*Ohio Public Service Company and Cleveland Electric Illuminating Company*) at less than one-half of your generating cost today at Elyria, Ohio and I view of this fact it would appear that the operations of said Elyria plant one day longer than possible would be a commercial crime."[35]

In December 1922, F. W. Wilson filed a request with the court to allow the company to make the necessary improvements at a cost of $350,000 to switch over to the Ohio Public Service Company, thereby converting their equipment to 60 cycle alternating current, with an estimated annual savings of $100,000 for power.[36]

Regardless of its eventual obsolescence, for most of that interim period, management ensured that the electric power needed to effectively propel the rolling stock was dependable and economical. In addition, they took great pains to expand the power and light side of the business and to acquire municipal, corporate, and residential customers, with varying success.

Unfortunately, in towns like Oberlin and Fairview, the company met tough competition from other power companies, for example, Cleveland Electric Illuminating (CEI), which already possessed local franchises. In the decades that followed, the Southwestern's power business was far more successful in acquiring new electric customers in rural communities than in the growing suburbs of Cleveland. However, like the circumstances in Norwalk, their successes could be precarious and sometimes litigious. In 1916, after termination of a contract to provide power to the community, the Norwalk electorate voted 10 to 1 to establish municipal lighting to replace the Southwestern. The company retained ownership, operation, and control of the Norwalk Gas & Electric Company continuously from 1901 to 1925 and provided power to Norwalk customers throughout, despite a rocky relationship with local officials and unresolved disputes that eventually landed the successor power company—Ohio Electric Power Company—before state and federal district court judges.[37]

Although power sales did become an increasingly important part of the operating revenues for the Southwestern, the company after 1914 separately reported the power sales that were not associated with railway operations. Hence, figures reported to the Public Utilities Commission of Ohio for the Southwestern's railway operations did not reflect the income from electrical power generation and distribution. After 1916, the earliest published accounts that offer any indication of the Southwestern's success in boosting electrical power sales appeared for the year ending December 31, 1925, following the court-supervised foreclosure and reorganization of the entire system. However, table 3.2 reveals a detailed listing of the power and light properties that the foreclosed properties published and provides a wealth of information about their market penetration in the region, compared to the continued growth of residential power use within Ohio and nationwide.

The growth of electric power sales, especially for residential purposes, was a nationwide phenomenon, not just an isolated effort by the Southwestern system to generate more revenues and pay for traction-oriented

Table 3.2. Cleveland, Southwestern & Columbus Railway power and light customers by community, 1924

\multicolumn{6}{c	}{CS&C Railway power and light properties in 1924}
Section name	Description served	Primary mileage	Customers	Voltage	Distribution type
Elyria	City of Elyria, Village of LePorte	10	295	2,300	distribution
Grafton	Village of Grafton, Village of Belden	5	12	2300	distribution
Oberlin	Oberlin Water Works	0.5	1	22,000	transmission
Birmingham	Village of Birmingham, Village of Wakeman, Village of Kipton	5	4	2300	distribution
Milan	Village of Milan (Mutual Light & Power at Milan)	1	9	2300	distribution
Norwalk	City of Norwalk	16	561	2300	distribution
Penfield	Village of Penfield	12	190	2300	distribution
Rockport	Villages of Rockport, West Park, Brook Park, Fairview, North Olmsted, Dover, Ridgeville, and Rocky River	50	1093	2300	distribution

| \multicolumn{6}{c}{CS&C Railway power and light properties in 1924} |
Section name	Description served	Primary mileage	Customers	Voltage	Distribution type
Berea	Villages of Berea, Prospect	6	60	2300	distribution
Strongsville	Village of Strongsville	8	106	2300	distribution
Brunswick	Brunswick, Valley City, Hinckley, and Bennett's Corners	28	800	2300	distribution
Medina	Ohio Gas & Electric Company at Medina*	0.5	1	22,000	transmission
Chippewa	Village of Chippewa Lake	1	29	2300	distribution
Seville	Villages of Seville, Creston, and Sterling	18	350	2300	distribution
Leroy	Lodi Light & Power Company	0.02	389	22,000	transmission
West Salem	Villages of West Salem (West Salem Electrical Supply Company) and Homerville	4	21	2300	distribution
Nankin	Village of Nankin	6	82	2300	distribution
Crestline	Village of Crestline	16	970	2300	distribution
Madisonburg	Village of Madisonburg	2	32	2300	distribution

CS&C Railway power and light properties in 1924					
Section name	Description served	Primary mileage	Customers	Voltage	Distribution type
Sullivan	Sullivan Light and Power Company	0.02	231	2300	distribution
Spencer	Spencer Light & Power Company	NA	123	2300	distribution
Rittman	Village of Rittman	8	432	2300	distribution
	Total	197.04	5,791		
* Medina Village customers not reported separately.					

Source: "Legal Notices," *Cleveland Plain Dealer*, February 20, 1924, 22; "Decree of Foreclosure," District Court of the United States, for the Northern District of Ohio, Eastern Division, General Electric Company, et al., vs. The Cleveland, Southwestern and Columbus Railway Company, et al., *In Equity No. 690*, entered February 9, 1924, D. C. Westenhaver, Judge, Exhibits various; *Report of the Public Utilities Commission of Ohio*, 1924, 270.

capital investments. As table 3.3 shows, the first three decades of the twentieth century saw an explosive growth in electric demand and accelerated decline in consumer costs. While electric power output in 1930 compared to 1902 grew over nineteen-fold, and the consumer price index grew over two times, the price for residential electric power was cut to 37 percent of that twenty-eight years prior. The table also illustrates that the power output expanded greatly in the 1920s, while aggregate consumption of that power did not. Corporate reorganization and consolidation of the industry provided the capital and the financial incentives—speculative as well as strategic—to enable the growth in capacity and lowering of unit costs for electricity.

In the 1920s, electric utilities throughout the nation increasingly consolidated their business operations into pyramid-like structures. Large holding companies were formed at the top to own or control a number of other subsidiary companies. Financially, the holding company structure helped the utilities reduce their construction and operation costs by taking advantage of economies of scale while also serving to increase energy sales, lessen the financing costs, and reduce the costs of materials and equipment through bulk purchasing at discounted prices. These were largely unregulated corporate activities, which led to numerous waves of purchases of smaller entities and consolidation of the industry.

Table 3.3. Index of national electric output and pricing

1902 = 100						
Year	Electric power output	Total energy consumption	Price of electricity (residential)	All prices (GNP)	Consumer price index
1902	100	100	100	100	100
1907	237	159	65	101	113
1912	415	180	56	103	120
1917	728	225	46	202	160
1920	948	227	46	336	250
1925	1,418	240	45	183	219
1930	1,921	255	37	152	208

Source: Leonard S. Hyman, *America's Electric Utilities: Past, Present and Future*, 3rd ed. (Arlington, VA: Public Utilities Reports, 1988), 72.

As an industry advocate argued in 1926, "The holding company is the vehicle for unification and finance in the public utility field and it is the vehicle for effective management which, in the broad sense, is the key to success in business."[38] However, as these holding company structures became interstate phenomena, the abuses of monopolistic behaviors and the futility of state regulation prompted calls for federal action in the 1930s. By then, just sixteen national holding companies controlled more than 75 percent of the electricity generated in the United States. Frequent published reports of stock manipulation, excessive financial charges, price speculation, exorbitant profits and fees extracted from subsidiaries, deceptive accounting, distorted earnings reports, and control by non-utilities like banks prompted action. In 1935, Congress passed the Public Utility Holding Company Act, which served to reorganize the electric and gas industries and create new laws and regulations in response to these corporate abuses.[39]

Before those national movements of massive corporate consolidation were addressed, the power and light sales of the Southwestern responded to the aggregate demand for electricity and would eventually become separate from the parent entity. Eventually, the Southwestern power and light territory, contracts, equipment, and properties were absorbed into the growing corporate public utility companies of the region—first the Western Reserve Power & Light Company in 1925, which sold the properties to Keystone Water Works & Electric Corporation in 1928, and then eventually the behemoth of Ohio Edison Company in 1930, based in Akron.[40]

One of the most significant changes in the business of supplying electric power to commercial and residential customers was migration from 25 cycle to 60 cycle alternating current in the 1920s. In 1922, Southwestern management recognized the efficacy of making the investments needed to supply 60 cycle AC to its customers. The conversion also enabled Southwestern to purchase power more economically from other companies in the region. As the court-appointed receiver for the property, F. H. Wilson reported the following benefits for the conversion:

- Better service to commercial consumers, due to better lighting current and cheaper prices of equipment.
- Same frequency as other Power Companies in this territory, making it practicable to sell, buy or exchange power for mutual convenience.
- Permitted the company to bid at a much better advantage for new power and light business.[41]

F. H. Wilson estimated the cost ranged from $400,000 to $450,000 to change equipment at sub-stations and install one additional sub-station that was needed. He also included the costs of changing motors and other electrical appliances in contracted industrial services, installing automatic switching at three sub-stations and semi-automatic switching at eight sub-stations, and thereby eliminating labor costs. In total, the estimated annual savings would be $50,000 to $75,000 per year, not including the one-time revenue from salvaging from the Elyria power plant and reduced costs of purchased power. On September 21, 1923 the Southwestern abandoned the Elyria plant and the power coming out of Lorain was now using the 60 cycle standard.[42]

Table 3.4. Cleveland, Southwestern & Columbus Railway Company electrical power and light services

Reporting year	Operating revenues	Operating expenses	No. of customers
1910	$16,278	Not Reported	Not Reported
1911	$40,493	Not Reported	Not Reported
1912	$47,247	Not Reported	Not Reported
1913	$50,338	Not Reported	Not Reported
1914	$68,333	Not Reported	Not Reported
1916	$80,488	Not Reported	Not Reported
1921	$179,478	Not Reported	Not Reported
1925	$379,214	$270,219	4,862
1926	$390,788	$321,422	5,357
1927	$438,376	$346,969	5,894
1928*	$418,692	$334,716	Not Reported

Sources: Report of the Railroad Commission of Ohio, 1910, 1911; Report of the Public Service Commission of Ohio, 1912; Report of the Public Utilities Commission of Ohio, 1914, 1915, 1916, 1926–29; In Equity No. 690, F. H. Wilson, "Preliminary Report of Receiver," filed January 13, 1922, 5.
* *Note*: 1928 figures for 11 months only.

As presented in tables 3.2 and 3.4, the data suggest that the Cleveland, Southwestern & Columbus Railway's strategy to enter the power and light marketplace was marginally successful. The Southwestern interurban line served customers in seven counties south and southwest of Cleveland, but the population was often very sparse. In the large towns and villages on the west side of Cleveland, the company was unable to crack the public utility market of Cleveland Electric Illuminating. It also had strong competition in other cities on their route. Consider an electric light company of comparable size, such as the Wooster Electric Company in Wayne County. This public utility served 5,142 customers in 1928 and had operating revenues of $365,605 and operating expenses of $239,924. This lone power company in Wooster was doing almost as much business as the Southwestern system, which stretched from Cleveland to Bucyrus, Wooster, and Norwalk. The few cities and villages in which the Southwestern had established a presence—for example, Brunswick, Medina, West Salem, Sullivan, Burbank, and Nova—had potential for slight growth. In the 1920s, however, that market in those small communities remained relatively weak. Prime cities like Ashland, Lorain, and Mansfield would become centers for high-powered tension lines of the Ohio Public Service Corporation, under the Doharty Syndicate interests, that serviced the region in the mid-1920s, dwarfing the capacity of the Southwestern properties. Described as a "Super-Power electrical system," the growing corporate colossus would eventually absorb the Southwestern power and light properties during the consolidation of the industry and the growing demand for power in northern Ohio.[43]

Regardless, the Southwestern's push to electrify the rural communities along its route in the 1910s and 1920s did have a noteworthy salutary effect. The company ushered in an era of "rural electrification" for small communities in Ashland, Medina, northern Wayne, and southern Lorain Counties long before the New Deal program of the 1930s attempted the same task in many parts of rural Ohio.[44]

EDWARD F. SCHNEIDER: PROGRESSIVE MANAGER FOCUSED ON SAFETY

Edward F. Schneider took over the reins as general manager of the Southwestern system in 1910 and served in that capacity until it was reorganized in 1924. Elected as secretary of the company in 1903, he was listed as secretary and purchasing agent from 1906 to 1910. He was the longest-serving manager in the history of the Southwestern, but in prior histories of the system he is rarely recognized for his notable influence on the profit of the system, as well as on its safety record.

Amazing as it might seem, his background wasn't in banking or railroads. He was a wholesale druggist. Born in Toledo on October 1, 1862, he received a public school education and graduated from German Wallace College in Berea, Ohio, and the Philadelphia College of Pharmacy. For twelve years he worked for Beyton, Myers & Company wholesale druggists before joining up as an investor with the Pomeroy & Mandelbaum syndicate's consolidated Northeast Ohio railway interests, the Cleveland & Southwestern Traction Company. Apparently, he was drawn into the enterprise via family connections. His wife, Helen, and the wife of F. T. Pomeroy, Mary, were sisters and the daughters of Col. H. N. Whitbeck, a Civil War veteran and former Cuyahoga County treasurer. Family

> "No life has ever been a total failure, for no man has been wholly without virtue. Wisdom is knowing what to do. Skill is knowing how to do it and virtue is doing it."
>
> "Another Talk With Trainmen," E.F. Schneider, *Electric Traction Weekly*, Volume 7, Number 33, August 19, 1911, 956.

Figure 3.14.

connections in the industry were not uncommon, as traction syndicate-building practices and development of interlocking directorates often involved social, financial, and political connections. In addition, Edward was a Freemason and member of the Order of Knights of Pythias.[45]

Schneider became the leading nationwide promoter of the "Safety First" movement in the street railway industry. His pathway to that initiative started with the worst tragedy that the railway company ever experienced on Memorial Day evening in 1907, in which a special car rammed into the back of another car on Middle Avenue at 5th Street in Elyria. The motorman was entirely at fault, and the distraction of a dead dog on the tracks led to the death of eight people—seven immediately at impact—and seventeen limbs amputated. The local hospital was overwhelmed with victims of the crash. As Schneider later described it, "the hospital looking more like a slaughter house than anything else, and everywhere the white faces or the drawn countenance surrounded by the blanched faces and wistful eyes of the dear friends watching and praying for them, while the surgeons were fighting among themselves for cases, and in the background was that human hyena waiting for a chance to grab off a damage claim against the company."[46] Obviously, as most railway managers understood at the time of his presentation, he was not a fan of personal injury lawyers.

While relating the emotional energy that drove his crusade for safety, Schneider also clearly conveyed the intellectual, financial, and moral justification for his subsequent initiatives that saved lives and careers. His approach was comprehensive and methodical, typical of the scientifically based management principles of that age, but with a Victorian sense of morality added for good measure. As he stated clearly to his peers, "I believe in man; I believe in human agency and the human element; I have faith in human beings. I don't want a cigar sign or an automaton for a motorman or conductor, but what I do want is to have that human element, that human agency educated—not educated necessarily in the sense of book learning, but educated in his business so that he knows."[47]

Following the Memorial Day tragedy, Schneider took three days off and met with every trainmen, power-house and substation workers, carbarn men, line men, and track men throughout the entire 217 miles of trackage in the Southwestern system. To cover the entire line, it took six separate meetings. He talked in specifics about accidents and the need for safety first, but also apparently listened, took actions to resolve employee concerns, and didn't overuse employee penalties for disciplining mistakes. "He put their shortcomings up to them face to face, tells them what they might have led to, and shows them that the service of the road must be a moral education."[48] He continued the practice every three months for years afterward. The successful response was obvious and depicted in figure 3.16. As reported five years after the Elyria tragedy, the accident account for the road went from 6.35 percent of the gross revenues to 1.25 percent, and the line had only two lawsuits with accident claims over the period. Importantly, he listened to his motormen and understood that the safety lessons had to be also taught to the riding pubic, as well as school-age children.[49]

His often-repeated mantra was that the brief success in safety was not his victory, but that of the Southwestern employees. All of them. As he told his employees at a gathering in the Elyria carbarn in 1911:

> So, we on the Southwestern can say we have saved the lives and limbs of a great many people by not having the accidents. You men never will know, you men never will realize, you men never will appreciate, you men never will be able to contemplate the number of lives you have saved, the number of injuries you have avoided, the amount of pain, the amount of suffering, the amount of sorrow, you, by your own efforts, by your co-operation, by your foresight, by the goodness of your hearts have saved, and I feel prouder of you every day.[50]

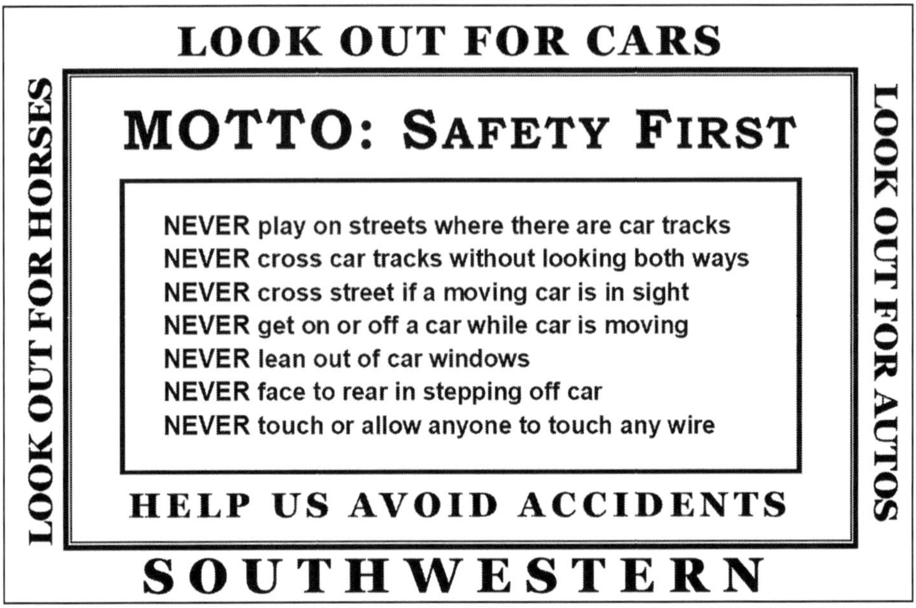

```
LOOK OUT FOR HORSES    LOOK OUT FOR CARS    LOOK OUT FOR AUTOS
                       MOTTO: SAFETY FIRST

                       NEVER play on streets where there are car tracks
                       NEVER cross car tracks without looking both ways
                       NEVER cross street if a moving car is in sight
                       NEVER get on or off a car while car is moving
                       NEVER lean out of car windows
                       NEVER face to rear in stepping off car
                       NEVER touch or allow anyone to touch any wire

                       HELP US AVOID ACCIDENTS
                       SOUTHWESTERN
```

Figure 3.15. Southwestern manager E. F. Schneider's "Safety First" blotter (adapted from *Electric Traction Weekly*, November 1912, 1080).

Dedicated to the proposition that the Southwestern was going to run without accidents, Schneider then took the effort along with his Superintendents to school age children. As he related, he and his team traveled to every public and parochial schoolhouse in every city and district and every grade from kindergarten to high school along the entire system. He made over 360 addresses and spoke to over 40,000 students in talks that lasted from ten to thirty minutes, depending. He handed out 50,000 nine-by-four-inch desk blotters reminding them of the proper behavior needed to avoid accidents. Reflected in figure 3.15 above, as the motto preached: Safety First.[51]

Measured success and promotion of his local advocacy at meetings of the Central Electric Railway Association gained Schneider some national notoriety within the interurban industry and some steam railroad lines. Presentation of his paper "The Prevention of Accidents" at a regional conference in early 1910 resulted in national distribution of copies to all electric traction lines, as well as its inclusion in two industry publications. Initially his paper was also distributed to motormen and other employees of electric railways throughout the country, but the efforts with public education stood out above the rest of the industry. His targeted educational approach with children through school classroom and multiclass presentations was replicated in other lines such as the Portland Railway, Light & Power Company in Oregon; Lehigh Valley Transit Company; Cincinnati Traction Company; and the United Railways & Electric Company of Baltimore. His efforts were even recognized by James O. Fagan, a renowned contributor to *The Atlantic* magazine and well-recognized critic of safety and claim management practices of the railroad industry. Fagan reportedly wrote E. F. Schneider in 1910, "I look upon your pamphlet as the most practical word on the subject from any quarter that I have yet come across." Notably, there were some favorable communications with the general solicitor of the Boston & Maine Railroad, as well.[52]

Schneider didn't stop with track safety, but also pursued the needs of his dairymen customers. In 1912, Schneider employed the services of a Cleveland veterinary surgeon and specialist to conduct an educational tour on the care of horses, sheep, and cattle. In the prior year the safety requirements of the milk inspection at Cleveland had become so rigid that hundreds of gallons of milk had been dumped into the sewers by the Cleveland health board. Of course, enlightened self-interest in preserving the milk business factored into the decision to underwrite the full costs of the lectures and tours, but education was once again the preferred means to benefit the farmers, the railway, and the public.[53]

As depicted in figure 3.16, despite the concerted efforts of the Southwestern management and employees, serious accidents would eventually return to plague the line. Increased activity reflected in more revenue passengers in any given period didn't necessarily equate to increased accidents for the year. Sometimes these were related to employee errors. For example, the head-on collision of two interurban cars in 1917 at the s-curve on the border of Strongsville and Brunswick, known as the Buckeye Pump Station, killed four and injured over thirty people, according to the *Medina County Gazette*. Medina County Coroner R. A. Brintnall declared that it was undoubtedly caused by the freight crew who forgot to take a siding to avoid the passenger car, despite having worked that run for seven years prior. Tragically, a few days later a line repair car crashed into a standing northbound Southwestern passenger car at Madisonburg near Wooster,

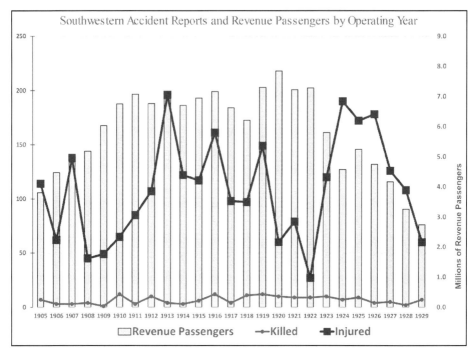

Figure 3.16. Southwestern, reported accidents by year. *Sources: Report of the Public Utilities Commission of Ohio, 1912–31; Report of the Railroad Commission of Ohio, 1906–11.* (Chart by author)

killing the motorman and injuring two others. In this case, a wooded curve and a thick haze were thought to be the cause of the fatal mishap.[54] As revenue passengers declined after 1922, the number of serious accidents unfortunately increased for a few years. Impacts with automobiles and trucks rather than collisions between interurban cars occurred more frequently, as increasing numbers of motorists flooded the roadways. Traffic congestion within some of the city tracks, as well as vehicles blocking and dodging the interurban cars at crossings, added to the tensions between the motormen and the traveling public. Of the system's trackage at its peak, about 85 percent of the line ran over private rights-of-way. That percentage decreased in the later 1920s as long sections of the line were abandoned, leaving a greater proportion of the line within public rights-of-way and therefore per revenue mile operating more prone to conflicts with ever-growing city automobile and truck traffic.[55]

FREIGHT IS GREAT

From the very beginning, the Pomeroy-Mandelbaum syndicate sought express traffic for both the Western and the Southern Divisions of the Southwestern system. The company stood as a charter member of the Electric Package Agency formed in 1898. Over time the Southern Division became the strongest of the two divisions for both express and freight traffic, while the Western Division's Elyria-Oberlin-Norwalk line suffered from competition with the LSE. The yearly statistical data reported for the entire system over the decades of operation must be examined carefully when making generalizations about the changes in revenues over time.

Before the Southwestern worked out a traffic agreement with the Cleveland Electric Railway Company in 1907, the Southwestern accounting methods classified some express services as "freight." The city of Cleveland prohibited electric railways from hauling freight over city lines, but did not restrict express shipments. After 1907 the Southwestern properly reclassified these express revenues to avoid the objections of Cleveland officials. Therefore, the early reporting of freight revenues prior to 1907 as illus-

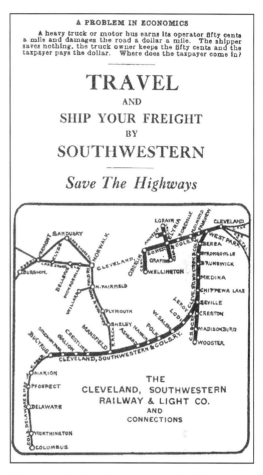

Figure 3.17. A sign of management battling the economics of competing truck lines—1925 Cleveland, Southwestern Railway & Light Co. timetable urging customers to "Save the Highways." (Author's collection)

trated in figure 3.18 should not be compared with the staggering growth of freight income starting in 1916.[56]

In May 1916, less-than-carload-lot (LCL) freight services were initiated between Cleveland, Bucyrus, and Wooster. According to M. A. Tatum, the superintendent of the Southwestern, the service was intended "to be of real benefit to merchants in central towns who desire to do quick business with Cleveland wholesale merchants." The company built new switches and sidings, and it purchased four new motor cars with attached trailers to accommodate the service. According to Tatum, Cleveland merchants had long sought approval of the extension of freight service. The merchants worked through the Manufacturers and Wholesale Merchants Board of Cleveland to have the service initiated.[57]

The Southwestern's interurban freight service became a direct competitor to the region's steam railroads for short-haul and express, but it also became a feeder to connecting systems' long-haul traffic. Although electric railways charged slightly higher rates than did steam railroads, they could transport goods short distances with greater speed. Perishable items such as fruits and vegetables suffered less damage during transport, resulting in lower costs to the merchant and thereby justifying the slightly higher unit rates for shipment. The Southwestern considered the transportation of milk and other express items such as bread and newspapers to be separate from its freight operations, since it had always provided these daily services.[58]

Figures 3.9 and 3.18 show that freight revenues increased substantially starting in 1916 and continued to grow as a percentage of the total operating revenues until 1929. This growth followed the inauguration of carload freight services on October 2, 1916, with five freight motors, six boxcars, and several flatcars. By 1926 the number of freight motors grew to thirty-four. Each division had daily scheduled freight trains operating in each direction, and interchange agreements were made with four steam railroads at eight different points along the Southwestern system.[59]

There appear to be at least two reasons for the newfound "friendly" relations with connecting steam railroads in 1916. First, federal control of the nation's steam railroads loomed over the heads of the industry throughout late 1916 to December 1917. The need to improve the flow of freight traffic and to convince the federal government that the steam rail-

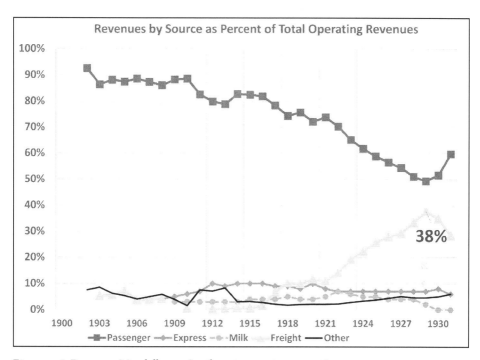

Figure 3.18. Pomeroy-Mandelbaum Southwestern system operating revenues as a percentage of total by source, 1900–1931. Companies include Cleveland, Elyria & Western Railway Company (1900–1902); Cleveland & Southwestern Traction Company (1903–6); Cleveland, Southwestern & Columbus Railway (1907–23); Cleveland, Southwestern Railway & Light Company (1924–31). "Other revenues" are the combined total of income from power sales (1902–14 only), switching revenues, property rental, and net amusement park earnings. (Chart by author)

road industry could do the job itself prompted Northeast Ohio railroads to be more cooperative with the Southwestern's interurban freight services than usual. Leaders in the railroad industry recognized by 1916 that problems encountered in meeting the demands of wartime shipments came primarily because the nation lacked an integrated system of transportation. The Army Appropriations Act of August 29, 1916, granted President Woodrow Wilson the authority to initiate federal control over the nation's railroads, but he did not exercise this option immediately.

The managers of the nation's railroads did their best to give President Wilson few reasons to use his newly established authority. Led by Baltimore & Ohio Railroad president Daniel Willard, the nation's largest steam railroads, as a special Committee on National Defense created by the American Railway Association, advocated from 1916 to 1917 an industry approach to improving coordinated operations. Operating from April 1917 to December 1917, the executive committee chosen by the presidents of fifty steam railroad companies moved to integrate the nation's rail system. "In scores of ways it took action looking to the more effective utilization of cars and railway facilities generally, the reduction in the number of trains, the reciprocal use by roads of each other's tracks and terminals."[60]

In the view of the Interstate Commerce Commission (ICC), the industry failed to accomplish this task. In a special report to Congress on December 1, 1917, the ICC called for the complete unification of the railroads in the country. On December 26, 1917, President Wilson chose to act on one of the ICC's recommendations by asserting government control over the railroads through the United States Railroad Administration (USRA), starting on January 1, 1918. Although the Southwestern did not fall under the control of the USRA, its efforts to expand interline freight shipments proved fruitful because of a national crisis in rail transport. This was probably not the intent of the steam railroads, but faced with the uncertainty of government control or even nationalization, doing business with interurbans would seem the lesser of two evils.[61]

A second reason for the Southwestern's friendly relationship with at least one major steam railroad can be explained by examining the board of directors of the Van Sweringen syndicate. Oris Paxton and Mantis James Van Sweringen joined with a syndicate of Cleveland area bankers in July 1916 to take control of the Nickel Plate Railroad. Among the Van Sweringen's syndicate members were representatives of both the Everett and Moore properties and the Pomeroy and Mandelbaum syndicate. F. E. Myers, chairman and president of the board of the Southwestern, and board member Otto Miller joined the Nickel Plate's directorate. Edward W. Moore and J. R. Nutt also became business associates in the Van Sweringen's railroad and Cleveland terminal project ventures. Through these board connections the negotiation of interline freight agreements with the Southwestern would be straightforward. Certainly, the interurban syndicate promoters could convincingly argue that they acted more as feeders to the connecting steam railroad system than as a competitor for traffic.[62]

First bolstered by steam railroad connections and a growing demand for freight services brought on by a wartime manufacturing boom, the Southwestern continued to increase its freight revenues over the ensuing decade. Revenues from freight services in 1916 amounted to $19,227 or 1.5 percent of the total operating income. By 1929 the CS&C made $364,635 or 37.8 percent of its total operating revenues from hauling freight. These figures remained strong until abandonment in 1931. A good part of the growth in less-than-carload freight traffic, even after World War I, came as a result of interoperational agreements with steam railroads and interurban lines alike, thereby giving the Southwestern the ability to move freight all the way to Indiana and Kentucky, as well as to Michigan and Pennsylvania.[63]

On April 1, 1922, the Southwestern joined with the Northern Ohio Traction & Light Company, Cleveland-Alliance and Mahoning Valley, Stark Electric, and Pennsylvania-Ohio Electric Company to initiate coordinated freight services in Northern Ohio. Within a year, the combine was joined by the Lake Shore Electric; the Columbus, Marion & Bucyrus; the Detroit United; the Cleveland, Painesville & Eastern; and the Columbus, Delaware & Marion Electric. The system also made arrangements with two major boat lines—between Cleveland, Detroit, and Buffalo—and scored a major coup by securing a contract with the Nickel Plate steam railroad which enabled freight delivery among all of the coordinating lines from northern Ohio to Buffalo, Detroit, Chicago, and other major manufacturing centers in the Midwest. As the publicity manager for the Northern Ohio Traction and Light Company boasted in the *Electric Traction* trade magazine, "Already this new freight system has brought relief to shippers along the lines of the allied companies and installed a 12-hour delivery service from these points to hundreds of cities and towns in Ohio, New York and Michigan."[64] Noting that the freight services for the NOT&L only required an additional investment not exceeding $50,000, the article reported outstanding improvement in yearly revenue—express business alone that previously totaled $20,000 monthly went up to $70,000 monthly for combined express and freight.[65]

The Southwestern made optimum use of its rolling stock and single-track mileage by scheduling freight and express shipments during off-peak hours. Much of these cargoes moved nightly on trains over the Southern Division destined for Columbus through a connection with the

Columbus, Delaware & Marion Railway at Bucyrus. In this way the demands on the system's electric power plants for hauling freight did not interfere with peak rush-hour demands for passenger traffic. This leveled out the electrical power demand curve over a twenty-four-hour period and reduced the total capital and unit operating costs of the line.

FREIGHT WAS GREAT, BUT NOT ENOUGH

During most of its life, the bulk of the Southwestern's revenues came from passenger fares and not freight revenues. It was not until 1929 that passenger revenues dipped below 50 percent of the railway's total operating revenues. As figure 3.18 illustrates, the percentage of total revenues produced by the passenger service dropped steadily from 92.5 percent in 1902 to 49.3 percent in 1929. The data show that the decline of the passenger revenues was steady, even dramatic, and that an increasing amount of the operating revenues came from freight, mail, and express operations. After World War I this was a common trend throughout the industry, for the greatest cause of this decrease in ridership was the rapid adoption of automobiles and competing bus lines.

As a result of declining ridership in the 1920s, most interurban managers expanded their short-haul freight services to compensate for the falling passenger revenues. The physical plant required little upgrading or expansion to accommodate the services, and additional investment was minimal. The Southwestern was clearly ahead of the industry in taking this approach to the problem in 1916, when the number of passengers and passenger revenues were still growing, as illustrated in figures 3.9 and 3.18.

Although the Southwestern management provided ample support to its freight services, efforts in the 1920s were primarily targeted in a different direction. Southwestern management sought to recapture the declining ridership revenues, but they were fighting a losing battle against the growing use of the automobile and the seemingly uncontrollable expenses of operating the electric railway line.

The Southwestern faced increasing costs during and after World War I, which were part of a national trend. The rises in wages for street and electric railway employees were especially dramatic. For example, nationally the wages per hour in May 1925 were equal to 222 percent of the average maximum hourly wage before World War I. The Southwestern felt a similar increase, as shown in figure 3.20. The average annual wage or salary paid

The Cleveland, Southwestern & Columbus Railway

Figure 3.19. Southwestern Car No. 214, built by Cincinnati Car Company, purchased in 1924, and refurbished for the Western Division parlor service. (Courtesy of Northern Ohio Railway Museum)

per Southwestern employee grew from $617 in 1912 to $907 in 1917 and to $1,515 in 1922. In the five-year period after 1912, wages grew by 47 percent, and in the ten-year period by 146 percent. From a business management standpoint, increases in average total wages and salaries per employee are acceptable provided there is a similar increase in productivity corresponding to increased operating revenues. In other words, if the productivity or revenue generated per employee increases in a similar fashion, then such increases in salaries and wages are acceptable and sometimes preferred.

The best way to measure this relationship is to calculate the percentage of total operating revenues made up by the wages and salaries. As shown in figure 3.20, there existed from 1912 to 1923 a cyclical trend upward in the percent of operating revenues taken out in wage and salary payments. As far as the management of the Southwestern was concerned, there was a cyclical decline in productivity. The line made less and less money for more and more wages. In spite of a drastic decline in operating revenues in 1924, there was a significant improvement in productivity because of being forced into receivership by creditors and reorganization of the company.

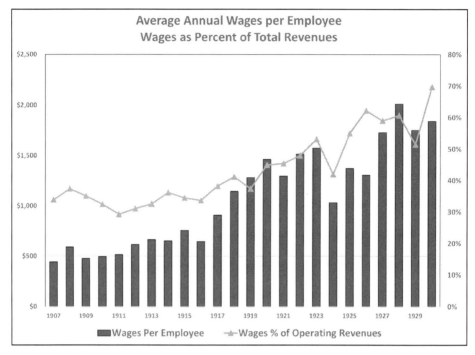

Figure 3.20. Southwestern average annual wages per employee and wages as percent of total operating revenues (1907–31). Companies involved: Cleveland, Southwestern & Columbus Railway (1907–23), and Cleveland, Southwestern Railway & Light Company (1924–31). (Chart by author)

The number of employees dropped from 503 in 1923 to 450 a year later, and the total wages paid decreased from $791,551 to $463,588.[66]

Concurrent with this rise in wages, material costs—the other major component of an electric railway's operating expenses—rose sharply from 1915 to 1921 and afterward decreased only slightly. Although no operating data exist indicating what specific material items dramatically increased in cost during the period for the Southwestern, they were probably much like those for comparable lines in the region. The Stark Electric Railroad, for instance, saw from 1917 to 1918 an increase of 45 percent in the unit cost of its coal, a major component in the line's operating costs. By 1919 the cost per ton of hard coal increased another 29 percent over the 1918 price. Other items typically used in great quantities on all electric railways included trolley wire, chestnut poles, rail bonds, and armature rewinding wire. From 1919 to 1920 these items increased per unit cost by 61 percent, 28 percent, 18 percent, and 44 percent, respectively. The Southwestern presumably would have had to pay for similar increases in materials needed to operate the interurban line. Much of the increased cost of materials came from wartime inflation, which abated slightly following the end of the conflict. However, these small decreases were not enough to offset the continuing growth of wage costs.[67]

Late in the line's boom period, the rising costs of operating the Southwestern outpaced the growth of revenues. Once gross revenues started to decline after 1920, the margin between the two grew even slimmer. Over the next several years it went through receivership and reorganization because of a declining ridership and rising costs. A 51 percent increase in operating expenses, as compared to only a 21 percent increase in revenues, pushed the Southwestern into the red in 1917 and 1918. Operating costs in the subsequent years did not lessen, and further losses in ridership revenues in 1921 and 1922 forced the Southwestern into receivership in the later year. Fred T. Pomeroy took over once again as president in 1922, but Frank H. Wilson, Southwestern's general manager since 1921, continued to run railway operations. The Southwestern failed to pay even its bond interest in 1923, and a major creditor, General Electric Company, forced foreclosure in early 1924. Bouncing back, the company reorganized under the name of the Cleveland and Southwestern Railway and Light Company.[68]

Given new life, the Southwestern made dramatic efforts to increase ridership. Immediately, the company invested in a fleet of twelve lightweight Cincinnati-built cars designed both to reduce labor and power costs and to provide a smooth ride over an ever roughening roadbed. Part of the financing for the cars came from $97,500 in car trust bonds; that is, bonds that are secured by a lien on rolling stock. In July of 1924, the number of cars running from Berea to Kamm's Corners on Cleveland's city limits increased while the price of ticket books for Bereans decreased to the lowest rate in five years.[69]

Aside from these actions to increase revenues, management attempted several cost-cutting measures. It abandoned an unprofitable portion of the Western Division from Oberlin to Norwalk and provided for a feeder bus service to its railway operations. In later years, as passenger traffic further declined, other unprofitable sections were similarly closed, while

Figure 3.21. Southwestern bus in Elyria around 1925. (Courtesy of Northern Ohio Railway Museum)

the Southwestern feeder bus service would be expanded to include more and more communities. The result was that in 1923 the company generated a $209,036 profit. It was the last time in its corporate life that the Southwestern made money, and it was principally due to increased gross revenues, rather than decreased operating expenses. As illustrated in figures 3.9 and 3.18, rising operating expenses in the 1920s became an unrelenting problem for the interurban line. It was one problem that was well outside the realm of the interurban manager's immediate control.[70]

Nationally, one principal reason for the significant rise in wage costs and minimal decrease in material costs was the rapid industrial and commercial growth that occurred after World War I. Demand for labor increased as industries expanded, and numbers of immigrants decreased starting in 1922. This resulted in a scarcity of labor and an increase in general wage levels that were required to attract and retain personnel. As American industries increased their output, productivity of each worker also rose because of economies of scale and new labor-saving equipment.

Figure 3.22. *Cleveland Plain Dealer* advertisement promoting a new parlor car service from Cleveland to Galion. (*Cleveland Plain Dealer*, April 10, 1925, 7; adapted by author)

From 1917 onward, higher costs of living and the organization of labor also created additional pressure for escalating wages. Much of the interurban industry was unable to match the swelling worker productivity, and therefore they were pressured into increasing fares to keep up with rising costs.

The Southwestern's labor force, unionized since 1904, contributed to increasing financial stress on the Southwestern's bottom line. The company was not only unable to improve worker productivity markedly in the 1920s, it actually was forced to deal with a decline. With fixed costs, decreasing ridership normally requires fare increases, but such actions hasten the decline in the number of passengers. With irrepressible rising costs, the interurban was pinched between the "rock" of higher costs and the "hard place" of ridership decline. In response, the Southwestern's managers attempted a mixture of cost-cutting methods and innovative marketing techniques to minimize their costs and boost income from passenger fares. As seen in 1923, they did have some modest, but only temporary, success.[71]

After recurring losses in 1924 and 1925, the Southwestern management intensified efforts to boost passenger ridership. In 1926 and 1927 it increased the number of parlor cars along the Southern Division, and the immediate results looked relatively promising, building on its new parlor

Figure 3.23. Introduced in 1910 as a semi-parlor car and used for special services, such as chartering for parties, railway officials, and dignitaries, CS&C Car No. 200 Alvesta was rebuilt in 1927. In 1910, CS&C had an agreement with Lake Shore Electric Railway so that chartered cars could be through-routed over both roads at a charge of 30 cents per car-mile. (Courtesy of Northern Ohio Railway Museum)

car services introduced in 1925. Parlor cars provided passengers with far more comfortable and spacious accommodations than the standard interurban car, as well as reservations in advance for specific seating preferences (see fig. 3.23). Patterned after the steam railroad's Pullman cars, the parlor cars had padded and leather-covered seats in a single file on each side of the aisle.

The first year of parlor car operation attracted 32,000 riders, who paid $11,500 in excess fares to ride them. In addition, on March 31, 1927, the Southwestern had a much-publicized "Dress-Up" day for all its employees. Complementing the many newly reupholstered seats and refurbished cars, redesigned uniforms for all employees featured dark-gray whipcord and gilded buttons.[72]

Figure 3.24. CS&C Car No. 200 Alvesta in Elyria with a group of businessmen. (Courtesy of Northern Ohio Railway Museum)

In a similar effort to attract riders and decrease costs, all Southwestern cars were painted orange. Thus the company abandoned the hallmark green cars that had characterized the railway since the start of the century. The increased visibility of the orange cars was an attempt to limit the growing number and associated cost of collisions with automobiles. As demonstrated in figure 3.26, the three highest annual accident rates per million revenue passengers on the Southwestern system occurred in the three years prior. By 1927 severe accidents occurred monthly on the busier sections of the railroad in Elyria and Lorain. In such mishaps, Southwestern cars and passengers fared much better than the automobiles and their occupants. This resulted in numerous high damage claims for the loss of lives and limbs.[73]

In their efforts to save their company, the management of the Southwestern did not stop at catering to the affluent first-class ridership, issuing snappy uniforms to employees, and overhauling color schemes. They also took measures to improve the efficiency of the operation as well as the quality of the ride. The company replaced and reballasted sixty miles of track in 1927 for a much-needed smoother ride and a reduction of the elec-

Figure 3.25. Pictured running at Kamm's Corners, CS&C Car No. 212, built in 1924 by Cincinnati Car Company, was painted orange and refurbished for safety and comfort in the Western Division parlor service. (Courtesy of Northern Ohio Railway Museum)

trical current loss from deteriorated grounding tie joints. In the same year, the Southwestern strung over 100 miles of electrically efficient aluminum high-tension wire, rebuilt several bridges, solicited and received free newspaper publicity, and gave agents commissions on improved ticket sales.[74] The company rewarded employees for good performance and used mass-marketing techniques to bring the people into the cars. It seems that almost every conceivable cost item was examined and reduced if possible. But the management did not stop there. Driven by necessity, they went beyond the ordinary and offered new and unusual services to their customers.

Southwestern president F. H. Wilson initiated what would be his company's last bold offensive to revitalize ridership. On May 5, 1928, the Southwestern became the first railroad in the United States to offer a through-coordinated rail-plane service. Taking advantage of a deal with the Detroit-based Stout Air Services, Southwestern passengers could

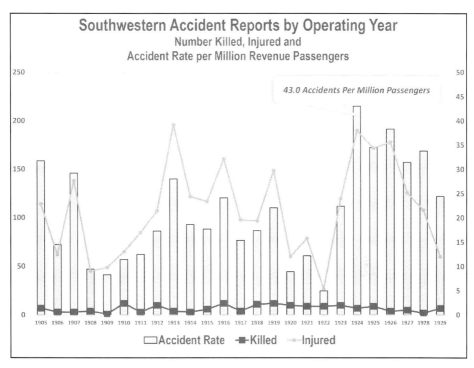

Figure 3.26. Southwestern accident reports by operating year, showing a peaking of the accident rate and number of people reported killed or injured on the Southwestern system in the 1920s. (Chart by author)

purchase an airplane ticket to Detroit at any one of ten major Southwestern terminals. Stout Air Service provided two flights daily to the Michigan city from the Cleveland Airport; they took 100 minutes to complete. How much of the Cleveland–Detroit air passenger traffic can be attributed solely to the Southwestern connection cannot be confirmed, but undoubtedly the interurban facilitated the public's use of this truly twentieth-century mode of transportation. In addition, the Southwestern sold excursion tickets for a fifty-mile sightseeing flight above Cleveland in a Ford Tri-Motor.[75]

In spite of these innovations, the company's total gross revenues for the year increased only around $7,300, while its operating costs rose by approximately $12,200. The relationship between revenues and costs continued to worsen over the subsequent years. Management then took more drastic measures, which reduced its income and quickened the pace of its demise, but this came as the result of a change in company ownership.[76]

Although Southwestern's management continued to face declining revenues and proportionally increasing costs, its high asset value and low stock price made it particularly attractive to a takeover. Efforts to increase ridership seemed futile; 1928 figures showed one million fewer riders on the interurban system than in 1927—a decrease of 22 percent. In mid-1928 the Atlantic Public Utilities, Inc., a Boston-based holding company, purchased 80 percent of the capital and common stock of the Southwestern's holding company, the Cleveland & Southwestern Company. Management of the Southwestern properties came under the control of Chase & Gilbert, Inc., of Boston, the principal syndicate behind Atlantic Public Utilities (APU), although F. H. Wilson stayed on as president and general manager of the interurban. Under the direction of the APU holding company, the Southwestern closed nonprofitable portions of the electric line, substituted marginally profitable Southwestern bus services for some lines, and sold assets to meet operating expenses. The APU, typical of other holding companies, took steps to separate the failing interurban railway from its successful properties, the electric power and light operations. As mentioned earlier, in November 1928 the Southwestern sold its power and light properties to its own subsidiary, Western Reserve Power & Light Company, which in turn became the property of another APU subsidiary, the Keystone Water Works & Electric Corporation, on December 1, 1928.[77]

The sale of the power and light properties benefited the holding company, but not the Southwestern. Their sale in November 1928 for $2,087,165 was just enough to retire the line's bonded debts dating back to 1895. Even with this sale, the company's books showed a deficit of $113,052 for the year, the largest to date. It was also the first year that operating expenses exceeded total gross revenues, a sign that the end was near. Divested of the only profitable segment of its operations, the Southwestern struggled along until October 1929, when it once again fell into receivership. That year it posted a loss of $107,169. The merciful death blow came when Guardian Trust Company of Cleveland filed a foreclosure suit on $2 million worth of unpaid bonds. The Southwestern finally ceased operations in January 1931, putting 250 people out of work.[78]

The Southwestern's thirty-six-year lifespan had a significant impact upon the people, towns, and cities of northern Ohio. The greatest beneficiaries of the road were the farmers and, to a lesser degree, town merchants. The character of rural life in the region changed dramatically during the first three decades of the twentieth century. The Southwestern played a major part in bringing the benefits of an increasingly urban and industrialized society to the doorstep of the farmer and his local community. Although not completely or easily measured, its impact on rural Ohio is unmistakable.

4

Communities of the Southwestern

AGRICULTURE

THE STORY OF the Cleveland, Southwestern & Columbus Railway (Southwestern) illustrates an appreciable link between the city and the country. The company's triumphs and trials paralleled those of its sister interurbans, but they also reflected the Southwestern's economic and social impact on a segment of society that was soon to be in descendancy: farmers. From 1900 to 1920 Ohio's farmers enjoyed a period of unparalleled prosperity and a relative pattern of stability. But in the years that followed World War I the fortunes of Ohio agriculture joined the roller-coaster pattern of America's agriculture as a whole. Seemingly, the affluence and decline of the Southwestern corresponded with the fluctuating fortunes of the farming communities it served.

According to the US Bureau of the Census, America's population passed the threshold of urbanization in 1920. From that year onward, more than one-half of the American people lived in urban communities. America, the country that was once proud of its homesteads, farms, and agrarian values, became an increasingly urbanized society as the twentieth century progressed.[1]

Ohio was in the forefront of this transition. In 1900, Ohio's urban population was 48 percent of the state total; this rose to 68 percent in just thirty years. During that same period, Cleveland grew from a city of 380,000 to an urban center of great economic power with 900,000 resi-

Communities of the Southwestern

Figure 4.1. Pictured at the West Salem Substation and used for limited service between Cleveland, Ashland, and Mansfield at West Salem Station, CS&C Car No. 135 was built in 1906 by the Niles Car & Manufacturing Company, based in Niles, Ohio, and promoted as "The Electric Pullmans." (Courtesy of Northern Ohio Railway Museum)

dents. These increasing numbers of urbanites brought about significant changes throughout the state, well outside their immediate communities. The city dwellers required increasing amounts of agricultural products from the hinterlands, while the farmers demanded more manufactured goods from the cities. For many Northeast Ohio rural communities, interurbans were a catalyst for changes within and upon these social and economic circumstances. With increased prosperity attributable to urban food demands, town residents took special excursions to see the opera or baseball games in Cleveland, while their children attended the colleges in Ashland, Berea, Cleveland, Oberlin, or Wooster.[2]

Ohio's interurbans played significant but unheralded roles in the transition from a rural to an urban state. In particular, the Southwestern was one of the supporting actors in that drama. It helped feed the growing population of Cleveland and contributed to the expansion of businesses and the decline in population density at its center. More importantly for Ohioans along its routes, it provided an essential link between the traditions of nineteenth-century rural parochialism and twentieth-century metropolitanism.

The region serviced by the Southwestern was dotted with small farming communities, as well as a considerable number of lightly industrialized centers such as Ashland, Medina, Elyria, Lorain, Norwalk, and Mansfield. The Southwestern also provided transportation to four college towns—Ashland, Berea, Oberlin, and Wooster—and to three major amusement parks—Chippewa Lake Park, Puritas Springs, and Seccaium Park—and a few minor ones. Consequently, this electric marvel afforded the farmers and villagers ready and dependable access to institutions of higher education, thrilling entertainment, and great numbers of manufactured goods and services.[3]

Even before the growth of the Southwestern tracks out of Cleveland, the earliest interurban systems benefited the milk production of the region. In 1901, the *Street Railway Journal* reported that nearly 10,000 gallons of milk a day were being transported into Cleveland via the various lines. The Northern Ohio Traction line reportedly averaged 2,500 gallons daily, while the Cleveland & Eastern Railway brought in nearly 3,000 gallons on special cars. The expansion of the Southwestern system west and southwest of Cleveland added dramatically to this "milkshed."[4]

One of the Southwestern's most profound contributions was to the continued growth of the region's dairy industry. In 1906, the Southwestern system was hauling only 800 cans of milk a day and earned about $20,000 in gross revenues for the year. However, with the growth of business over time, in 1915 the Southwestern carried 20,000 gallons of milk daily to Cleveland dairies, compared to the Eastern Ohio Traction Company's 5,000 to 6,000 gallons. The Southwestern alone transported almost one-half the amount consumed daily by the city dwellers. E. F. Schneider, general manager of the Southwestern, reported in 1919 to the Federal Electric Railways Commission that it was hauling 50,000 ten-gallon milk cans per month into Cleveland, for an average distance of twenty-five miles. In addition, the Green Line also hauled into Cleveland approximately 105,000 dozen eggs and 40,000 pounds of butter monthly. "We undoubtedly could increase the business in dairy and farm products," added Schneider, "if we were not limited in equipment, which at the present time we are unable to procure on account of limitation of our finances."[5]

The Medina County Creamery Company (MCCC) located in Cleveland became one of the beneficiaries of the interurbans radiating from the city. Started by a group of businessmen and farmers in the office of Medina attorney Frank Heath in December 1905, it received much of the milk carried by the Southwestern and the other interurbans. The initial directors of the company included J. K. Arnold, J. B. Stouffer, W. W. Watson, George Boult, and Z. H. Boult. By the mid-1910s the creamery claimed to be the largest manufacturer and wholesaler of creamery products in the city. It started with only 250 farmer suppliers in the fall of 1905 and in just three years acquired nearly 1,500 more. In 1911 alone, the firm paid Medina County dairymen $300,000 for cream and $20,000 for eggs. By 1912 more than 3,500 farmers supplied their milk over 105 different interurban cream routes scattered throughout the surrounding thirteen counties to the MCCC. For this one creamery, that was a supplier growth rate of over 1,300 percent in a little less than seven years! The speed and the frequency of the interurban service enabled the tremendous growth of this particular business and played a major part in furthering the economic prosperity for the farmers of the region. In 1920, the MCCC was bought out by the Fairmont Creamery Company of Omaha, Nebraska, the largest creamery company in the nation. A. E. Stouffer, formerly of Medina, remained the manager of the Cleveland plant for a few years before embarking on a career path that led to the founding of world-famous Stouffer Food Company.[6]

The growth of the regional dairy industry came from increasing urban demand and the farmers' quick recognition of the advantages in serving those markets. Headlines of an April 4, 1906, edition of the *Wooster County Democrat* read "FARMERS SHOULD SPECIALIZE." It advised, "Farmers who wish to succeed should make a specialty of some particular line suited to their farms and locations as to markets." Farmers along the Southwestern route heeded the message because it made sound economic sense. Generally, the costs of transportation are inversely associated with the degree of agricultural specialization and trade. The lower the transportation costs the greater the degree of specialization. The experience of the farmers along the Green Line supported the validity of this agricultural location theory.[7]

Aided by access to speedy transportation and motivated by increasing demand for dairy products from the growing urban centers, farmers along the interurban line purchased more dairy cattle, built larger barns,

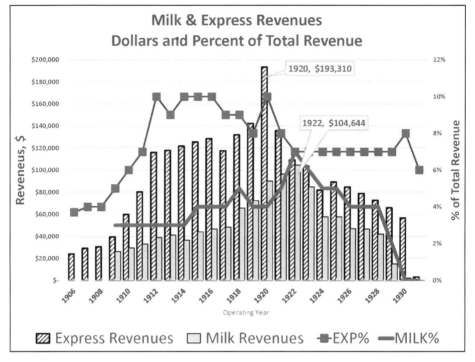

Figure 4.2. Southwestern operating revenues from transportation of milk and express and percentage of total operating revenues, 1907–31. Companies involved: Cleveland, Southwestern & Columbus Railway (1907–23) and Cleveland, Southwestern Railway & Light Company (1924–31). (Chart by author)

and expanded their milk production capabilities. Many farmers along the Southwestern formed associations to promote their newly found investments. For example, in February 1913 the Medina County Dairymen's Association began with twenty charter members; it grew to over 200 members by 1916.[8]

The temporary chairman at the first meeting of the association, Farnum H. Gibbs, was one of the many farmers who could attribute his newfound prosperity to the Southwestern. The Green Line crossed over Gibbs's land in Brunswick and built a substation just a few hundred feet from his home in 1902. Seizing on the opportunity, he opened a store next door to the station and expanded his dairy herd. By March 1916, Gibbs became treasurer of the Northern Ohio Milk Producer's Association. In just a few years, he became a prominent local dairyman and often boasted of the honors received by his Holstein and Jersey cattle at the local county fairs. As it did for Farnum Gibbs, the Southwestern provided other farmers opportunities to specialize and gave them pride in their enterprises and profitability that was long overdue.[9]

For the communities it touched, the Southwestern also played a significant role in changing the character of their small-town businesses. Merchants in towns like Oberlin and Medina at first expressed fears that the increased accessibility of larger and more competitively priced stores in the cities would destroy them. In Wooster, others complained that the trolley line would interfere with horse traffic patterns, making it unsafe for farmers to drive their teams into town. But jeers turned to cheers as other merchants soon lobbied to have the interurban routes pass in front of their particular establishments.[10]

AMUSEMENT PARKS

According to historians Dale Samuelson and Wendy Yegoiants, "With the turn of the twentieth century, the stage was set for the rapid national spread of amusement parks. Americans were ready to play, and there were people and machines ready to help them. There were three distinct influences on this growth: the natural draw of the seashore; electric railway companies' desire for weekend revenue; and the ability and willingness to quickly replicate a proven process."[11] While many parts of the country, like Ohio, do not have ocean shores to foster the emergence of amusement parks in their areas, they do have prominent water features like rivers, falls, and lakes that drew crowds of people seeking scenic beauty and natural comforts. As in much of the rest of the country, Ohio electric railways and resorts went hand in glove into the twentieth century.

In 1908, proprietors and managers of some major outdoor parks formed the National Amusement Park Association. The initial board of directors was headed by James R. Pratt, United Railways & Electric Company of Baltimore, Maryland, and populated by representatives of many such parks that had ownership and management ties to trolley syndicates—like Kennywood Park near Pittsburgh, Pennsylvania; Idlewood Park, Richmond, Virginia; White City, Trenton, New Jersey; and Lagoon Park, Cincinnati, Ohio. As the National Amusement Park Association stated in the *Street Railway Journal*, "it is fundamentally true that, while the street railways could live without the parks, upon the other hand the very existence of the parks depends upon the street railways." At the time the association posited that out-of-door parks were a necessity of American life, consisting of hundreds of such parks scattered throughout the country and investments totaling over $180 million in capital. In Ohio, the symbiotic relationship between electric railways and established as well as emerging parks was even more evident.[12]

Like the other interurban lines in Northeast Ohio, the Southwestern benefited from recreation and amusement parks along its lines to boost ridership, especially on weekends and holidays. During its lifetime, the Green Line owned two parks: Puritas Springs in Cleveland and Seccaium Park between Galion and Bucyrus. It also served parks over which it had no direct financial control: Fleming's Falls between Ashland and Mansfield, Luna Park in Mansfield, and Chippewa Lake Park near Medina. The two largest parks on the CS&C line were Puritas Springs and Chippewa Lake Park.[13]

Luna Park in Mansfield

Amusement parks historian David Francis characterizes the two Luna Parks in Ohio that emulated Thompson's Coney Island original as similar but unique in character and appearance. While Cleveland's Luna Park was the largest of the derivative parks, the Mansfield facility was the world's smallest of Luna Parks and least like the original, according to Francis. Casino Park, which adjoined Luna Park, provided an outdoor amphitheater venue for a series of popular summer performances, while Luna Park provided a pavilion called the White Maple Dance Hall, roller coaster, swings and a swimming pool, as well as small-craft boating. As reported in the *Mansfield News* in 1911, regarding Luna Park, "Here, the hand of man, rather than the hand of nature, was more instrumental in the making." Continuing the review of all the parks in the Mansfield area, "Luna park is meant for pleasure and sociability, not for reverie or nature worship."[14]

Fleming(s) Falls

Lying in Mifflin Township a mile south of Windsor, between Ashland Village and Mansfield, Stop 83 on the Cleveland, Southwestern & Colum-

Communities of the Southwestern

Figure 4.3. Luna Park, Mansfield. (Courtesy of Dennis Lamont Collection)

bus line included Fleming Falls. Sometimes referred to as Flemings Falls, at its prime it comprised a hotel, dancing pavilion, baseball grounds, and scenic falls. Advertised as a "nice place for Sunday School, Church and family picnics," it provided only a comparatively modest draw for the Southwestern. At the confluence of two streams above the falls, John Fleming built a grist mill using the waterfall to run his operations for a number of years, but it was destroyed by a flood. Purchased in 1911 by a young German immigrant, Paul Maurim, it was promoted as "The Beauty Spot of Ohio," with hotel accommodations that provided "homestyle dinners and suppers" along with concerts, dancing, and restful scenery. Eventually it was acquired by the Boy Scouts of America and then sold in 1940 to the Lutheran Church and operated as Camp Mowana.[15]

Seccaium Park

In 1899, W. E. Haycox, general manager and promotor of the Central Ohio Traction between Bucyrus and Galion, purchased fifty-seven acres of pastureland being used for the Crawford County Home and developed a resort amusement park to capture traffic between the two cities. Haycox

Figure 4.4. Postcard of Flemings Falls Resort, circa 1913. (Courtesy of Dennis Lamont Collection)

reportedly named the park after hearing a story about a Native American village called Seccaium. According to early pioneer history of the area, the village was prosperous and peaceful, but the occupants were murdered and plundered by another unfriendly tribe sometime before 1700 CE. Benefiting from being the portage between the Olentangy and Sandusky Rivers, it was a central place of contact between northern and southern Indigenous peoples for exchange of furs and wares, as well as for holding conclaves and powwows. Further explaining its importance to Ohio history, "On a prominent rise in the park stands a monument erected by the Historical Society, to commemorate and mark the battle ground where Colonel Crawford's men in 1782 fought their last battle with the Indians in Crawford's campaign against the Sandusky tribe. It was in this campaign that Colonel Crawford, after whom the county is named, was captured and burned at the stake."[16]

For a number of years the company operated the park that included a summer theater, dance halls, refreshment pavilion, bowling alleys, and boating in a man-made lagoon adjoining the Olentangy River. Eventually, the Southwestern retained ownership but leased the property out to varying individuals who intermittently attempted to revive the venue. The company's interest in the operation waned over time. According to

Communities of the Southwestern

Figure 4.5. Photo of Crawford County Pioneer Picnic excursion in 1906, via Southwestern car to Seccaium Park. (Courtesy of Northern Ohio Railway Museum)

various newspaper accounts, the Southwestern refused to provide a steady investment or maintenance of the property other than the dance hall and dining room, despite its early popularity. At one time, a tree fell on the bandstand, and the performing arts casino needed to close because of storm damage. The manager was forced to repair and reconstruct the structure over several seasons.[17]

In 1916, Bucyrus businessman Ralph A. Jolly leased and operated Seccaium Park for the Southwestern quite successfully for about decade and then purchased it outright for $6,000. Combined with the talents of his bandleader brother, Carl, the Jolly brothers expanded the facilities for dance and music that drew audiences from all over to hear performers like Jelly Roll Morton, Fletcher Henderson, Jean Goldkette, and Guy Lombardo. It was promoted as the place to dance—"A Fun Place to Go, Just for Fun." In addition, the park featured forty amusement rides, including a Ferris wheel, a roller coaster purchased from Luna Park in Cleveland called Pippin, Dodgem cars, a miniature railroad, and one of the first large concrete pools—fed by water from the Olentangy River. Measuring 175 by 85 feet and holding 660,000 gallons of water, the artificial pool opened on July 4, 1922, and was promoted as the largest concrete pool in Ohio, if

Figure 4.6. Puritas Junction to the six-mile loop connecting Southwestern-owned Puritas Springs Park. (Courtesy of Northern Ohio Railway Museum)

not the Midwest, capable of accommodating 1,200 bathers at once. The pool was drained, scrubbed down, and refilled every Sunday, and fresh water flowed in at a rate of 550 gallons per minute, helping keep the pool water clean and refreshed, and conditions sanitary.[18]

Puritas Springs

The Puritas Springs Park was a popular amusement park on the west side of Cleveland for sixty years, outlasting the interurban line that promoted it by nearly three decades. The park especially catered to the urban working classes of Cleveland city. In January 1898, the Pomeroy-Mandelbaum syndicate, under the Cleveland, Berea, Elyria & Oberlin Railway, through the Cleveland Trust Company issued an additional $125,000 in bonds to construct a six-mile branch line into the park. Owned by the Southwestern's subsidiary, Puritas Mineral Spring Company, from 1898 to 1915, the eighty-acre resort was described in advertisements in terms that especially appealed to the Cleveland city market. The park was located "seven miles southwest of Cleveland on grand bluffs, overlooking from

Communities of the Southwestern

Figure 4.7. Chippewa Lake Park entrance at the B&O Railroad and Southwestern Stations. (Courtesy of Northern Ohio Railway Museum)

Point Puritas, the magnificent and picturesque garden valley of Rocky River, south of Lake Erie, away from the smoke and dust of the busy city, where the air is clean, the waters pure, and the scenery grand."[19] One man who personified the spirit of the park and was largely responsible for its success was John E. Gooding. He leased the entire park in 1901 from the Southwestern and bought it outright in May 1915. He built it into a major regional amusement park over the decades, and after his death in 1937 at the age of seventy-two, his family operated the park for another thirty years.[20]

Chippewa Lake Park

Much further south of Cleveland, the Southwestern carried passengers to another park at Chippewa Lake in Medina County. This park served the recreation needs of neighboring rural towns and villages, as well as a more affluent patronage than the urban parks in the region. The Southwestern did not own the Chippewa Lake Park resort, but ran special excursions as well as providing regular service because of its popularity with many Northeast Ohio residents. During the heyday of the park, attendance

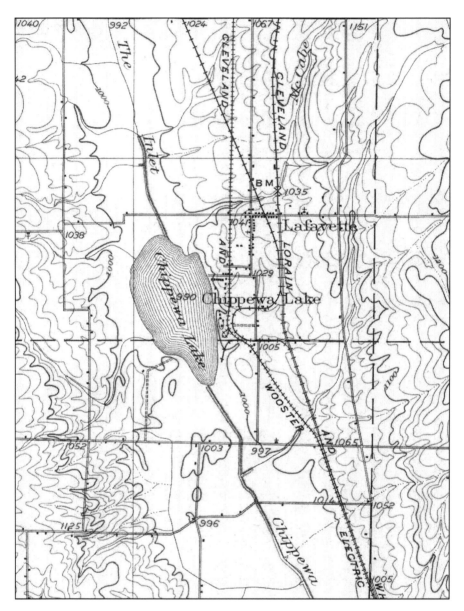

Map 4.1. Surveyed in 1904, United States Department of the Interior Geological Survey of Medina Ohio Quadrangle section depicting electric and steam rail services to Chippewa Lake Park. (United States Department of the Interior Geological Survey)

on Southwestern Sunday excursions and company picnic charters during the summer ranged anywhere from twenty to forty thousand daily. Besides the excursion and Sunday traffic, the Green Line benefited from seventy or more Cleveland families that spent their summers at cottages along the lake, leaving the "man of the house" to travel daily back and forth to work. As the Southwestern promotion claimed, "At this resort the busy man or woman finds restoration of strength and buoyancy of brain and body which are required to meet successfully the demands of modern life." Considering Chippewa Lake Park's appeal to the upper middle class, one could describe it as a resort for Progressive Era young urban professionals.[21]

Chippewa Lake Park was by all measures the strongest and longest-lasting resort on the Southwestern system. Served not only by the interurban line, it also benefited from regular service via the Baltimore & Ohio Railroad (Cleveland, Lorain & Wheeling RR). Branded as the "Million Dollar Amusement Park" in the 1920s, it boasted the most up-to-date attractions, thrill rides, hotel accommodations, athletic grounds, fishing, boating, and water features, as well as the finest and largest dancing pavilion in Ohio. Even after the rise of the automobile and manifestation of public funding for improved roadways, the park benefited from nearby access to two major federal highways—US Route 42 and US 224. Each provided ready access to motorists coming to and from the Cleveland and Akron metropolitan areas.

If Seccaium Park had any claim to big-name performers during its peak time, Chippewa Lake Park's reputation for famous bands and performances, as well as sizable audiences, was unparalleled in Northeast Ohio from the 1920s into the 1950s. Prominent visitors included the likes of Henry Ford, Harvey Firestone, and Thomas Edison in the early 1900s. After a decrease in interurban services starting in 1930 and eventually a total closure of rail travel the following year, Seccaium Park was reliant on automobile and charter buses in the subsequent years. For Chippewa Lake Park, many of the glory days occurred after final service by the Cleveland, Southwestern & Columbus Railway in 1931, and patrons arrived via the automobile, charter buses, and the B&O RR. Given its proximity to Cleveland and Akron populations, as well as regular steam railroad service and improved highways, the amusement park was able to continue for decades. The Big Band Era saw greats like Guy Lombardo,

Figure 4.8. A company picnic and excursion of the Ohio Brass Company to Chippewa Lake via the Southwestern, circa 1927. (Courtesy of Northern Ohio Railway Museum)

Vaughn Monroe, the Dorseys, and Glenn Miller come to the Ballroom. The first radio broadcast of the Lawrence Welk Band occurred in the Chippewa Lake Ballroom in 1933. Other live radio broadcasts from Chippewa Lake added to the prestige and notoriety of the park well after Seccaium closed its doors.

The development of Chippewa Lake Club adjacent to the park added to the attractiveness and access to the park for those who could afford to lease cottages at the lake. For $300 and upward per lot in 1919, you could lease it for 99 years, build a cottage, and have use of Chippewa Lake for boating, bathing and fishing, as well as walking distance to the Amusement Park. Sewer, water, natural gas, and electricity were all available to each lot. Applicants had to provide first-class references, "it being the aim of the Company to insure a selected family community."[22] Chippewa Lake Park owner and manager A. M. Beach successfully married the real estate development to the resort and amusement park business. Transportation by rail and road helped to facilitate and prolong the economic vitality of the operations well into the 1970s. The Southwestern benefited more from the Chippewa Lake connection in its early years of operation, but never to a degree that would guarantee its survival beyond the 1920s, especially after the development of a publicly funded road system dedicated to enhancing private automobile use and commercial truck traffic.[23]

PLAY BALL!!

America's historic love affair with organized baseball teams did not escape the attention of the interurban lines, including the Southwestern. Electric railway syndicates were connecting cities, villages, and towns in Ohio in the first decade of the twentieth century. At the same time, the business of organized baseball was taking root locally, regionally, and nationally. Business interests and promoters were forming teams and creating leagues to promote intercommunity rivalries in the hopes of generating regular and profitable attendance at weekend baseball games.

In this decade, the National League and American League business interests of America's largest cities were engaged in what is described as "all-out warfare in which the rival leagues wrestled over star players, territorial disputes and other politically motivated shenanigans."[24] In the ending days of the struggle between the two major leagues, the formation of minor leagues and independent leagues was particularly rampant in a way that helped promote a hierarchical system of amateur, semiprofessional, to professional league teams. As one observer noted in 1907, "The value of the organization under the supreme, all embracing national agreement may be judged upon the fact that in addition to the two great major leagues there are in operation under the National association the twenty-eight leagues enumerated above—together with a half dozen less important leagues—with a total of 196 clubs."[25] The headline summarized the popularity, as well as the profitability—"More Than 4,000 Players Employed and Almost 11,000 Games Scheduled for the Season of 1907— Safe Investment for Capital."[26]

TROLLEYS BOOM BASEBALL

> There is a new factor in baseball which is doing wonders toward organizing leagues in towns and villages. It is the trolley line. Trolley leagues are springing up in every direction. On some lines of electric railroad there may be half a dozen towns. The fare from one extreme of the system to the other is so small that the players can easily afford to pay it, and they are encouraged to put up small grounds and small stands,

not without any particular desire for revenue, but with the idea of affording summer amusement to the places in which they live and of course with the added eagerness of winning the championship of their section for their own particular village.

Ten years from now the United States will be covered with a myriad more of trolley leagues, from which in time will spring some of the great players of that epoch in professional baseball.

("The Pennant Races Revive 'Frenzied Baseball,'" *Mansfield News-Journal*, September 26, 1908, 11.)

At the same time, American's favorite pastime became an easy way for interurbans to enable this competition among the communities they served and gain passenger traffic on the most expensive days of the week: Saturdays and Sundays. The Southwestern system was no different and helped form a Cleveland and Southwestern (C&SW) Trolley League in 1904. Trolley leagues got their names because fans and players traveled to and from ballgames by way of the special trolley cars, as well as regular passenger services. Such leagues became breeding grounds for future professionals, as well as hosting the final game days for aging or unsuccessful aspirant professionals. In the earliest years, players were typically paid on a percentage basis from attendance, rather than a fixed salary. Sometimes the pot was sweetened a bit with prize money for the winner of a particular contest.[27]

Organized by J. O. Wilson, the general passenger agent for the system in 1904, the C&SW Trolley League lasted only three seasons. It started with eight community teams—Wooster Giants, Medina Stars, Norwalk, Wellington, Oberlin, North Amherst, Elyria Eagles, and Grafton—but within the first year, Wellington and Grafton dropped out. An Oberlin-Berea team formed mid-1904, but changes in team membership by 1905 whittled the league down to four anchor teams: Elyria, Wooster, Norwalk, and Medina. During the last season in 1906, the teams were Elyria, Wooster, Chicago Junction (later called Willard), and Medina.

These teams frequently played other teams in various independent leagues that sprang up in northern Ohio, but the Cleveland and Southwestern Trolley League produced some of the most spirited rivalries and profitable attendance, especially between the Elyria Eagles and the Wooster Giants. Unfortunately, one of the reported key factors for its early demise was that it was a Saturday-only ball league, because most of the cities prohibited Sunday baseball games with paid players. The larger cities accommodated Sunday games and thriving clubs couldn't prosper only on seasons of just Saturday double-headers.[28]

In 1905, the Elyria Eagles were presented the shiny silver engraved Trolley League Cup for the season by Secretary Wilson of the Cleveland and Southwestern Traction Company. Notably, E. G. Johnson, the so-called dean of the Lorain County Bar Association, attorney for the company, and prominent Republican political figure, was the featured speaker of the event. In the opinion of many, the Trolley League baseball team was the pride of the community and a boon for local business. As the article reminded readers, "So successful were they that their games kept the local fans at home where previously they had attended the league games at Cleveland. Not a game was played but what was not well attended."[29]

One of the most notable figures to play in the C&SW Trolley League was Charles Follis from Wooster. A Wooster native, Follis broke the color barrier in professional football, as well as playing semiprofessional baseball. At the turn of the century, after leading the Wooster High School Football team for an undefeated season, he began playing for the Wooster Athletic Association team, where he caught the attention of the manager of a team from Shelby, Ohio. Follis was 6 feet tall and 200 pounds—one of the biggest players in his day and reportedly very fast. The president of the Shelby Athletic Club, businessman Frank C. Schiffer, signed him up for a club that would become a professional team in the Ohio League called the Shelby Blues. As halfback, Follis led them to a state championship in 1902 and to win seven out of eight games in 1903. In 1904, he signed a contract with the Blues, creating the first documented evidence of an African American playing professional football—a historic first. His nickname was the "Black Cyclone" and sometimes "Follis the Speedy." Back then the game was played without protective equipment, and broken bones and other injuries were commonplace. Targeted on the field by his rivals because of his prowess, Follis was compelled to permanently leave football in 1906. He switched exclusively to semi-pro baseball, which he had been playing part-time off-season since 1904 for the Wooster Giants in the C&SW Trolley League.[30]

Follis passed away at the age of thirty-one from pneumonia after a short illness while playing for the Cleveland Cuban Giants in 1910. He played for the Wooster Giants from 1904 to 1906, first as catcher and then as short stop, and had a strong batting average in the Trolley League. In 1905 and 1906, he played for both the Wooster Giants and the Cleveland Starlight Champs. Interesting enough, the C&SW Trolley League teams were multiracial but never played on Sundays because of local sabbath-day restrictions. Competing in a different league, the roster of the independent Starlight Champs consisted of all Black players and played on Sundays in the cities that allowed for-profit ventures on Sundays. Occasionally they would also play in cities like Shelby, Ohio, where players were sometimes arrested and had to pay minimal fines after performing in the Sunday games. Upon the demise of the C&SW Trolley League, Follis played exclusively for the Cleveland Starlight Champs for several years and then the Cuban Giants until his untimely death. In death notices that appeared in the *Cleveland Plain Dealer* and the *Crestline Advocate*, it was widely recognized that his advancement to professional baseball was blocked entirely by his race. "He had few superiors behind the bat. Had it not been that his color barred him from major leagues, there is little doubt but that he would have been one of the star baseball players of the country."[31]

In 2018, the 132nd General Assembly passed House Bill 229, sponsored by Representatives Mark Romanchuk (R-Mansfield) and Scott Wiggam (R-Wooster), declaring the third day of February as "Charles Follis Day" in honor of the first African American professional football player who was born on that day in 1879. According to testimony on HB 229 from sports historian and playwright Jim Stoner before the Ohio House State and Local Government Committee, Charles Follis encountered and was befriended by a young Branch Rickey. Years later Rickey, as owner of the Brooklyn Dodgers—originally called the Trolley Dodgers—never forgot his friend Charles Follis and carried his memory forth in later years when he helped break the race barrier in modern sports by signing Jackie Robinson in 1947.[32]

No doubt the building of the electric railway system in Northeast Ohio not only facilitated frequent interurban travel for business purposes, but enabled communities within the region to celebrate a healthy dose of friendly sporting competition as a newfound diversion in their previously less-traveled lifestyles. Proudly in hindsight, the Trolley League teams of the Southwestern and their respective communities were seemingly color blind, at least when it came to local baseball team competition.

> **LIGHTNING STRIKE KILLED ONE AND KNOCKED DOWN TWO: FOLLIS HAS NEAR MISS**
>
> While practicing before a game with the Atlantic City team at Inlet Park, New Jersey, three members of the Cleveland Cuban Giants team were too close to a lightning strike on August 26, 1909. The Black second baseman, William Bedford, was killed when the bolt hit the ground near him and the electric charge was conducted into his body by his metal cleats. Cuban Giants catcher, Charles Follis, and short stop Walter Gordon were knocked down by the strike, but emerged shaken but unharmed. The 1,000 spectators in the stands at the time reportedly felt the shockwave and were thrown into a panic.
>
> ("Lightning Bolt Killed Negro Second Baseman," *Norwich* [CT] *Bulletin*, August 27, 1909, 3; "Notes," *Medina Sentinel*, September 3, 1909, 5; "Lightning Kills Player," *Washington Post*, August 27, 1909, 8.)

TO THE GRAVE SERVICE: DOLORES

In 1910, the general manager of the Cleveland, Southwestern & Columbus Railway, E. F. Schneider, ordered the construction from the trucks up of a custom funeral car in the company shops in Elyria. Two funeral cars of the Cleveland Railway Company had operated over the Southwestern system for a few years prior. Demand occurred so frequently that management decided it was worth building their own special car and offering its services over their vast network. For a cost of $3,600, above the trucks and motors, the car was a Mercedes gray trimmed in black, with only a thin gold line and number 43 and "Southwestern" name on the exterior. It had a rated total capacity of forty passengers, weighed 30 tons, and was 51 feet in length. "It was the idea of its designers to make Dolores as far removed from the ordinary trolley car as could be. To that end, everything savoring of the railroad has been eliminated and the car made to compare favorably in its appointments and fittings with a private equipage."[33]

The car was called the "Dolores"—a biblical name meaning pain or sorrows—and was described as quite elaborate, with interior woodwork in quarter-sawed early English oak wax finish and a color scheme of green and purple. Seats were upholstered in dark-green plush, curtains and window shades were purple fabric, and chairs in the pall bearers' compartment were wicker that matched the dark woodwork with green leather upholstery. The floor was laid with white and black linoleum and a dark-green runner going down the center aisle. The specially built car for funerals and the grieving had enough room for two caskets, with loading on either side, and had fold-down shelving for floral arrangements. The pallbearers' compartment had seating for eight people, separated by a door from the passenger compartment that had seating for twenty-six, and six in the observation part, but also contained additional folding chairs. The car had a toilet room and lavatory with pull-down washbowl, as well.[34]

It was advertised at the time that the Southwestern system provided the services of Dolores to more than thirty sizable cities, ran very close to a number of cemeteries, and had sidings adjoining several of them. According to reports, once initiated it was quite busy, averaging eight or nine funerals for a typical six-day week. Initially, charges were the regular chartered car rate, plus $5 or $10 depending on the distance traveled. In 1911, it earned about $2,000 over the regular chartered car rates, making it a very profitable source of revenue. However, by 1921, the Southwestern had raised the rate to a flat $50 but was forced to reduce it by half in August of that year, reportedly because of the increasing use of automobiles and decline in service requests. It served the families of the Southwestern communities until 1925.[35]

ANOTHER DOLORES

The Baltimore & Northern Electric Railway—later the United Railways—had rebuilt an 1896 Laclede Car Co. parlor car in 1900, which provided a luxurious funeral car, also named "Dolores." Although not equipped with the Southwestern's preferences for dark-green accented materials, it had similar refined but tasteful features. Street railways in most major cities throughout the country provided this specialized service to the grieving families, while interurban systems tended to leave that service to the big city rail companies, rather than invest in their own specially modified car, like the Southwestern. This Dolores was retired in 1927, another victim of the automobile era.

(Raymond F. Crapo, *The Environment of the Traction Era* [Short Beach, CT: Bradford Electric Railway Historical Publications, 1978], 28; Bob Boetticher Sr., "Death Takes to the Rails: A Look Back at the Rise and Fall of the Funeral Trains and Streetcar Era," *American Funeral Director*, April 2021, https://www.nmfh.org/wp-content/uploads/2019/09/Funeral-Trains.pdf, accessed April 14, 2022.)

Figure 4.9. CS&C RR funeral car "Dolores." (Courtesy of Northern Ohio Railway Museum)

IMPACT ON SMALL-TOWN LIFE

Often small political battles, or at least modest debates, erupted between competing business factions over the routes of interurban lines through the towns. In 1902 a Medina Trade Committee, composed of councilmen and business leaders, issued a special report on the potential influence of the proposed Southwestern route. The document discussed the impact on local businesses of the Southwestern's route through Berea, Elyria, Oberlin, North Amherst, and Wellington. The committee's Majority Report observed that in Elyria most businessmen believed that the best locations were along the electric line, while in Oberlin, "all the business men wanted a street car line in front of their places of business, and there were found two instances of business concerns located towards the extreme end of the street not touched by the electric line vacating their old quarters and moving down a narrow street located on the electric railway."[36]

The Southwestern line typically received a mixed reception from the business community, ranging from antipathy to enthusiasm and dependent upon the anticipated results of its arrival and continued operation. The Majority Report of the committee in Medina concluded, first, that there was a significant tendency for businesses to centralize along the route of the electric railways; and second, "that a line passing a great part of the business houses only favors that portion of a town to the detriment of the other part." The Minority Report of the same committee also recognized the tendency for rents to be higher near interurbans but believed that the interurban's specific location within the town had little significant impact on the general business community. Some economists observed a few years later that this impact was typically more dramatic for certain types of businesses, for example dry-goods merchants, than for others like hardware retailers.[37]

Sometimes, the electorate was able to weigh in directly on the railway's path. In Medina Village, there was an organized plea to voters by a group of South Court merchants to continue building the Southwestern track along the western edge of the public square to West Smith Road, rather than turning the corner westward at North Court and West Liberty Street. The group arguing for the South Court route suggested that it was a better bargain for the local taxpayers to have the company regrade Smith Road and replace pavement disturbed by building south on Court Street, and that having one curve in the village was better and safer than three. Additionally, they contended that business interests in the entire community would be better served, rather than just the "north siders." With the visible support of the largest employer in the village, the A. I. Root Company, the voters chose the West Liberty Street route 329 to 289 in a large turnout at a spring election in April 1902. It was a narrow win for the company, northside businessmen, and A.I. Root Company, as it was much cheaper to construct and kept the interurban traffic and depot on the north side of the village.[38]

Even the major urban center from which the Green Line radiated was not isolated from these opposing reactions. Cleveland residents mostly believed that the Southwestern, and other interurbans, were not assets to their community, but burdens upon the city's taxpayers. Though the interurbans paid rental fees for access to the city, most people suspected that those fees provided insufficient income to repair tracks and street pavements damaged by their heavy interurban cars. After over a decade and a half of interurban operation, there was a move in 1916 by several members of Cleveland City Council to prevent all suburban electric railway cars from entering the city. The companies were accused of dam-

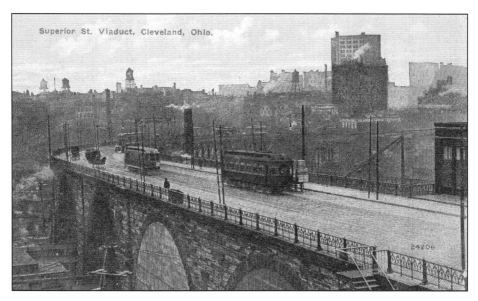

Figure 4.10. A 1914 postcard of Cleveland's first high-level bridge, the Superior Viaduct, which provided easy access to downtown for streetcars, pedestrians, horse-drawn vehicles, and private automobiles from the westside. (Author's collection)

aging the property of the city-owned streetcar line. The move would have required interurban passengers and express freight to be transferred just as they entered the Cleveland city limits.

Thousands of patrons along the lines and merchants in the city protested vigorously against the regulation. Along with the support of Traction Commissioner Fielder Sanders of Cleveland, city merchants argued that it would cost the Cleveland Railway Company at least $100,000 a year in lost revenues and seriously diminish business from out-of-town patrons. Fortunately for the interurbans, the measure failed. It demonstrated that significant divisions, however, occurred within the central city over the perceived benefits derived from interurban operations. In a sense, it also depicted a triumph of metropolitan-oriented commercial interests over residential-based parochial concerns. The interurbans would not always fare so well in other localities.[39]

Once the railway line had operated for several years, local enmity seldom decreased. Rather, it frequently increased and took on several menacing forms. Local citizens and politicians were often openly hostile.

Franchise renewals became occasions for heated public debates. Typically, the controversies involved local fares, street paving costs, electrolysis damage to nearby water and sewer pipes, local regulation of the number of cars and running times, and complaints from motorists who found the streetcars a nuisance. Interurban companies were often charged with being negligent absentee landlords and associated with the large public utility companies that people categorized as malevolent enterprises. Formidable political figures, such as Cleveland's reform mayor Tom L. Johnson, attacked the corruptive influences of the light, water, and streetcar companies and urged municipal ownership of such concerns in the public interest. Interurban companies rarely escaped similar attacks and often publicly suffered from the "guilt by association" that the assailants encouraged.[40]

The Southwestern fell victim to this animosity toward "big companies." Unfortunately for the firm, these actions tended to increase operating costs at a time when they were already damaging its future solvency. Starting in 1914, a hostile faction of the Berea village government waged a constant battle with the Southwestern over renewal of the company's franchise. For two years proposals and counterproposals followed court battles and State Public Utilities Commission meetings. Neither side emerged from the ordeal unscathed. The main issue between Berea's Village Council and Southwestern management involved fares. The Southwestern proposed in 1914 a cash fare of fifteen cents and a ten-cent commuter fare from Berea to the Lorain Street depot in Cleveland. After two years of arguments, the interurban dropped the proposed commuter fare down to nine cents. The Village council originally proposed a ten-cent cash fare and a commuter fare of eight cents. A citizen committee charged by council to study the issue and make recommendations in June 1916 yielded to the Southwestern's proposed fifteen-cent cash fare but held out for the eight-cent commuter fare. Residents argued that Berea commuters should not have to pay for the company's losses incurred by overextending its lines into less profitable areas. Other sore points involved the interurban's share of paving costs, repair of electrolysis damage to water pipes along the railway, and council's regulation of interurban traffic through the village.[41]

With the village's franchise expiring in less than six months, the Southwestern's board of directors rejected Berea's franchise proposal on July 25, 1916, and voted to reroute the line to the east of the village. Beyond the one-cent difference on the commuter fare rate, it refused to pay for the resurfacing of a double track width down the main street because the line used only a single-track section for its operations. Management felt that the town was trying to extort corporate revenues to pay for street improvements that would primarily benefit the villager's motorists and ultimately hurt the interurban. Also behind the move was the company's desire to improve freight service and running time into Cleveland by constructing a more direct route and bypassing the congested local streets. The company was also fearful of similar franchise demands from Brook Park and West Park in the future.[42]

After securing a temporary franchise through the court system, the Southwestern built the bypass and abandoned Berea in the summer of 1917. The interurban now bypassed the community that had been its birthplace. Opening on August 4, 1917, the new route went through the Cuyahoga County Fairgrounds and the Rocky River Valley to the south of Berea, bypassing the main section of the community. It was an extra cost and loss of revenues that the Southwestern did not want to endure, but local animosity forced the relocation.

The interurban directors did see advantages to the bypass around Berea. The management of the Southwestern saw a reduction in running time and improvement in freight service as a desirable alternative. In the short run it abandoned the ridership of Berea in hopes of a more profitable operation. Given no other profitable alternative, the Southwestern's decision was, from its perspective, in the best interests of the stockholders and its future relations with other communities. It improved the interurban's future bargaining position as it proved the board of directors was not bluffing. Other towns along the line would have expected similar franchise arrangements if the Southwestern had accommodated Berea's demand. In fact, Medina did make a similar request in April 1918. But that community later backed down and reached an agreement with the line rather than let the Southwestern carry through with their threat to leave the community. If Medina or other places had not mitigated their demands, the Southwestern would have had to make the decision that it ultimately did in Berea: abandon the line or bypass the community.[43]

Southwestern's effect upon rural Northeast Ohio was measurable and significant. To the farmer and townspeople along its routes, the Southwestern gave a taste of increased mobility that was to become more fully attained with the adoption of the automobile. In addition, it helped bring about a period of prosperity to the farm. Though relatively short, this period enabled the farmers to modernize. Economically and socially, it propelled farmers into the growing middle-class of American society. In short, the interurban, with its access to twentieth-century higher education, amusement and commodities brought the hinterlander closer to the urbanite.

Political scientist, H. E. Hoagland observed in 1912 the dramatic changes that Illinois farmers had witnessed over the previous decade, owing to a multitude of factors which included electric railways. Although he was describing the conditions of rural life in "The Land of Lincoln," his comments are just as applicable to Ohio's experience.

> No previous decade in the history of the state has witnessed such rapid strides in the direction of bringing the city to the farmer ... the development of the telephone, the more general utilization of the country meat and grocery wagon and the automobile, the extension of trolley lines, and the introduction of numerous other devices which are fast becoming part of life on the farm, to show that instead of the farmer being continually made to feel the isolation of country life, he sees that he is being brought closer and closer in touch with urban life.[44]

Interurban lines radiating from Cleveland brought elements of urban life out into the Ohio countryside early in the century. The farmers and villagers of northern Ohio were not strangers to the peculiarities of immigrant labor or the benefits of industrialization. Gangs of immigrants constructed the thousands of miles of interurban track from the 1890s to the 1910s. Seasonal workforces needed by area fruit orchards and the grain, vegetable, and dairy farms were also filled by urban residents and immigrants searching for economic success in the "land of opportunity." Many farmers along the interurbans had business dealings with foreign-born merchants, wholesalers, or retailers in Cleveland. Even urban newspapers were carried daily by express to the various interurban stops. Consequently, unfamiliarity and ignorance, integral components of conflict, could have been diminished with the help of the interurban. The Southwestern was instrumental in bringing urban civilization to many farmers along its line and in "cultivating" them, so to speak. Professor of economics at Princeton University, Ernest L. Bogart, observed in 1906, "Not less important in its influence upon the endurableness of farm life is the socializing effect of the electric road; the contact with town and city life has contributed greatly to the breadth of view, the culture, and the happiness of the farmer's family."[45]

Certainly, the urbanizing process that was underway in the 1900s and 1910s had social consequences by the 1920s. The farmers of the hinterlands became more like the middle class of the city. After a generation of close contact, socialization reduced the differences between the rural inhabitants of Ashland, Huron, Lorain, and Medina Counties and the citizens of Cleveland and its metropolitan communities. This was especially true as middle-class urbanites moved into the outlying communities. In some respects this also symbolized the movement of urban attitudes and values out into previously rural environs. The metropolizing of the communities around Cleveland is unmistakable, and the interurban lines like the Southwestern radiating out from its borders played a dynamic role in that process.[46]

5

Financing Northeast Ohio Electric Railways

THE ROLE OF OVERCAPITALIZATION IN THEIR RISE AND DECLINE

THIS CHAPTER WILL answer two important questions about the Cleveland, Southwestern & Columbus Railway and some other selected Northeast Ohio electric railways. These are: How did these roads compare to other lines in the industry, and why did the systems overcapitalize? The importance of answering these two queries is that they address a critical issue in explaining the rise and decline of electric traction within the region. In all likelihood, they shed light on the demise of the industry elsewhere.

This study concludes that the financing, construction, and operation of the region's railways closely emulated those elsewhere in the nation. However, the concurrence of market demand and experienced capitalists in Northeast Ohio provided the impetus for building a network of electric railways that were individually larger and more expensive than those found in most other sections. The expansion of the electric railways beyond the boundaries of the cities was enabled by improvements in electrical technology after 1896; a reorganization and betterment of the financial climate after 1898; and the demographic pressures that were dispersing the urban populations of the region's major cities. Although these factors enabled the traction syndicates to finance and construct the region's electric railway systems, they cannot explain entirely the reasons for overbuilding and overcapitalization.

The longer average mileage per line depicted in figure 5.1 represents the region's heavy concentration of interurban roads. Ohio was the leading state in interurban mileage in 1912 with 2,747.42 miles, followed by Indiana, New York, and Pennsylvania. In that year, interurban lines accounted for 68 percent of all electric railway track mileage in the state, second only to Indiana with 77 percent.[1]

Northeast Ohio, much like the rest of the state, had several conditions that favored interurban development. The 1902 US Census report summarized the traffic and geographical conditions that encouraged interurban growth:

> From the standpoint of traffic the favoring conditions are (1) a comparatively dense population, arising from many and populous towns and villages; (2) connection with a large city, which attracts travel from the smaller towns and rural districts, and from which also summer traffic may be carried to resorts and rural districts; (3) general material prosperity and intelligence. From the standpoint of cost the important consideration is that the territory to be served shall be comparatively level, and otherwise free from physical obstacles to economical construction and operation.[2]

Northeast Ohio communities, geography, and business culture provided conditions that were conducive to the development of considerably larger and better-funded electric railway companies than typically found elsewhere in the nation. Figure 5.1 numerically confirms that observation throughout the entire era of Electric Traction.

Interurban historians George Hilton and John Due state that the presence of these essential factors account for Ohio's early rise to prominence in the interurban industry. These conditions existed in Northeast Ohio to varying degrees depending on location. However, in as much as some of the factors listed by the US Census were essential to interurban growth and development, they only hint at two equally important factors: human needs and organizational behavior.[3]

Two conspicuous forces stood behind the building of interurbans and other electric railways in Northeast Ohio. The first compelling force was the insatiable and changing transportation needs of the region's residents and businesses. The second force driving the vast expansion of electric roads into the rural areas of the region included the various business organizations that were willing to fill those needs in hopes of making a

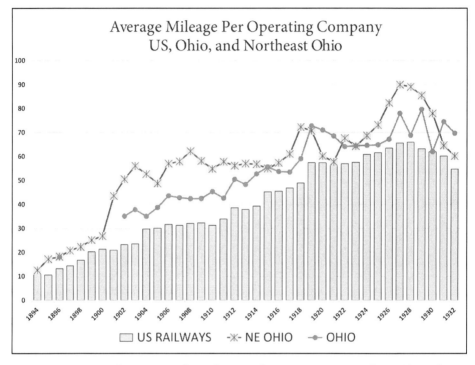

Figure 5.1. Average mileage operated per electric railway company in Northeast Ohio, Ohio, and the United States. *Sources: Statistical Abstract of the United States*, 1931; *Street Railway Journal*, 1902–32; *Report of the Public Utilities Commission of Ohio*, 1912–31; *Report of the Railroad Commission of Ohio*, 1906–11. (Chart by author)

profit from those endeavors. Northeast Ohio had an aggressive business culture that nurtured a financial community willing to risk capital to meet those demands. Based upon their recent successes in steam railroad construction and the region's iron and steel industries, confidence in their ultimate profitability was high early in the promotion of these enterprises. The institutional ties of electric railway promoters allowed access to greater wealth than the region itself possessed, as investment bankers from New York, Pittsburgh, Boston, and Philadelphia backed up securities issued on electric railway projects in the region. What determined the eventual length and financial structure of these interurbans was the interaction of these two variables. Changes in either component, the demand, or the financing altered the pace of construction and sometimes the eventual outcome of the railway project as well.

Table 5.1 shows the annual change in electric railway track mileage in Northeast Ohio and the country. The two great bursts in interurban building described by Hilton and Due, in 1901–4 and 1905–8, are easily identifiable. The electric railway track mileage in Northeast Ohio had its greatest and primary surge from 1900 to 1904, while the Cleveland, Southwestern & Columbus Railway system saw its cyclical growth between 1900 and 1909. Subsequent gains in Ohio mileage were minor in comparison to percentage increases in national urban and interurban railways. The Northeast Ohio electric railway figures represent changes in the total track mileage that companies actually operated during the year and not the amount built.

The amount of track added to the region's operating companies after 1904 reveals that it was mainly incremental and not cyclical. Following the initial primary surge of track coming online from 1900 to 1903, the region expanded its trackage in smaller increments. The largest interurban railways chiefly increased in size through mergers and consolidation rather than new track expansion after 1904. Following 1905, subsidiary relationships appear to replace corporate mergers as the principal method of consolidation, thus reflecting a change in business philosophy.

Evidence indicates that the electric railway industry in Northeast Ohio after 1904 grew at a slower but steadier pace than the average national rate of development. Several interurban projects started comparatively late, but the region's growth in total mileage was dispersed throughout 1904 to 1914. The building of new tracks inspired by so-called interurban mania happened early in the history of the industry. Trackage additions and extensions grew steadily as firms merged to form interconnecting systems and networks while urban systems improved service by double trackage. Notably, 80 percent of the trackage that Northeast Ohio electric railways would ever operate was completed by 1910, compared to 1907 for the nation as a whole. It would take the region only five years to reach 90 percent of its all-time total, and by 1919 it peaked at 1,697 total miles. The nation, in comparison, reached its electric railway peak a year earlier in 1918 with 48,484 miles of track, while the total interurban mileage reached its high point in 1916 at 15,580 miles.

Some historians and railway enthusiasts have hinted that this quick rise in electric railway track mileage was the result of that interurban

Table 5.1. Percent annual change in total track mileage, Interurbans in Northeast Ohio, Ohio, United States and Cleveland, Southwestern & Columbus RR, 1900–32

Year	\multicolumn{4}{c}{Percent change in track mileage by year}
	NE Ohio	Ohio	US interurban	CS&C RR
1900	35%	18%	37%	82%
1901	17%	23%	48%	11%
1902	16%	21%	48%	57%
1903	11%	21%	33%	13%
1904	3%	-1%	18%	0%
1905	1%	11%	10%	0%
1906	3%	17%	13%	21%
1907	2%	-1%	16%	3%
1908	2%	0%	10%	0%
1909	2%	-5%	5%	31%
1910	3%	-3%	6%	0%
1911	1%	-2%	4%	0%
1912	1%	2%	4%	0%
1913	2%	0%	5%	0%
1914	4%	2%	4%	2%
1915	1%	2%	3%	0%
1916	4%	0%	0%	0%
1917	2%	0%	0%	0%
1918	5%	-1%	-1%	0%
1919	2%	-1%	0%	0%
1920	-11%	-1%	-1%	0%
1921	0%	-2%	-1%	0%
1922	-5%	-2%	-1%	-9%
1923	0%	-1%	-1%	-5%
1924	-3%	-3%	-1%	0%
1925	-4%	-1%	-2%	-7%

Percent change in track mileage by year				
Year	NE Ohio	Ohio	US interurban	CS&C RR
1926	-6%	-5%	-4%	-6%
1927	-5%	-1%	-3%	0%
1928	-1%	-8%	-7%	-5%
1929	-4%	-1%	-7%	0%
1930	-2%	-3%	-9%	0%
1931	-23%	-11%	-12%	-50%
1932	-7%	-9%	-14%	

Sources: *Statistical Abstract of the United States*, 1931; *Street Railway Journal*, 1902–32; *Report of the Public Utilities Commission of Ohio*, 1912–31; *Report of the Railroad Commission of Ohio*, 1906–11.

mania, the consequences of which are purported to be an overcapitalization and overbuilding of the industry. Since Ohio led the nation in interurban mileage early in the growth of the national industry, it could be presumed that this mania was possibly more rampant or more contagious in Ohio than elsewhere. As shown above, the greatest surge in interurban building in Northeast Ohio, however, occurred before 1904. Subsequent "building booms" measured in track mileage were relatively small in comparison with the national averages.

Many contemporary observers and subsequent historians saw overcapitalization as the foremost problem of city and interurban electric railway lines. Hilton and Due contend that this overcapitalization sowed the seeds of a future disaster. They reasoned that interest payments on the debt ate increasingly into operating revenues. This left little net income for equipment depreciation and dividend accounts.[4]

At the time, critics of the industry believed that the overall debt figure equaled nearly 50 percent of the operating income and went primarily for promoters' profits. Some contended that this inadvertently arose from overconfidence on the amount of future ridership that the additional track miles would generate.[5]

Others saw more devious purposes for overcapitalization. Ernest L. Bogart, a professor at Princeton University, argued in 1906 that there were three causes of this phenomenon:

First, the desire of the roads to deceive the public as to their earnings; for, as soon as too large dividends are declared, the public demands either lower rates of fare or higher rates of taxation. Second, the fact that the stock sells better if the rate of interest is moderate, the investors feeling that a high rate of interest may denote a risk in the undertaking. Third, stockwatering brings large profits to the promoters and managers.[6]

Contemporary observers, like industry analyst John Moody, saw the seeds of electric railway overcapitalization in the experiences of bankers and builders with the steam railroad industry. A local observer, the *Canton Repository*, reiterated the resemblance, "The way in which these lines have been pushed is a present day parallel of the building of the steam railroads." The successes of steam railroad promotion were still fresh in the minds of capitalists just as the crunch in the securities market was eased. The new financial institutions such as trust companies and more aggressive investment banking houses in the later 1890s facilitated the early growth of the industry in the region as well as the country. In addition, the building and financing practices of the steam railroad industry, which developed in the 1870s and 1880s, provided an effective model for similar development and promotion of electric railways.[7]

In the first electric railways of Northeast Ohio, railroad men built and operated the lines and, more importantly, were responsible for their financing. Understanding why the railway builders overcapitalized their projects and the reasons for the great cycles of expansion requires grasping steam railroad financing and promotional methods. It also means recognizing that there were different concepts of overcapitalization and differing opinions as to the meaning of those concepts. These variants did carry over into the electric railway industry, as politicians, economists, and capitalists dealt with issues of taxation, regulation and, for some, public ownership of the lines.

William Z. Ripley, an economist at Harvard University in the 1910s, suggested that the word "capitalization" in steam railroad enterprises had three different meanings. The financial components are depicted graphically in figure 5.2. Ripley contended that the disparate viewpoints of the accountant, financier, and economist clouded the actual meaning of the term so that analysis of capitalization was somewhat confusing. Accountants look at capitalization from the viewpoint of permanent corporate

Financing Northeast Ohio Electric Railways

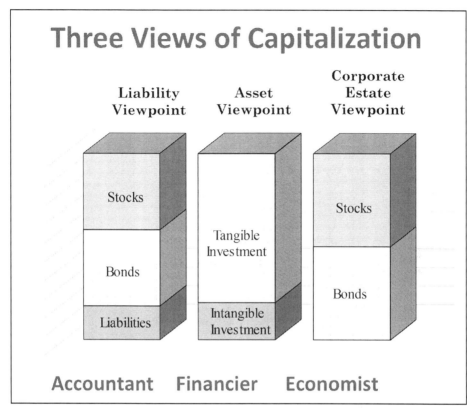

Figure 5.2. Ripley's three views of capitalization. *Source:* William Z. Ripley, *Railroads: Finance and Organization* (New York: Longmans, Green, 1915). (Chart by author)

liabilities. On the other hand, economists, when speaking of capitalization, describe the aggregate paper certification of value as reflected in the par value of the corporate securities, or in other words, the sum total of outstanding capital stocks and bonds. Ripley referred to this as the corporate estate viewpoint.[8]

Ripley contended that railroad financiers looked at capitalization substantially differently than economists or accountants. Unlike the economists' and accountants' conception of capitalization as a liability, the financier viewed capitalization as the book value of the capital account. To him it was the sum total of all assets, tangible and intangible. Financiers argued that what was important was the "true value" of the property. This meant the earning power of the properties as reflected in the actual capital acquired from the sale of the securities. In other words, promoters suggested that the potential earning power and intangible investments made by the promoters had to be figured into the final number for the sale of stocks and bonds. Therefore, their capitalization number tended to be higher than that which would have been calculated by the economist.[9]

The distinction, then, between the economists and the financiers in reporting the capitalization of steam railroads was that the former viewed it as the sum total of all outstanding securities at their face value. To the latter, capitalization was the sum total of all capital realized from the sale of stocks and bonds represented by the potential value of the property. To further confuse the debate, economists and legislators defined overcapitalization as the "amount by which the represented shares and capital liabilities of a corporation exceed the value of its capital assets." Since the financier claimed a higher true value than the accumulated face value of all securities, he became an easy target for charges of "watering" the stock and overcapitalizing.[10]

Of course, steam railroad builders had a long-standing reputation of "playing loose with the facts" when it came to disclosing financial details. They earned this notoriety during the great expansion of steam carriers after the Civil War. The Crédit Mobilier scandal involving the Union Pacific did much to expose the dark side of the relationship between railroad construction companies and steam railroads. Although the scandal exaggerated the abuses of the system, it illustrated accurately how great fortunes for the promoters and builders could be produced deceitfully. Frequent exploitation of the dubious relationship between promoters and builders by unscrupulous businessmen continued in the decades that followed. Ripley described in 1912 how a railroad construction company operated legally, but to the decided advantage of the promoters.

> A corporation is formed with a cash capital sufficient in amount to undertake the preliminary work. This company enters into an agreement with the railroad by which it is to receive stated amounts of bonds and stock upon each section of road as completed. It proceeds forthwith to build the line to the limit of its cash resources; and progressively receives the securities from the railroad as provided in the contract.... The construction company more often makes use of the railroad securities as issued to secure temporary loans, based upon these as collateral.[11]

Once completing the road, the construction company sold the bonds. Sometimes the promoters used stocks as a bonus to clinch the sale of the bonds, which they needed to pay off the construction loans. If promoted successfully, the value of the bonds exceeded the cost of construction and reflected the "intangible value" and future earning power of the enterprise. Therefore, the profit in cash from the sale of bonds allowed the construction company owners to retain capital stock holdings in the road. If they held on to enough of these securities, they exercised some control over its management.[12]

Often the construction management accounts came under the direction of the same people supervising the accounts of the railroad, a dangerous arrangement that led to dishonest business practices. Without independent reviews of the transfer of property and money between the corporations, an exaggeration of the reported costs of construction was possible, if not encouraged. The aggregate costs per mile of track could be inflated to equal the amount of money available from the sale of bonds, instead of reflecting the actual costs of construction. The construction company could likewise increase its reported costs of materials or labor, reflecting the promoters' own gains in personal income rather than a response to local labor or material markets.[13]

Besides this wasteful or fraudulent method of financing construction, the construction company encouraged an overcapitalization and overextension of the road. The promoters made their fortunes in building the road rather than in operating it. They retained control of the capital stock, while the value of those securities reflected no contribution to the capital of the corporation or its earning power. Thus the more miles of track the promoters built, the more money they made.[14]

The merger of railroads also created attractive opportunities for promoters. There could be sound economic or business reasons for consolidation, and often financial opportunities for their exploitation as well. Combining railroad properties could improve their efficiency through the centralization and downsizing of management, purchasing, and traffic control. In addition, mergers could eliminate harmful competition or encourage more traffic volume and revenues because of coordinated service and through-traffic agreements.

Consolidation of railroads usually involved the issuance of new securities. These certificates provided opportunities for promoters to exploit the newly gained "operating efficiencies." The owners of the railroad used the new value of the securities, based upon their "probable" incomes, to fund the consolidations. Without increasing the tangible value of the properties, railroad owners could issue securities that reflected the speculated future earnings of the merged corporation. This became another method of stock watering available to railroads financiers.[15]

During the lifetime of the steam railroad and electric railway industries, hundreds of companies failed to pay their fixed bond costs and had to reorganize their debt structure. Under these circumstances the financial reorganization could also bring about an increase in capitalization without enlarging corporate assets. Under reorganization of a firm, because of the inability to pay the fixed charges upon the indebtedness, the old bondholders could be induced to forgo their right of foreclosure by accepting new bonds and preferred stock. Bondholders had to cooperate with the reorganization plan developed by a reorganization committee that represented the interests of all holders of bonds and stocks. Bondholders who did not agree with the committee-approved reorganization plan only had the right to share in the cash proceeds from a foreclosure sale. The proceeds would typically be of less value than the bonds and stocks in a going concern that had successfully acquired an underwriting syndicate to finance the reorganization. Bondholders could be asked to sacrifice their lien on the property, a portion of the bond principal, or even the interest. In this way the new fixed-interest payment imposed upon the company emerging from reorganization was reduced, but only in the short term. Typically, its total capitalization increased and in the long run the funded debt payments grew. In addition, syndicates underwriting the new securities received large bonuses, which further offset any gains made in the reorganization.[16]

Not only did promoters of steam railroad projects use these innovative methods of corporate financing, but financiers of other corporate endeavors of the time, including electric railways, also employed them. The Connecticut Railway and Lighting Company issued $9.35 million in bonds and shares of stocks equaling $15 million to consolidate nine roads in 1909 that had a prior aggregate total capitalization of $8.2 million.

William Ripley contended that using $24.25 million in securities to purchase properties previously capitalized at $8.21 million was a common situation in the state, besides being a prime example of flagrant overcapitalization. Not all segments of the business community agreed with this unfavorable characterization of corporate finance. In the minds of the promoters, the new securities reflected the true value and earning power of the combined properties.[17]

Determining the "true value" of electric railway properties became a hotly debated issue between governments and railway owners during the first three decades of the twentieth century. In order to efficiently regulate street railway fares, set rates of taxation, or determine standard levels of service, local and state governments needed to come to grips with the value of public service corporations. By nature, these firms represented private enterprises operating through exclusive rights granted by government. Standardized engineering and appraisal methods easily determined the tangible values of electric railway properties. The intangible values, however, became by definition the total value of the property as a business minus its physical or tangible worth.

It is not necessary to dwell on the complex and detailed accounting practices used to assign values to the intangible portions of an electric or steam railway business. Quite often its value was negotiated and reflected political rather than economic considerations. Instead, a simplified contemporary definition describes the perceptions of the time most appropriately. Frank Ford, a consulting engineer from New York City, defined it in 1911 as follows: "The intangible property represents the cost of acquiring rights and capital for producing the tangible property and for placing the company in a potential position for doing business efficiently as a going concern." The value of the intangible properties then equaled the sum of either the first costs or the costs of reproducing the electric railway company that had to do with government franchises, financing the physical properties, and starting operations.[18]

Identifying each part of these intangible costs reveals the areas that syndicates like PomeroyMandelbaum and EverettMoore could use for their own financial benefit. This ill-defined area of costs allowed them to further the speculative investment beyond the point of reasonable rate of return. The intangible investment comprised the various expenses incurred from the promotion of the enterprise, incorporation of the organization, franchises from municipal authorities, consents from property owners and state utilities commissions, improvements of technical standards, and development of business methods. It also included the costs associated with consolidation and control of other businesses, financial expenses for bond and stock underwriting, financial negotiations, and sale of securities. Lastly, the promoter frequently added in his expenditures from the development of inventions, purchases of patents, or the licenses required prior to commencement of operation.[19]

In much the same way as previously described for steam railroad construction practices, electric railway promoters preyed upon this intangible property to set the value of their securities. As syndicate members financed the construction of interurban lines, they commonly paid to the new company previously subscribed installments. The completed construction work and the cash installments were used as collateral to borrow additional funds. When the line was completed and sold to another corporation of the same syndicate, the sale price covered more than construction costs. It also included a hefty profit margin for the original investors that paid for the tangible properties and the intangible assets they contributed. The price further represented a considerable amount of money for the anticipated or speculated earning power of the road. The parent company authorized bonds for consolidation based on the tangible and intangible value of the acquired properties. Some of the stock representing the newly consolidated company was typically given to the original investors or as a bonus to buyers of the mortgage bonds.[20]

This financial arrangement produced electric railway syndicates that gained more from building and financing lines than from running already established ones. The earlier an investor became involved in the syndicate, the greater the rewards as each new line was opened and consolidated. In an overcapitalized property, however, the capital stocks issued against the property would be nearly worthless in the longer run because the fixed charges from the bond payments and interest would leave nothing to be distributed to the stockholders.

What actually limited overinvestment in the electric railways was merely the expectations of future earnings. This was unfortunately an insufficient safeguard for some interurban ventures. Industry observers like Frank T. Carlton, who was associated with the Toledo University School, concluded in 1904, "In many, probably in the majority of cases, they [interurban railway stocks] represent a capitalization of the prospects of future earnings, and these prospects in many instances assume a roseate tint only when seen through the spectacles of the promoter."[21]

Evidently the syndicates that constructed electric railways of Northeast Ohio operated within the same business and financial parameters as the steam railroads. As mentioned earlier, many of the principal syndicate leaders had substantial experience with steam railroad building and finance. They learned their trade when the steam railroad industry was in its ascendancy and applied these business practices to other and, they hoped, more lucrative projects involving electric traction.

There were significant and substantial linkages between steam railroad promoters and various electric railway syndicates in Northeast Ohio. Dozens of promoters associated with the interurban and street railway projects of the Everett and Moore, Hanna, Pomeroy & Mandelbaum, and Johnson syndicates invariably had investments in steam railroad projects. The interlocking directorates between these syndicates and steam railroad projects came in all sizes and degrees of success. Northeast Ohio electric railway syndicate members had prior and contemporary investments in such roads as Ashland & Western Railroad Company; Lake Shore & Michigan Southern; Nickel Plate; Pittsburgh, Youngstown & Chicago Railway Company; Valley Railway; Union Pacific Railroad; and the Wheeling & Lake Erie Railroad Company.

The connections between steam railroads and the early electric railway industry in Northeast Ohio provided obvious and significant benefits to the task of financing, promoting, and building these railway systems—steam and electric. Individuals with experience and interest in building railroads dominated the largest financial institutions of the region and were located in Cleveland. The interurbans that emerged in the latter 1890s offered the same opportunities for promotion and profit. Just as the financial system encouraged the overextension and overcapitalization of the steam railroads, so, too, did it encourage the same behavior in building and financing the interurbans.

Identifying the principal promoters of Northeast Ohio's electric railways and linking them to companies involved in steam railroad construction, finance, or operation provides only circumstantial support for suspecting overcapitalization of the regional industry. No evidence exists that can clearly demonstrate an association between the overbuilding and overcapitalization of the nation's steam railroad industry and the extent of capitalization or track building of the region's electric railways. What the industries had in common, however, were similar financial, construction, and operating methods. These moved easily from the steam railroad industry to Ohio's interurban railway industry through active members in both industries.

The business and financial methods employed by the steam railroads could be easily transferable to the electric railways. In other words, it could be said that the steam railroads figuratively "graded the roadway" in advance of interurban expansion. With tried and tested methods of railroad finance and construction available to electric railway promoters, they had only a few obstacles to overcome before the first great surge in building from 1900 to 1904 began. The evidence suggests that this one great surge was enough to overcapitalize most of the region's roads. Those firms which expanded too far into unprofitable territory in the subsequent years doomed themselves from the start to an early death under the crushing burden of debt.

The question about overcapitalization and overbuilding must be answered by looking specifically at each company and comparing it with other similar operating firms, either nationally or regionally. Fortunately, there are several financial indicators that can be used to distinguish between roads that may be overcapitalized and those that were not excessively burdened by that particular problem. When calculated over the lifetime of each road and compared to industry averages, the pattern of capitalization is clear and relatively distinct. As will be discussed, these measurements also provide in total an indication of how the industry functioned regionally.

The four financial indicators to be used provide discrete measurements of asset management, track capitalization, passenger traffic density and debt management. The financial indicators to be used are the capital intensity ratio, capitalization per mile of track, total revenue passengers per mile of track, and debt interest as a percent of total operating revenues. The indicators calculated for each Northeast Ohio electric railway will be compared with industry averages by operating class according to

Interstate Commerce Commission (ICC) criteria, thereby making adjustments for differing scales of operations. The ICC divided the electric railways into three separate operating classes based upon the annual income from railway operations. Class A companies had incomes of more than $1 million, Class B firms had income from railway operations of more than $250,000 but not in excess of $1 million, while Class C carriers earned no more than $250,000 per year from railway operations.[22]

A description of each factor follows and the results for three of the four factors in the analysis for northeast Ohio railway companies are presented in table 5.2. For the purpose of clarity, it should be understood that the total capitalization figures used for this analysis are only partially comparable to published national statistics that aggregated results from the entire industry. The selected reported values indicate comparatively higher levels of capitalization for individual firms than that revealed individually by the US Census in 1902 and 1907. The capitalization figures indicated by the US Census for electric railways reflect the *economist's view*. "Capitalization, therefore, includes the par value of securities issued to represent capital stock, common or preferred, funded debt, inclusive of negotiable debt between companies and receiver's certificates, and real estate mortgages." In comparison, the "Total Investment in Road and Equipment" reported to the Ohio Railroad Commission and the Public Utilities Commission of Ohio for individual firms represents the financier viewpoint. In comparing values derived from the two methods, the individual value is typically higher than that computed using the economist's method.

If any one figure can represent overcapitalization of an individual firm, it is the total amount invested in road and equipment. Therefore, the analytical step using the road and equipment figure as a discriminator between those roads which may have overcapitalized and those that probably were not is skewed in favor of placing more in the former category than in the latter. Some firms may be wrongfully identified as being overcapitalized on the basis of average capitalization per mile of track for that particular operating class. That can be accounted for at the end of the analysis when all the factors are considered. The purpose of the comparison is to provide a list of electric railways that are likely to have been overcapitalized. All four factors must be weighed against one another before a judgment can be made on that issue.

Table 5.2. Capitalization analysis of Northeast Ohio electric railways ranked by average capital intensity

Electric railway company	ICC operating class	Average capital intensity	Average capitalization per track mile	Average revenue passengers per track mile
Cleveland Railway Company	A	2.47	$ 85,324	$ 808,085
Youngstown Municipal Railway	A	2.86	$ 81,129	$ 404,050
Youngstown, Park & Falls Street Railway	C	4.46	$ 99,854	$ 555,936
Ashtabula Rapid Transit Company	C	4.78	$ 81,003	$ 350,178
Mahoning Valley Railway Company	B,C	6.76	$ 83,558	$ 273,177
Stark Electric Railroad	B,C	7.19	$ 67,402	$ 72,553
Northern Ohio Traction & Light Company	A,B	8.27	$ 150,003	$ 262,863
Cleveland, Southwestern & Columbus Railway	A,B	9.31	$ 52,136	$ 27,772
Lake Shore Electric Railway Company	A,B	10.51	$ 88,888	$ 31,985
Youngstown & Ohio River Railway	B,C	10.80	$ 92,381	$ 20,000
Youngstown & Southern Railway	B,C	12.78	$ 94,307	$ 56,436
Mansfield Railway, Light & Power Company	C	13.00	$ 80,409	$ 68,380
Youngstown & Sharon Street Railway	C	13.71	$ 149,187	$ 97,767
Lorain Street Railway	B,C	14.54	$ 170,959	$ 238,390
Pennsylvania & Ohio Railway	C	14.76	$ 50,248	$ 38,692

Electric railway company	ICC operating class	Average capital intensity	Average capitalization per track mile	Average revenue passengers per track mile
Cleveland, Painesville & Eastern Railroad	B,C	14.98	$ 87,931	$ 50,509
Cleveland, Painesville & Ashtabula Railroad	C	15.36	$ 78,601	$ 23,309
Mahoning & Shenango Railway & Light Company	A	15.96	$ 219,294	$ 313,839
Eastern Ohio Traction Company	C	17.71	$ 53,445	$ 13,542
Sandusky, Norwalk & Mansfield Electric Railway	C	18.60	$ 37,712	$ 8,129
Sandusky, Fremont & Southern Railway	C	25.68	$ 134,589	$ 12,560
Cleveland, Alliance & Mahoning Valley Railway	C	30.38	$ 71,893	$ 11,178
Sharon & New Castle Street Railway	C	41.17	$ 82,165	$ 9,633

Source: Stephen D. Hambley, "The Vanguard of a Regional Infrastructure: Electric Railways of Northeast Ohio, 1884–1932" (PhD diss., University of Akron, 1993), table 9.1, 416.

Capital Intensity Ratio

Capital intensity is the amount of assets required to finance each dollar of sales. It provides an indication of the amount of investment needed to generate added sales revenues in comparison with other companies or industries. It is used to evaluate comparatively how well firms manage their assets to produce income. In past economic writings it has often been referred to as a measure of the turnover of fixed property investment. Across industry types it also indicates the relative amount of capital needed for operating the business. For example, public utilities are said to be more capital intensive than retail or service firms because they require far more expenditures in materials, equipment, and property

Table 5.3. National capitalization factors, 1902–32

Average capital intensity by class			
Total capitalization / Total operating revenue			
Year	Class A	Class B	Class C
1902	8.90	9.51	10.90
1907	8.23	10.06	12.13
1912	7.69	9.57	10.79
1917	7.54	8.84	8.28
1922	5.25	5.79	5.95

Average capital intensity by industry			
Total capitalization / Total operating revenue			
Year	Telephone	Electric	Steam RR
1902	4.5	5.4	6.2
1907	4.7	5.6	5.0
1912	4.3	6.4	5.5
1917	3.9	5.2	4.5
1922	3.2	4.2	3.6

United States			
Total capitalization per track mile			
Year	Class A	Class B	Class C
1902	$ 178,063	$ 77,515	$ 47,872
1907	$ 159,241	$ 80,616	$ 64,913
1912	$ 155,029	$ 86,524	$ 63,600
1917	$ 161,909	$ 92,287	$ 57,728
1922	$ 161,229	$ 78,035	$ 50,092
1927	Not reported	Not reported	Not reported
1932	Not reported	Not reported	Not reported

Financing Northeast Ohio Electric Railways 179

United States			
Revenue passengers per track mile			
Year	Class A	Class B	Class C
1902	$358,372	$ 118,998	$ 75,484
1907	$361,701	$ 123,390	$ 74,788
1912	$399,058	$ 150,218	$ 74,009
1917	$358,840	$ 121,161	$ 83,248
1922	$420,996	$ 110,519	$ 78,151
1927	$443,695	$ 99,517	$ 63,154
1932	$369,460	$ 80,985	$ 33,717

Source: Stephen D. Hambley, "The Vanguard of a Regional Infrastructure: Electric Railways of Northeast Ohio, 1884–1932" (PhD diss., University of Akron, 1993), table 9.1, 416.

to produce and sell their product. This means that to increase sales or revenues by even a small amount requires a great deal more outside capital than for firms or industries with lower capital intensity figures.[23]

Economist Martin Glaeser calculated capital intensity (CI) ratios across a mix of public utilities and industries for representative years from 1902 to 1924. He found that the average industry capital intensity ratios of electric railways were higher than for all other types of utilities except for water. Table 5.3 provides a comparison of the capital intensity ratio for electric railways with steam railroads, electric power utilities, and the telephone industry. Notably, capital intensity ratios for these three selected industries were far lower than that observed for the electric railway industry, regardless of operating class.[24]

Likewise, Glaeser calculated the capital intensity ratios by groups of representative companies of various other nonpublic utilities industries. Again, according to his calculations, the electric railways had significantly higher ratios. The sampled bituminous coal mining firms had the highest ratio of the group, with a value of 2.94 dollars of fixed property investment per dollar of sales. Rubber and tire manufacturing firms had an average capital intensity ratio of 0.52 dollars of fixed property investment per dollar of sales. The sample of iron and steel manufacturing firms produced a capital intensity ratio of 1.43, while petroleum companies had a ratio of 1.33. The average ratio for ninety-four companies from 1916 to 1921 was

0.55 dollars of fixed property investment per dollar of sales. In comparison, as shown in table 5.2, the average capital intensity ratio for Class A electric railways in 1917 was 7.54, the lowest of the three railway operating classes.[25]

Glaeser's comparison of CI values across industry types shows that for the most part, the nation's electric railway industry required more capital per unit of sales than any other type of industry or public utility, except for water operations. He concluded that electric railway companies were typically more capital intensive than telephone, electric and gas utility companies, although some deviation between individual companies did exist. Criticisms that all electric railways experienced overcapitalization need to be evaluated against other measures of capital intensity, like capitalization per mile of track.

Capitalization per Mile of Track

In the 1890s the first chief statistician of the Interstate Commerce Commission, Henry Carter Adams, employed the calculated capitalization per mile of track to compare uniformly the different reported costs of construction and investment of the nation's steam railroads. The US Bureau of the Census and the investment and banking industries also used this calculation to analyze the relative capital investments in electric railway companies. It provided a modest, if imperfect, gauge of the relative expenses incurred in constructing an electric railway line while making adjustments for total road length. All other factors being equal, railways built at the same time should have approximately equal capitalization per mile of track figures. However, all intrinsic factors are rarely ever equal even in the same industry, let alone across industry types.[26]

Comparing steam railroad and electric railway industries or electric traction companies themselves using this factor should be done with caution. Total investment in road and equipment for electric railroads sometimes included the values of limited franchises secured from municipalities or counties for operating over public roads. The differing philosophies governing investment in electric railway and steam railroad rolling stock were also not reflected in the miles of track operated figure that was used to compute the factor. Steam railroads chose to invest in tracks or rolling stock depending on conditions that had little to do with factors that influenced electric railway investment. In addition, an interurban often reported the value of its electric power generating and distribution network in the total capitalization figure. This of course had an imprecise and often inconsistent relationship with total track mileage. The total operating expenses reflected the costs of constructing and operating these power plants. The sales of power sometimes appeared in the operating or gross revenues, depending on the year of the reporting information and the agency collecting the data. As an added asset to the total value of an interurban, the electric power plant bolstered the financial performance of the company and therefore reduced the price it paid to finance long-term debt. The boosting effect of the power properties on the salability of mortgage bonds became especially noticeable as the electric industry prospered in the 1920s while the traction companies declined.[27]

Whether a specific firm's total capitalization figure represented electric power plant properties became a question for stockholders as well as public utility regulators. Investment analysts warned public utility investors in the 1920s that mortgages could be spread over properties of varying type or separated, depending on the owner of the properties. Therefore the par value and dependability of bonds let against such properties could vary significantly between companies. Recalling that the US Census data used this par value to estimate total capitalization calls into question the total reliability and comparability of the factor across firms.[28]

Keeping these limitations in mind, the total capitalization per mile of track factor will be used to help identify overcapitalized railway lines. Since the factor became a conventional method of comparing relative capital investment for the electric railway and steam railroad industries, its use is reasonable. Provided other factors are considered in making the final judgment, the average capitalization per mile of track by railway class will help identify companies normally identified as overcapitalized by other firms within the industry.

Notably, the Cleveland, Southwestern & Columbus Railway system had a comparatively low average capitalization per track mile of $52,136—third lowest amongst all of the systems in Northeast Ohio. Only the Pennsylvania & Ohio Railway (P&O) and the Sandusky, Norwalk & Mansfield Electric Railway (SN&M) were lower, but both were ICC Class C operations and had significantly high capitalization ratios of 35.4 percent and 63.4 percent, respectively.

Total Revenue Passengers per Mile of Track

The number of revenue passengers per mile of track gives an indication of the density of traffic. It provides a means of indexing the growth or decline in passenger traffic because it adjusts for track extensions or abandonments. However, in comparing various railway companies, one notable characteristic emerges. Urban lines had higher traffic densities than interurban or suburban operations. This is because railway lines extended into rural areas tended to have fewer people to draw upon in comparison with roads operating in urban areas where more people rode the railway. The US Bureau of the Census explained in 1912 this relationship, "The extension of lines into rural districts, where travel is relatively light, tends to reduce the average number of passengers carried per mile of track and is a factor that affects comparative averages." This indicates that comparing the traffic density figure between different types of railways should be done with caution.[29]

The traffic density figures, however, provide a means of evaluating claims that electric railway promoters built more miles of track than future traffic could support. Examining the issue of overextension reveals its critical relationship to overcapitalization. They both fed upon the speculative fever of electric railway construction and promotion. In addition, when capitalization and track extensions were not held within reasonable bounds they both contributed to the eventual demise of the electric traction firms.

George Hilton and John Due have contended that in the first interurban railway building boom starting in 1900s many railway promoters overestimated the rate of long-term future traffic growth. But in many rapidly growing cities this might not have been as unreasonable an assumption as some have asserted. Hilton and Due, as well as urban transit policy historians like David W. Jones, have plainly stated that the cyclic overexpansion of electric railways into regions where population growth could not possibly have supported their continued existence doomed much of the industry to an early grave. The basis of their contention is that overexpansion cut into the much-needed profits required to depreciate adequately the equipment and expand auxiliary operations. The traffic density factor will help identify which Northeast Ohio lines may have overextended their lines and subsequently might provide some rationale for their ultimate demise.

The results of the analysis using the financial indicators presented in tables 5.3 and 5.4 show that with a couple of exceptions Northeast Ohio electric railways were overcapitalized. Since annual national data are not available, average values over the life of the roads were compared to the averages calculated from the US Bureau of the Census reports. The comparison shows that the interurbans tended to be overcapitalized while some urban lines avoided that problem. The electric railways that did not appear overcapitalized operated within the region's largest cities: Youngstown Municipal Railway and Cleveland Railway Company and its predecessors, Cleveland City Railway and Cleveland Electric Railway Company.

There is at least one factor that explains why these two electric railway companies had above-average ridership, lower capital intensity ratios, and lower capitalization per mile of track figures than the national average for ICC Class A companies. The Cleveland Railway Company and the Youngstown Municipal Railway operated under service-at-cost agreements with their respective municipalities that provided for tight supervision of their methods of operations and financing. Undoubtedly, this public oversight of electric railway capitalization helped limit the amount of bonds and stocks issued by the corporations and therefore their debt payments. How this materially inhibited overcapitalization requires further explanation.

A pioneering effort in the municipal regulation of street railways, Cleveland's service-at-cost agreement under the Tayler plan became a model for other cities throughout the nation. Witnesses before the Federal Electric Railway Commission in 1919 testified that they considered the service-at-cost plan in Cleveland responsible for keeping the road well maintained, providing first-class service to riders while protecting the interests of its investors and restoring credibility with the public and creditors. Other cities—for example, Cincinnati, Dallas, Montreal, and Youngstown—adopted similar plans of operation in the 1910s. Its principal benefit, according the FEC testimony, resulted from removing the shadow of speculative gain that had tainted local public opinion against street railway operators.[30]

Under the Tayler Grant franchise agreement, Cleveland reserved the right to determine the level of street railway service, scheduling of runs, routes, and the terminal locations for connecting interurban lines. In return, company investors received guarantees of fixed returns: an annual

6 percent return on capital stock, 6 percent on floating indebtedness, and 5 percent annually on the total bonded debt of the corporation. As John J. Stanley, president of the Cleveland Railway Company, explained, "The scheme was to deduct from the receipts the operating costs, the maintenance costs, taxes and interest. The interest cost was, of course, the 6 per cent on our stock. The balance would go into the interest fund. When that interest fund became $700,000 or more, the fare was reduced. When it came down to $300,000 the fare was increased. So the interest fund is the barometer."[31]

In order to make the agreement work, the issue of capitalization and the opposing views of how much the intangible investments should be worth had to be resolved up front. According to Newton D. Baker, city solicitor at the time of the Tayler Grant franchise, capitalization of the Cleveland Railway Company represented its physical valuation. The city agreed to allow the capitalization of the unexpired franchise value at the time of consolidation, but it stipulated that it be reduced each year thereafter to nearly zero by 1919. This meant that the funded debt interest payments became tied to a diminishing level of intangible asset valuation. The provision effectively drained out the "water" in the corporate securities and subsequently affected the company's operating and fixed costs.[32]

The original service-at-cost plan in Cleveland imposed two significant problems that influenced the long-term viability of the railway operation. First, the fixed accounts for extensions and improvements of the railway as stipulated in the Tayler Grant agreement proved to be too restrictive. The agreement prohibited the Cleveland Railway Company from selling its stock below par value; it remained below par from 1918 to 1925. In order to pay for improvements, other methods of financing included increased fares or special allowances granted by Cleveland City Council. That body did not like to issue special allowances or grant increased fares to pay for capital improvements, so it made an attempt to find a politically viable solution to the problem. In 1925 a special committee of the Cleveland Chamber of Commerce at the request of the Street Railway Committee of the Cleveland City Council studied the franchise problem and its effects on the fares. These participants concluded in a published report that "this method of financing does not increase the capitalization and fixed charges of the company, but has a tendency to increase the rate of fare to a greater extent than would result if new stock were issued for such a purpose, since such financing comes out of the fare box."[33]

Second, the fixed return on the capital provided no added inducements for improving the economics of the operation. If the company management had successfully implemented strategies to reduce the costs of transportation in the system, it would not have been rewarded. In fact, the franchise agreement would have required a reduction in fares. As Newton Baker pointed out in 1919, it would have been better for both parties if the return on capital could have been boosted an additional one-half of one percent as long as the company did not reach the maximum fare stipulated in the franchise.[34]

To address these weaknesses, the Cleveland Chamber of Commerce report made several recommendations that consisted of compromises both parties could tolerate. Cleveland City Council adopted several of these compromise positions on April 26, 1926, when it amended the original plan and extended the franchise to 1951. The local lawmakers granted the Cleveland Railway Company the right to operate buses and increased the maximum fare to ten cents cash, fifty cents for six tickets, one cent for transfer, and no rebate. They also adjusted the levels of the interest fund account to a minimum of $500,000 before fares would be increased and to a maximum of $1.1 million, which would subsequently cause a reduction in fares. The settlement resolving the issues satisfactorily for both parties lasted well into the worst years of the Great Depression. The settlement worked so well that until 1938, stockholders received the guaranteed returns, unlike the experiences of other Northeast Ohio electric railway companies.[35]

The success of Cleveland's service-at-cost plan provided an inspiration to other municipal leaders in Northeast Ohio to emulate the joint private-public arrangement. Beginning January 16, 1919, the Youngstown Municipal Railway (YMR) operated under a service-at-cost franchise with the city of Youngstown. Guided by the Cleveland approach, the terms of the YMR arrangement reflected the same restrictions first used nearly a decade earlier in the Forest City. Just like the Cleveland City street railway commissioner, Youngstown's commissioner stipulated the company's level of service, reviewed all accounts, and supervised all expenditures. Youngstown's service-at-cost franchise guaranteed an annual rate of return of 7 percent to the firm on a capitalization that closely approximated the real physical valuation of the property. It likewise diminished the intangible value of the YMR's corporate worth, thus reducing public complaints and suspicion. The service-at-cost operation proved to be such a success that the company conducted an extensive modernization program in the 1920s. Its quality of service helped the YMR earn along with other lines in the Penn-Ohio system the transit industry award for excellence in 1926.[36]

The Federal Electric Railways Commission echoed the praises it heard about the benefits of service-at-cost plans. The commission suggested that the plan provided a better alternative than outright municipal ownership for solving the critical financial difficulties that plagued America's electric railways. The chief barrier to overcome in solving the nation's electric railway problem, according to the FEC and numerous witnesses to their hearings in 1919, required restoring public confidence in the industry. Newton D. Baker's testimony reiterated that important point when he said, "I do not think it is possible for me to emphasize too strongly, so far as the expression of my own belief is concerned, the feeling that no street railroad settlement can be a successful one which is not understood in its details and approved by the people. It is one of the most intimate of their services, and they resent and distrust and suspect the management unless they understand."[37]

Debt Interest Paid

The initial analysis using the first three discriminating factors produces a large list of electric railways indicating probable overcapitalization and overextension. To identify definitively those roads that were in fact overcapitalized requires applying the final and fourth factor. As shown in table 5.4, the debt interest paid or accrued per year as a percentage of total operating revenues provides an additional way of judging overcapitalization.

At least one financial reality operated against syndicates overinflating the values of their properties through bond sales. The more bonds the company sold, the higher its annual fixed interest costs. The more that the bonds actually stood for real assets, instead of water or speculation on future earnings, the greater the earning power and therefore the easier it would be to meet the annual interest payments. The presumption is that regardless of the reasons for taking on fixed debt, a well-managed and well-operated electric railway company should have been able to assume those fixed costs. If more capital investment went for rolling stock, additional trackage, or greater electrical generating capacity, firms should have also set aside the appropriate amounts in equipment depreciation accounts. The final proof, then, of whether a Northeast Ohio electric railway company overcapitalized or overextended its tracks is in the proportion of operating revenues dedicated to the payment of long-term interest. If the company management utilized the capital wisely, the firm should have been able to cover its fixed interest costs better than a firm that had overborrowed or overextended its track mileage.

Table 5.4 provides a listing of Northeast Ohio electric railways by the average debt interest paid or accrued (DIP) as a percentage of total operating revenues over their respective years of operation. Minimum and maximum DIPs observed over their respective years of operation as well as the standard deviation are also provided. The standard deviation is a descriptive statistic providing a measure of the dispersion of the data around the mean. It describes numerically the amount of variation from the average for the entire sample population. A small standard deviation of a few percentage points would indicate a more consistent pattern of a firm's debt management in comparison with a firm with a larger standard deviation. The Cleveland, Southwestern & Columbus Railway system over its thirty-one years of operation had an average DIP of 19.6 percent, with a standard deviation of 4.3 percent—a comparatively low variance, indicating a reasonably consistent pattern of debt management. As presented in table 5.4, the Pomeroy-Mandelbaum property performed better than any of the Everett-Moore lines—Northern Ohio Traction & Light Company, Lake Shore Electric, and the Cleveland, Painesville & Eastern Railroad—with respect to debt issued and managed.

The national statistics furnish a measure of the overall traction industry's debt management performance. According to US Census data, the average amount of revenues paid toward debt interest equaled 15.7 percent of the total operating income for the period from 1902 to 1922. The maximum DIP in any one year was 17.3 percent of the total operating revenues in 1912, while the minimum was 13.8 percent in 1922. These figures provide some guideposts for scrutinizing the DIPs of Northeast Ohio electric railways operating from 1900 to 1932.[38]

Table 5.4. Debt interest paid and capitalization analysis of Northeast Ohio electric railways

Electric railway company	Average for period	Number of years	Observed Minimum	Observed Maximum	Standard deviation	Factors met	Description
Cleveland Railway Comp / Cleveland Electric Railway	3.7%	28	1.4%	9.5%	2.7%	0	Low
Youngstown Municipal Railway	5.7%	9	4.3%	8.7%	1.3%	0	Low
Youngstown, Park & Falls Street Railway	7.0%	11	4.5%	11.6%	2.4%	1	Medium
Stark Electric Railroad	13.7%	26	6.6%	24.4%	5.5%	1	Medium
Mahoning Valley Railway Company	15.1%	15	9.2%	20.3%	3.7%	1	Medium
Youngstown & Sharon Street Railway	19.4%	13	6.5%	30.2%	7.3%	3	High
Cleveland, Southwestern & Columbus Railway	19.6%	31	10.5%	29.9%	4.3%	3	High
Youngstown & Ohio River Railway	20.4%	22	9.4%	43.5%	8.8%	4	High
Lorain Street Railway	21.8%	26	7.7%	45.0%	13.4%	3	High
Northern Ohio Traction & Light Company	23.5%	30	12.1%	35.0%	5.7%	4	High
Ashtabula Rapid Transit Company	23.5%	15	19.0%	32.9%	4.0%	2	Medium
Eastern Ohio Traction Company	23.7%	18	2.7%	47.3%	13.1%	3	High

Column group headers: Debt interest paid (DIP) or accrued per year as percent of operating revenues; Likelihood of overcapitalization

Financing Northeast Ohio Electric Railways

Electric railway company	Debt interest paid (DIP) or accrued per year as percent of operating revenues						Likelihood of overcapitalization	
	Average for period	Number of years	Observed Minimum	Observed Maximum	Standard deviation		Factors met	Description
Youngstown & Southern Railway	24.7%	25	5.4%	56.8%	11.8%	4	High
Lake Shore Electric Railway Company	25.1%	29	11.3%	50.4%	9.8%	3	High
Mansfield Railway, Light & Power Company	28.8%	11	20.4%	39.2%	6.3%	4	High
Mahoning & Shenango Railway & Light Company	30.6%	10	25.4%	59.7%	9.8%	3	High
Sandusky, Fremont & Southern Railway	30.8%	22	19.2%	51.9%	9.4%	4	High
Cleveland, Painesville & Eastern Railroad	31.1%	27	20.6%	50.4%	6.1%	4	High
Sharon & New Castle Street Railway	31.1%	12	11.3%	54.7%	16.8%	4	High
Pennsylvania & Ohio Railway	35.4%	15	26.2%	43.0%	4.9%	3	High
Cleveland, Painesville & Ashtabula Railroad	36.6%	21	13.4%	72.7%	11.7%	4	High
Cleveland, Alliance & Mahoning Valley Railway	45.6%	11	23.6%	99.7%	25.9%	4	High
Sandusky, Norwalk & Mansfield Electric Railway	63.4%	8	52.1%	69.6%	6.2%	3	High

Note: Average debt interest paid, ranked from lowest to highest.

The data reveal that the two electric railways operating under municipal service-at-cost franchises paid the lowest proportions of their total operating revenues to service their long-term funded debt. As suggested in table 5.4, the Cleveland Railway Company consistently had the lowest DIP of any other railway in Northeast Ohio. Throughout the twenty-eight years of data analyzed, the CRC's average DIP was 3.7 percent with an observed maximum of 9.5 percent and minimum of 1.4 percent.

The company with the next-lowest DIP was the Youngstown Municipal Railway, which operated from 1919 to 1940. However, the city did not take over ownership until 1921, and the interest payment for capitalization before that date was included with that of the Mahoning & Shenango Railway & Light Company. For the nine years of information available between 1922 and 1932, the YMR had an average DIP of 5.7 percent with a maximum of 8.7 percent and minimum of 4.3 percent of the total operating revenues.

Judging by the data, evidence indicates that the Cleveland Railway Company and the Youngstown Municipal Railway were not overcapitalized or overextended. They both survived relatively intact the lean years of the 1920s and the devastation of the Great Depression. Their survival, however, does not prove that overcapitalization, which plagued the industry, caused the demise of the other roads. It does indicate that those two properties survived the roughest operating years of the industry in large part due to their debt management practices and relatively low funded debt.

Based upon the four step analysis, it is uncertain whether the Mahoning Valley Railway; Stark Electric Railroad; Youngstown, Park & Falls Street Railway; and Ashtabula Rapid Transit should be considered grossly overcapitalized. Likewise, based upon the conservative indicators used to identify overcapitalization characteristics of the lines, the debt management of the Cleveland, Southwestern & Columbus Railway was also probably quite reasonable. Consequently, other operating and financial statistics of these companies should be individually examined for indications of gross overcapitalization.

Figure 5.3 shows the DIP of selected operating companies rated in table 5.4 with low to high likelihoods of overcapitalization. When looking at the DIP of urban and interurban operating companies with low to high likelihoods of overcapitalization, there are a few noteworthy observations. The general trend for the percentage of debt interest paid from the early

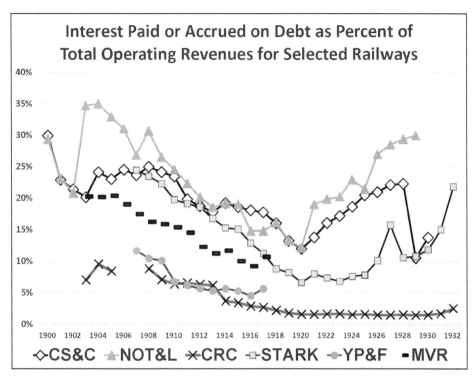

Figure 5.3. Selected railways with low to high likelihood of overcapitalization. *Legend:* CS&C: Cleveland, Southwestern & Columbus Railway Company; NOT&L: Northern Ohio Traction & Light Company; CRC: Cleveland Railway Company; Stark: Stark Electric Railroad; YP&F: Youngstown, Park & Falls Street Railway; MVR: Mahoning Valley Railway. (Chart by author)

1900s to the 1918–20 period was downward for all lines examined. The Youngstown, Park & Falls Street Railway had the lowest average DIP of the group examined in table 5.4, the third lowest for the entire region and well below the national average. Only one indicator suggested that the line might have been overcapitalized: the YP&F had an average capitalization of $99,854 per mile of track, compared to the national average of $56,841 per mile for an ICC Class C operation. However, it had the second-highest average annual passenger revenue of $555,936 per track mile in the region. That high traffic volume largely came from the sole rail connection to the popular Idora Park and exclusive street railway privilege in crossing the Market Street bridge over the Mahoning River in downtown Youngstown. The investment was no doubt financially prudent for the times and should not be considered overcapitalized.[39]

The values calculated for the average capital intensity (ACI) and average revenue passengers (ARP) per mile of track for the Youngstown, Park & Falls Street Railway (YP&F) indicate that the line had a relatively high traffic density and lower capital intensity than other Northeast Ohio electric railways except for the Cleveland Railway Company and Youngstown Municipal Railway. However, the YP&F was consolidated with the city lines of the Youngstown Municipal Railway line in 1922 and did not suffer from deficient debt management.

The YP&F primarily served two important transportation functions. First, the company operated the sole streetcar route to the popular amusement park, Idora Park, on weekends and holidays and also extended through one of the more affluent areas of the city. Consequently, the doubletracked YP&F line had one of the highest traffic volumes in the Mahoning & Shenango Railway & Light Company (MSR&L) network as reflected in the statistics. Second, the line had only eight miles of track from 1907 to 1922, and it was never extended beyond Idora Park. The parent company, MSR&L, which took control in 1906, made only minor capital improvements on the line. The company never issued additional mortgage bonds after its initial bonds in 1898, thereby keeping the capitalization number comparatively low.[40]

To the north of Youngstown another city railway system exhibited characteristics suggesting that it might have been overcapitalized. The fifteen years of data available for analysis indicate that the Ashtabula Rapid Transit Company (ART) only exceeded the industry average in two categories, the capitalization per mile of track and the percent funded debt interest paid from operating revenues. In the remaining two, the ART had a capital intensity lower than the industry average and carried more revenue passengers per mile of track than the industry average for a Class C operating company. The data suggest that this property was probably overcapitalized from the start. Yet, it managed to survive beyond the first industry decline in the early 1920s because of municipal ownership.[41]

Another company to the south of Ashtabula Rapid Transit Company, the Mahoning Valley Railway Company (MVR), did not become the property of a municipality, but instead was one component in a much larger electric railway system and the subsidiary of an interstate holding company. The statistics for the MVR reveal that during its years as an independent operating company it failed in only one out of the four factors used to identify possible overcapitalization. However, once absorbed by the larger corporation as the MSR&L, it shared in the problems of overcapitalization that plagued that network. The MVR operated from 1896 to 1917, when it formally merged with its parent company, Mahoning & Shenango Railway & Light. Like the YP&F and the ART, most of the MVR's track mileage had been completed early in its lifespan and mortgage bonds issued only once specifically on the property in June 1903. Under the control of the Republic Railway & Light Company, subsequent bonds issued over all of the Youngstown area properties did not become part of the funded debt interest payments of the MVR. The statistics can only evaluate the debt management practices of the MVR while it functioned separately as an independent operating company. According to operating and financial data, the DIP of the MVR declined steadily from 1905 to 1916, indicating management's desire to work down the bond interest.

The only indication that the Mahoning Valley Railway Company may have been overcapitalized comes from comparing its average capitalization per mile of track of $83,558 with the national average for a Class B operating railway of $82,995 per mile of track during the same period. Since these figures are close and the method used to calculate the MVR's total capitalization was conservative, the firm should not be deemed overcapitalized on solely this basis. The MVR's debt interest payments did fall below the national average DIP throughout most of its operating life. This fact and the results of the other indicators confirm that the line did not suffer from overcapitalization prior to its formal merger with the MSR&L in 1917.

Northeast Ohio's largest independent interurban system, the Stark Electric Railroad (SER), serves as a prime example of a responsibly promoted and well-managed electric railway company. It should be noted that unlike any other interurbans operating in Northeast Ohio, the SER did not recapitalize its debt during the 1910s or early 1920s. Without adding to the long-term debt of the SER, the owners and management demonstrated an unusually high degree of frugality in financing their operations. Working down the bond interest payment, the company kept its rolling stock operating over the line longer than many other interurbans in the region through a reputedly high standard of maintenance.[42]

However frugally managed, the Stark Electric Railroad's low traffic density as measured by the average revenue passengers per mile of track indicated a meager level of passenger earnings to support the debt payments. Considerable portions of SER's gross earnings came from power sales and freight services. At the end of 1927 the company sold its profitable power properties to pay off its outstanding mortgage bonds issued in 1903 that were due on January 1, 1928. The dramatic jump in the DIP after 1928 depicted in figure 5.3 was caused by the refinancing of the outstanding debt and dramatic decline in operating revenues. Entirely dependent upon passenger earnings for its income, the SER entered receivership in 1930, and survived nearly a decade of marginal earnings and no added capital investment. Even devoid of high fixed costs for funded debt payments, the SER could not survive the declining demand for passenger services brought on by the surge in popularity of automobiles and buses. Responsible debt management did not provide enough assurance of longevity for an interurban line like the SER.

The Cleveland, Southwestern & Columbus Railway (CS&C) is the only other interurban that could be considered less overcapitalized compared to others that operated in Northeast Ohio. But the overcapitalization did not occur during the great period of growth between 1901 and 1907. The data suggest that overcapitalization of the CS&C occurred in 1924, well after its period of expansion. It also shows that other factors played a more significant role in the demise of the interurban line.

Prior to 1924, officers of the Southwestern managed the funded debt of the line responsibly, given the nature of its operations and desire to expand its electric power sales. As depicted in figure 5.3, the Cleveland and Southwestern Traction started in 1900 with a debt interest payment approximately equal to 30 percent of its total operating revenues and reduced it to 20 percent by 1903. After a bump back to 24 percent in 1904, from then to 1907 growth in operating revenues kept the increased interest payment proportionally level. Following the merger of Cleveland & Southwestern Traction Company; Cleveland, Ashland & Mansfield Traction Company; and the Cleveland, Elyria & Western Railway Company to form the Cleveland, Southwestern & Columbus Railway Company in 1907, the DIP generally decreased until 1921. During that time the CS&C did not issue additional bonds and it continually worked down the bond interest.

The specter of financial troubles hit the Southwestern just as the United States prepared for entrance into World War I. The fundamental shift in the US economy that became manifest during the war brought about severe operating problems for the interurban. From 1917 to 1929, the CS&C went through a series of financial maneuvers designed to boost business and reduce costs. Sharp increases in operating expenses in 1917 followed by a decline in gross revenues in 1921 caused the company to lose money and forced it into receivership in 1922. The bondholders foreclosed on the line in 1924 and reorganized the debt.

During the reorganization, the Southwestern issued $2.2 million in general mortgage bonds, but insufficient earnings forced deferment of the first scheduled interest payment until 1929. The restructuring of the debt in this way started a financial time bomb that could only be defused by increasing revenues. However, as previously described, the CS&C's innovative methods of stimulating passenger revenues failed to bring the company back from the path of destruction. The continued rising share of operating costs and declining revenues throughout the remaining years of the 1920s forced the company to sell off its assets. In December 1928, the CS&C sold its profitable electric power properties to pay off the 1924 bonds scheduled for payment on March 1, 1929. The line fell into receivership in October and abandoned operations in January 1931. The Guardian Trust Company compelled that event when it foreclosed on $2 million worth of unpaid mortgage bonds.[43]

The foreclosure and restructuring of the Southwestern's debt in 1924 did not result from a mishandling of its earlier funded debt. Rather, it came as a consequence of declining sales and dramatically increased operating costs. In the industry, one of the common measures of fiscal health and management efficiency was the calculation of gross operating expenses divided by gross operating revenues, called the Operating Ratio. The smaller the ratio, the more efficient the company management is at generating revenue compared to total expenses. As shown in table 5.5, the operating ratio of the CS&C started to climb significantly in 1917, and it continued to increase throughout the 1920s. At the same time, a national study of 435 electric railways reported a shift of industry operating ratios from 65.14 percent in 1917 to 72.13 percent in 1918, largely owing to drastic increased costs of labor and supplies and to minimal increases in reve-

Table 5.5. Operating ratios for selected Northeast Ohio systems, 1900-1931

	Operating expenses / Operating revenues					
Year	All NE Ohio	CS&C	NOT&L	LSE	CRC	Stark
1900	57%	57%	61%			
1901	46%	55%	57%			
1902	59%	57%	55%	67%		
1903	62%	59%	57%	64%	62%	
1904	64%	62%	57%	59%	61%	
1905	60%	58%	56%	54%	61%	53%
1906	55%	56%	59%	55%		43%
1907	59%	58%	57%	53%		43%
1908	62%	62%	58%	54%	61%	54%
1909	63%	62%	55%	53%	60%	44%
1910	57%	60%	55%	43%	71%	43%
1911	62%	57%	55%	49%	77%	46%
1912	63%	59%	53%	55%	75%	49%
1913	69%	61%	58%	55%	76%	52%
1914	64%	62%	57%	59%	73%	53%
1915	67%	63%	65%	59%	72%	54%
1916	67%	61%	58%	59%	74%	54%
1917	73%	77%	58%	62%	80%	61%
1918	79%	76%	70%	68%	77%	76%
1919	78%	73%	79%	67%	75%	73%
1920	89%	79%	85%	71%	89%	77%
1921	94%	82%	84%	75%	79%	78%
1922	91%	83%	79%	69%	74%	85%
1923	94%	82%	87%	70%	88%	82%
1924	111%	81%	95%	74%	82%	86%
1925	103%	86%	86%	77%	85%	90%
1926	110%	90%	102%	83%	84%	99%
1927	91%	91%	100%	85%	79%	86%

Financing Northeast Ohio Electric Railways

Operating expenses / Operating revenues							
Year	All NE Ohio	CS&C	NOT&L	LSE	CRC	Stark
1928	92%	92%	97%	84%	82%	99%
1929	94%	100%	97%	102%	85%	93%
1930	110%	115%	102%	123%	77%	97%
1931	120%	140%	116%	149%	75%	109%

Legend: All NE Ohio: All electric railways of Northeast Ohio; CS&C: Cleveland, Southwestern & Columbus Railway Company; NOT&L: Northern Ohio Traction & Light Company; LSE: Lakeshore Electric; CRC: Cleveland Railway Company; Stark: Stark Electric Company.
Source: Hambley, "Vanguard of a Regional Infrastructure."

nues.[44] It is clear that operating costs after 1917 had a more dramatic effect on the CS&C's profitability than the debt interest payment that continued to decline until 1921–22. It is fair to say that the rapid escalation of operating expenses compared to operating revenues was a problem for every electric railway operation nationally.

When all external and internal factors influencing the viability of electric railway financing and operations are considered, it must be recognized that the owners and management of the electric railways ultimately determined the capital structure of the enterprise. A pattern emerges from the data presented in figure 5.3, tables 5.4 and 5.5, and figure 5.4 that leads to a conclusion about the quality of the Northeast Ohio's electric railway promoters and owners. Ownership of the various lines as they expanded in the early years and as they matured to become ongoing business concerns differed in their approaches to funded debt. The service-at-cost agreements forced upon the lines by Cleveland and Youngstown circumscribed the owners' decisions to use funded debt to expand trackage or improve the rolling stock. That direct public oversight did not occur until 1910 for the Cleveland Railway Company and until 1921 for the Youngstown Municipal Railway.

The syndicates responsible for the construction of the Stark Electric Railroad and the Cleveland, Southwestern & Columbus Railway effectively remained in control of the companies throughout most of their operating lifespans. The stockholders' decisions to incur additional debt were limited to the earliest years of expansion and appear to have been

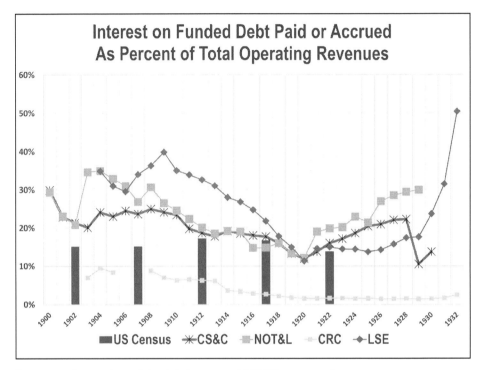

Figure 5.4. Comparison of the debt interest paid (DIP) or accrued per year as a percentage of total operating revenues for the Cleveland, Southwestern & Columbus Railway (CS&C); Northern Ohio Traction and Light Company (NOT&L); Cleveland Railway Company (CRC); and Lake Shore Electric (LSE); and national average documented by the US Census for all types of electric railways (urban, suburban, and interurban). (Chart by author)

reasonable, given the typical business expectations and attitudes of the time. Neither company was grossly overcapitalized when comparing their average investment per mile of track to the national and the regional industry. If there was "water" contained in the capitalizations of these two roads, it was a trickle compared to the "soaking" from such lines as the Lorain Street Railroad, Mahoning & Shenango Railway & Light Company, and Sandusky, Fremont & Southern Railway.

The data presented also indicates that the competing Everett and Moore syndicate typically overcapitalized every property that it promoted and operated. This was a pattern that emerged early in their interurban promotions which the syndicate carried over from its urban street railway and steam railroad building experiences. In all fairness, it can be said that some of the syndicate's properties were not as grossly overcapitalized as others. For example, Everett and Moore capitalized the Lake Shore Electric at $88,888 per mile, while their Northern Ohio Traction & Light Company had an average investment of $150,003 per mile. But the pattern makes clear that the cost of the syndicate's system building of the LSE and the NOT&L in 1905 and 1906 doomed both operations to proportionately higher debt interest payments than the Cleveland, Southwestern & Columbus Railway and the Stark Electric Railroad.

HOLDING COMPANIES

It should be noted that another form of corporate ownership and management lent itself to overcapitalization of two Northeast Ohio lines in the teens and twenties. The overcapitalization of these combined urban and interurban roads resulted from decisions made by the "absentee landlords" of the industry, the holding companies. How this came about has much to do with the character of the industry throughout the nation during these decades and its uneasy relationship with the public. If service-at-cost agreements improved the public's view of electric railways, holding companies heightened the problem. This, however, was not the original intent or necessarily the worst attribute of this particular form of corporate organization.

The modern holding company originated at a time that state legislatures looked to expand businesses access to capital and rationalize the bond and securities markets. Advocates of holding companies claimed that the securities of the large holding company and its subsidiaries would be far safer and more stable than those of small independent firms. In the midst of the hard economic times and short money supply of the 1890s, holding companies offered hope of renewed prosperity with stability to business-dominated state legislatures.

The modern holding companies that eventually stretched across interstate boundaries appeared following legislation in business-dominated states like New Jersey. Starting in 1895, several states liberalized their corporate statutes, allowing firms to sell and issue bonds in order to finance subsidiary corporations. Proponents of the holding companies later claimed them to be the answer to costly receiverships and financial reorganizations resulting from the sins of overcapitalization. The holding company form of corporate organization failed to live up to such overstated promises of widespread business reform.[45]

The holding company organization effectively produced the same business management benefits of consolidation without actually merging the corporate entities. The capital of the holding company consisted of the stocks and bonds of other corporations rather than physical property. This business structure facilitated the financing of extensions and improvements of local companies that had weaker credit. Through the centralization of purchasing and management training, it also enabled improved efficiencies in the operating costs of the subsidiary companies.[46]

Holding companies became the dominant method of corporate organization of the public utility industry in the 1910s and furthered in the 1920s. A legal brief on the Clayton Antitrust Act submitted to the Committee on Interstate Commerce of the US Senate in 1914 on behalf of several public utility holding companies described the great extent to which this type of organization had permeated the industry. According to the testimony, holding companies controlled 76 percent of America's electric light and power industry, approximately two-thirds of the nation's capital invested in artificial gas companies, and over two-thirds of the entire capital invested in street and interurban railways. Public utility holding companies controlled in 1914 a little over 61 percent of the nation's street and interurban track mileage. In Northeast Ohio, the holding company became a force in street railway properties starting in 1911 when the Republic Railway & Light Company purchased 98 percent of the common stock of the Mahoning & Sharon Railway & Light Company.[47]

The presence of holding companies added to problems between the public and the local traction operators and to the inability to diminish escalating operating costs in the 1920s. The Northern Ohio Traction & Light Company came under the thumb of a New York holding company, Northern Ohio Electric Corporation, in 1916, and later the Commonwealth & Southern Corporation. The NOT&L battled throughout the 1920s with Akron officials and public opinion over franchise provisions and fare rates. The public's attitude, as reflected through its elected representatives, was mistrustful of the millions in assets and revenues held by the NOT&L and its parent company in deciding what was an equitable agreement.

As John Moody, the famed utility analyst, described it in 1920, the holding company had two main disadvantages.

> One, a condition suggestive of absentee landlordism is the fact that properties are dominated and managed by interests far removed from the locality served, with a resulting tendency to cause local dissatisfaction. Another is a feeling likely to exist in such cases on the part of the community served, that the property is backed by unlimited wealth and the question of profitable local operation is immaterial if under the circumstances the public can gain the better of the situation.[48]

How then did holding companies influence the capitalization of Northeast Ohio's interurbans and city lines? Critics argued that holding companies commonly caused overcapitalization of street railway properties. Joseph B. Eastman, a member of the US Interstate Commerce Commission in 1919, charged that these corporations issued shares on an inflated capitalization that forced them "to draw every possible drop of income out of the underlying companies that could be secured in order to support earnings upon the inflated shares of these voluntary associations." In the case of Northeast Ohio, these holding companies did issue bonds on the combined electric and traction properties in the mid-1920s, which aggravated the debt interest payment problem of the railway portion.[49]

Heightened by a public that suspected covert motives behind their local investments, holding companies faced charges that they woefully neglected the traction portions of their properties. To many citizens and politicians, the holding company should be blamed for rush hour transportation problems because they refused to invest the money needed to buy and operate more streetcars. The firms had difficulty defending themselves against these charges largely because they contained hints of truth.

In the case of Northeast Ohio's electric railways, the holding companies over the Northern Ohio Traction & Light Company and the Mahoning & Shenango Railway & Light Company legally split off their traction and electric holdings, to the detriment of urban and interurban transit. In fact, investors of the larger holding corporation derived a major benefit from its ability to sell off portions of its subsidiaries that proved to be unprofitable or burdened with long-term debt. If timed correctly with fluctuations in the stock or bond markets, profitable subsidiaries could be recapitalized at better rates. At the same time, the holding company could consolidate the unprofitable departments of several properties under another subsidiary.

The "Great Breakup" of the Northern Ohio Traction & Light Company system in 1930 and the Republic Railway & Light Company dismemberment of the Mahoning & Shenango Railway & Light Company's properties in 1920 are both examples of this practice. These holding companies broke up their systems into woefully overcapitalized transportation and electric power properties that were exceptionally valuable to the parent company. In both cases the transportation lines were split up, sold off, and eventually abandoned. In aggregate the MSR&L traction and light properties did not appear to be especially overcapitalized. But once the city of Youngstown took over the city lines and the profitable electrical properties consolidated into the Penn-Ohio Electric Company, the interurbans revealed that independently they had been overcapitalized and overextended.

In effect, the holding company prospered more by separating the traction and light companies than by keeping them together. The traction firms were already overcapitalized, and the market would not absorb more capital stocks or bond without making the company pay a higher premium. On the other hand, the electrical industry needed the added capital to continue its tremendous growth. By separating them, the holding company could get the needed capital on the bond market without having to pay the price for shouldering the burdens of their traction operations.

SUMMARY AND CONCLUSIONS

This chapter placed the region's electric railways in the context of the national industry. The national patterns of growth and development were not exactly reflected in the statistics for the region's traction industry. Rather, they reflect the character of regional economic cycles, business organizations, and the changeable demands of the public. The region's lines tended to be longer and costlier per track mile than the national average. They also drew from a smaller than average traffic density in conducting their passenger business. This may help explain why these roads were at the forefront of the industry in innovative ways of boosting ridership and transportation-related services.

Historians Hilton and Due asserted that early overcapitalization and overbuilding of the interurbans into rural areas pushed the industry into an early grave. The evidence indicates that this became a significant problem for the region's electric railways, and with few exceptions a principal cause of their individual demise. Other factors contributed to the ultimate decline and death of the region's interurbans, but as an industry none became so pervasive or imposing.

A fundamental question arising from the capitalization analysis and preceding description of railway financing remains to be answered succinctly. Why did most of these electric railways overbuild and overcapitalize? Several answers discussed above alluded to the relationship between the profits of steam railroad promoters and those gained in electric railway construction. In addition, the loosening of credit enabled by industrial securities issued through aggressive financial institutions and the interurban network building accomplished by the Everett and Moore syndicate also explain part of the reason. But in the final analysis the real answer ostensibly boils down to two simple factors: first, the business and political culture of Northeast Ohio enabled this to occur; and second, the public needed speedy, dependable transportation.

The builders of Northeast Ohio's electric railways overbuilt and overcapitalized because the people wanted it and the promoters could do it. For a time, there was no other substantive way to meet the transportation demands and there were few legal or financial limitations on those promoters with access to the region's wealth. The people and businesses of Northeast Ohio desired the network of electric rails and so they were built to meet those personal and economic needs. Those with investments sought ways that would protect those interests, through consolidation, holding companies, and even service-at-cost agreements. But in the end, the economic and personal needs of the people and businesses of the region pushed away electric traction and embraced the automobile and truck. To them it was a passing romance before the true love affair with the automobile began in earnest.

6

Reflecting on the Industry and the Southwestern

THE PRECEDING CHAPTERS have focused attention on the businessmen and institutional affiliations that engendered the development of the electric railway industry in Northeast Ohio, as well as the Cleveland, Southwestern & Columbus Railway system. Uncovering these "wheels within wheels" of syndicate relationships of these men does not reveal their personal motivations and ambitions. However, examining the business climate and culture that took ambitious dreams and made them a reality provides a better understanding of how the industry rose and fell. The accomplishments, then, of the interurban system building were the consequences of individual actions empowered by the resources of a heavily industrialized region.

The urge to explain the demise of the industry is the logical outcome of attempting to explain its creation. The reasons for its beginnings were transitory, as were the people who worked on the roads or benefited from their services. The weaknesses of the region's interurban industry had more lasting effects. They resulted from the collective faults in its construction, financing, and operations. Many of the critical weaknesses of the interurban industry listed by George Hilton and John Due, as mentioned earlier, typify Northeast Ohio's electric railways. The Eastern Ohio Traction Company, weakest of the Cleveland interurban lines, never reached its planned destination; neither did the Sandusky, Norwalk & Mansfield or the Cleveland,

Alliance & Mahoning Valley Railway. The system building of the Everett and Moore syndicate succeeded in only two cases, the Lake Shore Electric and the Northern Ohio Traction & Light Company. But even the latter road failed to reach the originally intended Ohio River Valley destination. The Southwestern system came close to reaching its initial and ideal connection to Columbus and many of the major towns between but was limited by the lack of population density per track mile. It was never going to be the fastest or cheapest route from Columbus to Cleveland. It did, however, serve as the regional feeder to trunk lines that provided faster and cheaper services to the long-distance traveler. In summary, it served the small towns and rural countryside between major cities for at least a few decades.

All but the region's largest interurbans lacked any period of continuing prosperity. Even those roads which managed to make a profit during the peak years of railway operation could not weather the financial distress of the bad years. Profits from all of the largest lines, such as the Lake Shore Electric; Northern Ohio Traction & Light; Cleveland, Southwestern & Columbus Railway; Mahoning & Shenango Railway & Light Company; and the Stark Electric Railroad were diverted to investments in the electric light and power business. That was a wise decision, yet the electric railway departments declined in the 1920s and became a liability rather than a source of income. Consequently, the holding companies that owned these properties split them up and disposed of their unprofitable or marginally profitable railway businesses.

Although only mentioned in passing, all the region's electric railways suffered in the 1920s as automobile traffic burdened urban roadways. All but the Stark Electric Railroad lacked a high-speed entrance into the downtown district of its largest central city. The increased running times through the cities plagued the region's interurbans throughout the late 1910s and 1920s. These delays put them at a competitive disadvantage as the other forms of urban transportation, the car and the bus, crowded the streets. Just as the steam dummy lines could not interfere with the prevailing use of horses by tax-paying citizens over public streets, so too the streetcar had to give way to taxpayers' desires to drive their private automobiles into the increasingly vibrant downtowns. The sheer number of privately owned automobiles and competing buses in the later 1920s virtually squeezed the streetcar off city streets, including the interurban services.

Another congenital weakness identified by Hilton and Due maintained that the industry's gross overcapitalization and overbuilding doomed it to an early grave. The previous chapter concluded that for most of Northeast Ohio's lines those factors did play a large role in their individual decline. The Southwestern system did better than average for most of its life but could not escape the systemic trends of financing capital-intensive industries and consumer preferences. The evidence also identified two of the region's urban electric railway systems that avoided overcapitalization and managed to survive the crushing blow of the Great Depression. Public scrutiny through service-at-cost franchises ultimately protected these two lines from self-destructive debt management behavior and overbuilding.

The Southwestern system, as well as all of the electric railways of Northeast Ohio, suffered to varying degrees from adversarial relationships with local governments and the riding public. Only the Cleveland Electric Railway and the Youngstown Municipal Railway managed to escape from the crippling consequences of that opposition. Their service-at-cost operations assuaged the public's fears and government scrutiny and allowed meaningful negotiated settlements over disputed matters.

The interurbans of Northeast Ohio, on the other hand, suffered from an endemic mistrust of the industry by the people. The interurbans unwittingly entered a "twilight zone," as described by Martin Glaeser, where their system-building practices avoided public scrutiny for a time. Once the public perceived that the railway represented a monopoly and they recognized an ongoing need for its services, it emerged from the twilight zone as a publicly regulated utility. The system-building practices that successfully propelled the traction industry into a public utility also brought public condemnation and suspicion. The takeover of the region's principal lines by holding companies in the 1920s added to the general mistrust of the electric railways and effected a pervasive apathy to their problems in the twenties from competing automobiles, buses, and trucks.

In combination, all of the weaknesses identified by Hilton and Due were found in the Southwestern as well as the other Northeast Ohio electric railways. Their collective demise reflected widespread changes in the business culture that had nurtured their growth and the transportation expectations of the public. That is, the support of the business elite to initiate, build, and finance the early traction projects fell by the wayside after only a few decades of operation. The infrastructure of business institutions needed to keep the companies going failed to see much hope for the industry, given the decline in passenger traffic experienced in the 1920s. By the Great Depression only the most stubborn of traction men still believed that the electric interurban industry had a chance to survive.

The operating strategies of electric railway ownership changed by the 1920s, as did the traveling habits of the people. In short, the people making decisions on the direction of the traction business based them on short-term profits and not on long-term public needs. For example, the Cleveland, Southwestern & Columbus Railway and Northern Ohio Traction & Light Company bus lines both went from being the feeders to their railways to becoming their eventual replacements as the company abandoned rail service. The Lake Shore Electric and the Southwestern management attempted to stimulate passenger business or augment it with increased freight earnings. The LSE successfully exploited the freight traffic potential of its system. However, the LSE freight traffic depended upon interurban and steam railroad interline agreements that proved vulnerable during the Great Depression. The NOT&L's noted success at freight traffic proved insufficient to guard against dismemberment by its parent holding company, the Commonwealth and Southern Corporation. The Southwestern system, as seen, had some modest success at increasing freight revenues, but it just was not enough to offset the decline of passenger traffic.

The role of the traction industry in the region's development bears little relationship to these enumerated problems. Instead, the economic and social importance of the railways to the region's communities occurred during its initial growth, development, and subsequent "golden years" of operation. Its demise, although consequential, does not indicate the value or the impact of the railways' existence. The modernizing effects on the urban and rural populations of Northeast Ohio remain the legacy of the traction syndicates, regardless of their own profit motives or unfortunate methods of financing and promotion.

In a 1993 article, "The Wrong Track," George Hilton argues that the interurban railways of America faced doom from the start. He admits that they provided inventive solutions to early transportation problems and appeared to be the next logical big change in intercity transport. Yet Hilton concludes, "The interurbans were just too transitory. They were a clever idea that didn't go."[1]

In general, it is difficult to reasonably challenge Hilton's conclusions. The tenor of the article, however, may suggest to some that the transitory nature of the interurbans diminished their value to the people they served. This could not be farther from the truth. The interurbans were short-lived, but during the times that these electric cars glided over thousands of miles of rails, they provided essential functions to America's industrialized and developing communities.

If the role of government throughout the last century of transportation history in America is considered in broad terms, the interurban industry deserves more consideration than it received. Interurbans made as much economic sense in the first quarter of the twentieth century as does subsidizing the commuter rail system in the first quarter of the twenty-first century—the major difference in this comparison being the public's definition of what is the best role of government and what transportation industries should be public concerns. Few economists would suggest today that the nation could do without a passenger rail system. Likewise, many economists and public utility regulators argued in the late 1910s that the electric railway industry was a vital part of the American economy. Current advocates of passenger rail, as well as aviation, argue for government subsidies to these transport industries, while those in 1919 suggested the crucial role of the electric railway merited a relaxation of public regulation and fare restrictions.

The differences between today's and yesterday's values are surely matters of perspective. The unifying theme that bridges these differing views is the relationship of transportation to the public. Citizens and their government in the first quarter of the twentieth century had distinctly different views on public transportation than they did in the last quarter of the same century, or in the first quarter of the current one. The accepted roles of government in the transportation industry have changed. The expectations and desires of the people for differing modes of transportation have likewise evolved. What was desirable to the small-town resident in 1900 in the way of electric railway transportation would not be generally acceptable today. Few people now would see electric streetcars and interurbans operating on fixed routes and timetables as an improvement over the flexibility and freedom offered by the automobile over America's interstate and freeway systems.

The interurban industry in Ohio met the transportation needs of hundreds of communities, thousands of businesses, and millions of people. Its transportation and ancillary functions, although transitory, became crucial to the development of both the urban and the rural sections of the state. They enabled the dispersion of population from the urban core at a time when reformers suggested that this could provide the ultimate cure for urban problems. Health professionals also contended that suburbanization and out-migration from the crowded cities promoted the public health. For those who could afford to move out of the city, barring other contravening social forces, it empowered their choice of residence and mobility. Suburban and rural life in Northeast Ohio became enriched by the movement of people outward from the boundaries of the city. The electric railways in effect became the instrument of social and demographic changes for the region.

Economist Martin G. Glaeser suggested that public utilities are the consequences of civilization. If that is true, then construction of the electric railways into the farmlands of Northeast Ohio represented a higher level of civilization to the region's communities—so much so that they became necessities in the daily lives of the people. Although a short-term love affair, the relationship proved critical to communities as they built paved roadways and improved their living standards.

The electric railways of Northeast Ohio were built without public financing, but they became part of the public infrastructure. They provided an essential function to the citizens and businesses. Unlike electric power and the telephone, this essential function had a limited duration. What the public deemed a necessity in the late 1900s and early 1910s became a nonessential amenity in the late 1920s and could be later abandoned when replaced by a publicly funded system of highways, thoroughfares, and roadways. In the process of building and operating for decades, the electric railways of Northeast Ohio proved to be the vanguard of a modern regional infrastructure.

The Cleveland, Southwestern & Columbus Railway, or Pioneer Route, connected the city with the country at a time when the people of both worlds found the connection mutually beneficial. The Southwestern's effect on the economic and social development of the region may explain

Figure 6.1. Car No. 483, on the last day and last run to Elyria, leaving Kamm's Corner, February 28, 1931. (Courtesy of Northern Ohio Railway Museum)

why many mourned its demise, even though the general population had abandoned it. Certainly, the event and causes of its passing did not go unnoticed in 1931, as witnessed by newspaper reporter Roelif Loveland's following eulogy.

THE LAST CAR PASSES ON THE GREEN LINE

"Oh, the trucks and the buses and the automobiles
Have killed the merry rumble of the 'Green Line' wheels.
They grabbed up her fares; on her freight they fed—
Shed a tear, Old Settler, The 'Green Line's' dead."[2]

Notes

INTRODUCTION

1. James A. Toman and Blaine S. Hays, *Horse Trails to Regional Rails: The Story of Public Transit in Greater Cleveland* (Kent, OH: Kent State University Press, 1996), 8.

2. H. Roger Grant, *Electric Interurbans and the American People* (Bloomington: Indiana University Press, 2016), 57.

3. Joseph Quincy III, "Welcoming Address," in American Street Railway Association, *Report of the Seventeenth Annual Meeting of the American Street Railway Association*, Boston, MA, September 6, 1898, 19.

CHAPTER 1

1. C. Francis Harding and Dressel D. Ewing, *Electric Railway Engineering*, 2nd ed. (New York: McGraw-Hill, 1916), 10–11; Harold C. Passer, *The Electrical Manufacturers, 1875–1900: A Study in Competition, Entrepreneurship, Technical Change, and Economic Growth* (Cambridge, MA: Harvard University Press, 1953), 216–17.

2. Carl Hering, *Recent Progress in Electric Railways* (New York: W. J. Johnston, 1892), 201; Department of Commerce and Labor, Bureau of the Census, Street and Electric Railways, 1902 (Washington, DC: Government Printing Office, 1905), 170–71; Crosby and Bell, *The Electric Railway in Theory and Practice* (New York: W. J. Johnston, 1893), 246–47.

3. "Danger of the Trolley System," *Street Railway Journal* 10, no. 1 (January 1894): 37.

4. "Danger of the Trolley System," 37.

5. Passer, *Electrical Manufacturers*, 224.

6. Hering, *Recent Progress in Electric Railways*, 202.

7. Harding and Ewing, *Electric Railway Engineering*, 272–73.

8. Crosby and Bell, *Electric Railway in Theory and Practice*, 345–51; A. Morris Buck, *The Electric Railway* (New York: McGraw-Hill, 1915), 3; Hering, *Recent Progress in Electric Railways*, 15–16.

9. Crosby and Bell, *Electric Railway in Theory and Practice*, 255–59; Hering, *Recent Progress in Electric Railways*, 167–75; Department of Commerce and Labor, Bureau of the Census, *Central Electric Light and Power Stations and Street and Electric Railways, 1912* (Washington, DC: Government Printing Office, 1915), 201.

10. Department of Commerce and Labor, Bureau of the Census, *Statistical Abstract of the United States* (Washington, DC: Government Printing Office): 1924, Table No. 381; 1934, Table No. 421; 1938, Table No. 465.

11. Harding and Ewing, *Electric Railway Engineering*, 205; F. W. Carter, *Railway Electric Traction* (London: Edward Arnold, 1922), 204–8; Crosby and Bell, *Electric Railway in Theory and Practice*, 143–44.

12. Harding and Ewing, *Electric Railway Engineering*, 7–8; Crosby and Bell, *Electric Railway in Theory and Practice*, 107–10; Hering, *Recent Progress in Electric Railways*, 354–56; William D. Middleton, *The Time of the Trolley* (Milwaukee, WI: Kalmbach, 1967), 60–61, 64.

13. Middleton, *Time of the Trolley*, 71–72.

14. Passer, *Electrical Manufacturers*, 217, 251; Frank Rowsome Jr., Stephen D. Maguire, technical ed., *Trolley Car Treasury: A Century of American Streetcars- Horsecars, Cable Cars, Interurbans, and Trolleys* (New York: McGraw-Hill, 1956), 87–88; Middleton, *Time of the Trolley*, 72–73.

15. Buck, *Electric Railway*, 71–73; Crosby and Bell, *Electric Railway in Theory and Practice*, 87–90.

16. Crosby and Bell, *Electric Railway in Theory and Practice*, 350; Hering, *Recent Progress in Electric Railways*, 22; "Electric Street Railways," *Cleveland Plain Dealer*, October 29, 1889, 4.

17. Passer, *Electrical Manufacturers*, 238–48; Rowsome, *Trolley Car Treasury*, 82–83.

18. Department of Commerce and Labor, Bureau of the Census, *Street and Electric Railways, 1902*, 167–68; Harding and Ewing, *Electric Railway Engineering*, 10.

19. Department of Commerce and Labor, Bureau of the Census, *Street and Electric Railways, 1902*, 167–68; Harding and Ewing, *Electric Railway Engineering*, 106–7; Crosby and Bell, *Electric Railway in Theory and Practice*, 123–43.

20. Frank J. Sprague, "Mr. Sprague Discusses Early Steps in the Development of Electric Traction," *AERA* (February 1932): 852; George W. Hilton and John F. Due, *The Electric Interurban Railways in America* (Stanford, CA: Stanford University Press, 1960), 6–8.

21. "Sprague Discusses," 852.

22. "Sprague Discusses," 852–53; Passer, *Electrical Manufacturers*, 250.

23. Passer, 252–53.

24. Passer, 256–58.

25. Passer, 256–58; Benjamin Garver Lamme, *Benjamin Garver Lamme: Electrical Engineer: An Autobiography* (New York: G. P. Putnam's Sons, 1926), 48, 193–95.

26. Passer, *Electrical Manufacturers*, 256–58; Lamme, *Autobiography*, 48, 193–95; Arthur M. Schlesinger and Dixon Ryan Fox, eds., *History of American Life* (New York: Macmillan, 1936), vol. 9, *The Nationalizing of Business, 1878–1898*, by Ida M. Tarbell, 231–32.

27. Passer, *Electrical Manufacturers*, 136–38, 296, 306, 309, 306–10; Dumas Malone, ed., *Dictionary of American Biography*, vol. 17 (New York: Charles Scribner's Sons, 1935), 514–15.

28. Passer, *Electrical Manufacturers*, 136–40, 300–301, 337; Harding and Ewing, *Electric Railway Engineering*, 11, 106–14; James M. Blower, *Northern Ohio Revisited* (Akron, OH: By the author, 1968), 154; Lamme, *Autobiography*, 63–68, 81, 197–98; Harry Christiansen, *Trolley Trails through Greater Cleveland and Northern Ohio* (Cleveland: Western Reserve Historical Society, 1975), 3:54–55; Buck, *Electric Railway*, 355–57.

29. Hilton and Due, *Electric Interurban Railways*, 4–11; Harry Christiansen and Liz Christiansen, *New Northern Ohio's Interurbans and Rapid Transit Railways* (Euclid, OH: Trolley Lore, 1983), 730–35.

30. Alfred D. Chandler Jr., *The Visible Hand: The Managerial Revolution in American Business* (Cambridge, MA: Harvard University Press, 1977), 192–94.

31. Department of Commerce and Labor, Bureau of the Census, *Statistical Abstract of the United States* (Washington, DC: Government Printing Office, 1922), Table No. 235; William M. Gregory and William B. Guitteau, *History and Geography of Ohio* (Boston: Ginn, 1922), 206–13.

32. Keith L. Bryant Jr., ed. *Encyclopedia of American Business History and Biography: Railroads in the Age of Regulation, 1900–1980* (New York: Bruccoli Clark Layman, 1988), xvi–xvii; Chandler, *Visible Hand*, 143–48.

33. David Kotz, *Bank Control of Large Corporations in the United States* (Berkeley: University of California Press, 1978), 25; Thomas C. Cochran, *Business in American Life: A History* (New York: McGraw-Hill, 1972), 155; James P. Baughman and Richard S. Tedlow, "J. P. Morgan, 1837–1913," in *The Coming of Managerial Capitalism: A Casebook on the History of American Economic Institutions*, ed. Alfred D. Chandler Jr. and Richard S. Tedlow (Homewood, IL: Richard D. Irwin, 1985), 271–73; Larry Schweikart, introduction to *Encyclopedia of American Business History and Biography: Banking and Finance to 1913*, ed. Larry Schweikart (New York: Bruccoli Clark Layman, 1990), xxvi.

34. Benjamin Graham and Spencer Meredith, *The Interpretation of Financial Statements* (New York: Harper & Brothers, 1937), 116; Richard B. Morris and William Greenleaf, *U.S.A.: The History of a Nation*, vol. 2 (Chicago: Rand McNally, 1969), 95–99.

35. Chandler, *Visible Hand*, 171–75; Baughman and Tedlow, "J. P. Morgan," 278–79.

36. Kotz, *Bank Control*, 25–26; Albro Martin, *Enterprise Denied: Origins of the Decline of American Railroads, 1897–1917* (New York: Columbia University Press, 1971), 17–18; Morris and Greenleaf, *U.S.A.*, 97–98.

37. James Ford Rhodes, *The McKinley and Roosevelt Administrations, 1897–1909* (New York: Macmillan, 1922), 116; Martin, *Enterprise Denied*, 18; Rhodes, 116–17.

38. Albro Martin, *James J. Hill and the Opening of the Northwest* (New York: Oxford University Press, 1976), 274–75.

39. Charles W. Cheape, *Moving the Masses: Urban Public Transit in New York, Boston, and Philadelphia, 1880–1912*, Harvard Studies in Business History 31, ed. Alfred D. Chandler Jr. (Cambridge, MA: Harvard University Press, 1980), 1; Ronald R. Weiner and Carol A. Beal, "The Sixth City: Cleveland in Three Stages of Urbanization," in *The Birth of Modern Cleveland, 1865–1930*, ed. Thomas F. Campbell and Edward M. Miggins (Cleveland: Western Reserve Historical Society, 1988), 45–46.

40. Cheape, *Moving the Masses*, 1.

41. Cheape, 16–17.

42. Cheape, 9; David W. Jones, Jr., *Urban Transit Policy: An Economic and Political History* (Englewood Cliffs, New Jersey: Prentice-Hall, Inc., 1985); 31–32; Mark S. Foster, *From Streetcar to Superhighway: American City Planners and Urban Transportation, 1900–1940* (Philadelphia: Temple University Press, 1981), 36–45.

43. Jones, *Urban Transit Policy*, 33; Department of Commerce and Labor, Bureau of the Census, *Street and Electric Railways, 1907* (Washington, DC: Government Printing Office, 1910), 100–103; Wallace McCook Cunningham, "Stocks and the Stock Market: Electric Railway Stocks," *Annals of the American Academy of Political and Social Science* 35 (May 1910): 657–73.

44. Department of Commerce and Labor, Bureau of the Census, *Central Electric Light and Power Stations and Street and Electric Railways, 1912* (Washington, DC: Government Printing Office, 1915), 184, 223–25; Moody's Investors Service, *Moody's Analyses of Investments and Security Rating Books: Public Utility Securities*, ed. Maurice N. Blakemore (New York: Moody's Investors Service, 1924), xlviii.

45. Cunningham, "Stocks and the Stock Market," 658.

46. Cunningham, 190.

47. Cheape, *Moving the Masses*, v–vi.

48. J. S. Badger, quoted in Hering, *Recent Progress in Electric Railways*, 100–112.

49. Hering, *Recent Progress in Electric Railways*, 25; Hering, 24–25; Harold C. Passer, *Moving the Masses, Electrical Manufacturers, 1875–1900: A Study in Competition, Entrepreneurship, Technical Change, and Economic Growth* (Cambridge, MA: Harvard University Press, 1953), 253–54; Weiner and Beal, "Sixth City," 45.

50. Griffin's argument did not take into account the other factors which twentieth-century urban economists recognize influence residential land use—such as site rent, housing costs, competing land uses, land-use zoning, and geography. See James Heilbrun and Patrick A. McGuire, *Urban Economics and Public Policy*, 3rd ed. (New York: St. Martin's, 1987), 107–38.

51. Sam Bass Warner Jr., *Streetcar Suburbs: The Process of Growth in Boston, 1870–1900* (Cambridge, MA: Harvard University Press, 1962), 22–23; Ian S. Haberman, *The Van Sweringens of Cleveland: The Biography of an Empire* (Cleveland: Western Reserve Historical Society, 1979), 18–30; James Toman, *The Shaker Heights Rapid Transit* (Glendale, CA: Interurban, 1990), 11, 15–16; James M. Blower and Robert S. Korach, *The NOT&L Story* (Chicago: Central Electric Railfans' Association, 1966), 76–77; Weiner and Beal, "Sixth City," 45–46.

52. Edward E. Higgins, *Street Railway Investments. A Study in Values* (New York: Street Railway Publishing, 1895), 98.

53. Edward E. Higgins, "The Intrinsic Value of Street Railway Investments," *Street Railway Journal* 10, no. 1 (January 1894): 18.

54. Harold C. Livesay, "From Steeples to Smokestacks: The Birth of the Modern Corporation in Cleveland," in *The Birth of Modern Cleveland, 1865–1930*, ed. Thomas

F. Campbell and Edward M. Miggins (Cleveland: Western Reserve Historical Society, 1988), 54–69.

55. Samuel P. Orth, *A History of Cleveland Ohio*, vol. 1 (Chicago: S. J. Clarke, 1910), 646; Ronald Weiner, "The New Industrial Metropolis: 1860–1929," in *The Encyclopedia of Cleveland History*, ed. David D. Van Tassel and John J. Grabowski (Bloomington: Indiana University Press, 1987), xxx–xxxi; William Ganson Rose, *Cleveland: The Making of a City* (Cleveland: World, 1950), 430; Jon Moen and Ellis W. Tallman, "The Bank Panic of 1907: The Role of Trust Companies," *Journal of Economic History* 52 (September 1992): 614; *Moody's Manual of Investments*, various issues.

56. Moen and Tallman, "Bank Panic of 1907," 612–16; Larry Neal, "Trust Companies and Financial Innovation, 1897–1914," *Business History Review* 45 (Spring 1971): 35–51; Weiner, "New Industrial Metropolis," xxx–xxxi; Jacob Dolson Cox Sr., *Building an American Industry, The Story of the Cleveland Twist Drill Company and Its Founder: An Autobiography* (Cleveland: Cleveland Twist Drill, 1951), 150–51.

57. Henry V. Poor, *Manual of the Railroads of the United States for 1889* (New York: H. V. and H. W. Poor, 1889), xxii–xxiii.

58. Poor, *Manual*, xxii–xxiii.

59. John H. Garland, "The Western Reserve of Connecticut: Geography of a Political Relic," *Economic Geography* 19 (July 1943): 305–6; William M. Gregory and William B. Guitteau, *History and Geography of Ohio* (Boston: Ginn, 1922), 104–6.

60. Weiner, "New Industrial Metropolis," xxx; Weiner and Beal, "Sixth City," 29–30, 34–35.

61. Gregory and Guitteau, *History and Geography of Ohio*, 207–9.

62. Christiansen and Christiansen, *New Northern Ohio's Interurbans*, 754; Department of Commerce and Labor, Bureau of the Census, *Street and Electric Railways, 1902* (Washington, DC: Government Printing Office, 1905), 111–16.

63. Heilbrun and McGuire, *Urban Economics and Public Policy*, 64–79; Hilton and Due, *Electric Interurban Railways*, 183–84; Livesay, "Steeples to Smokestacks," 54–69.

64. Robert Leslie Jones, "Ohio Agriculture in History," *Ohio Historical Quarterly* 65 (July 1956): 244–52.

65. "Canton in the List of Trolley Centers," *Canton Repository*, May 11, 1905.

66. Paul Barrett, "Public Policy and Private Choice: Mass Transit and the Automobile in Chicago between the Wars," *Business History Review* 49 (Winter 1975): 477–80; Joel A. Tarr, Josef W. Konvitz, and Mark H. Rose, "The Evolution of Urban American Technology," *Journal of Urban Technology* 1 (Fall 1992): 1–18; Sam Bass Warner Jr., *Streetcar Suburbs: The Process of Growth in Boston, 1870–1900* (Cambridge, MA: Harvard University Press, 1962); John C. Teaford, *City and Suburb: The Political Fragmentation of Metropolitan America, 1850–1970* (Baltimore: Johns Hopkins University Press, 1979).

67. Martin G. Glaeser, *Outlines of Public Utility Economics* (New York: Macmillan, 1927), 6.

68. Glaeser, 6.

69. "Southwestern Files Answer: Other Villages May Protest," *Berea Enterprise*, January 16, 1914, 1.

70. Morton Keller, *Regulating a New Economy: Public Policy and Economic Change in America, 1900–1933* (Cambridge, MA: Harvard University Press, 1990), 59.

71. Keller, 45–49, 65.

72. Delos F. Wilcox, "What Shall We Do with the Street Railways?" *American City* 20 (April 1919): 336.

73. Glaeser, *Outlines*, 304–10.

74. Charles B. Galbreath, *History of Ohio*, vol. 2 (New York: American Historical Society, 1925), 678, 685; "Many People Sign Petition," *Akron Beacon Journal*, April 13, 1904, 1, 4; "That Franchise Bill," *Evening Independent*, April 12, 1904, 7; "Brannock Bill Signed By Gov Herrick Today," *Sandusky Evening Star*, April 19, 1904, 1; Eugene H. Roseboom and Francis P. Weisenburger, *A History of Ohio* (Columbus: Ohio State Archaeological and Historical Society, 1956), 320–23; Hilton and Due, *Electric Interurban Railways*, 105.

75. Keller, *Regulating a New Economy*, 3.

76. Hilton and Due, *Electric Interurban Railways*, 9, 42.

77. Department of Commerce and Labor, Bureau of the Census, *Street and Electric Railways, 1907* (Washington, DC: Government Printing Office, 1910), 271.

78. Ohio Public Utilities Commission, *Report of the Public Utilities Commission of Ohio to the Governor of the State of Ohio* (Springfield, OH, 1913–35), hereafter abbreviated as *Report of the Public Utilities Commission*, [year(s)].

79. Moody's Investors Service, *Moody's Analyses of Investments and Security Rating Books: Public Utility Securities*, ed. Maurice N. Blakemore (New York: Moody's Investors Service, 1931), 2220–21; Christiansen and Christiansen, *New Northern Ohio's Interurbans*, 814, 852; Central Electric Railfans' Association, *Electric Railways of Northeastern Ohio*, Bulletin 108 (Chicago: Central Electric Railfans' Association, 1965): 82–94; David D. Van Tassel and John J. Grabowski, eds. *The Encyclopedia of Cleveland History* (Bloomington: Indiana University Press, 1987), s.v. "Greater Cleveland Regional Transit Authority," 471; Toman, *Shaker Heights Rapid Transit*, 97–108.

80. As cited in Federal Electric Railways Commission, *Proceedings of the Federal Electric Railways Commission: Held in Washington, D.C. during the months of July, August, September, and October*, 1919, vol. 3 (Washington, DC: Government Printing Office), 1920.

81. Hilton and Due, *Electric Interurban Railways*, 208–9.

82. Hilton and Due, 239.

83. Hilton and Due, 208–239; Blower, *Northern Ohio Revisited*, 93.

CHAPTER 2

1. George W. Hilton and John F. Due, *The Electric Interurban Railways in America* (Stanford, CA: Stanford University Press, 1960), 8–9.

2. *Report of the Railroad Commission of Ohio to the Governor of the State of Ohio for the Year 1907* (Springfield, OH: Springfield, 1907), 393, hereafter abbreviated as *Report of the Railroad Commission of Ohio*, [year(s)].

3. *Report*, 393.

4. *Report*, 393; E. W. Bemis, "The Street Railway Settlement in Cleveland," *Quarterly Journal of Economics* 22 (August 1908): 543–47; Tom L. Johnson, *My Story*. Elizabeth J. Hauser, ed. (Kent, Ohio: Kent State University Press, 1993) 17–27, 158–62, 206–20.

5. Johnson, 278–9; Bemis, "Street Railway Settlement," 543–49

6. C. B. Fairchild, "The Cross-Country Roads at Cleveland, Ohio," *Electrical Engineer* 26, no. 540 (September 8, 1898): 221–27; *Electric Railway Systems: ICS Reference Library* (Scranton, PA: International Textbook, 1908), Line and Track, section 38, p. 36.

7. George W. Knox, "Remarks," *Proceedings of the American Electric Railway Association* 3, no. 3 (October 1914): 318.

8. Sam Bass Warner Jr., *Streetcar Suburbs: The Process of Growth in Boston, 1870–1900* (Cambridge, MA: Harvard University Press, 1962), 52–64.

9. Theodore Hershberg, Dale Light Jr., Harold E. Cox, and Richard R. Greenfield, "The Journey-to-Work: An Empirical Investigation of Work, Residence and Transportation, Philadelphia, 1850 and 1880," in *Philadelphia: Work, Space, Family, and Group Experience in the Nineteenth Century*, ed. Theodore Hershberg (New York: Oxford University Press, 1981): 128–73.

10. George S. Lee and Edward J. Martin, *Express and Parcel Post Services: The Traffic Library* (Chicago: American Commerce Association, 1921), 95–97; Ohio, Public Utilities Commission, *Report of the Public Utilities Commission of Ohio to the Governor of the State of Ohio* (Springfield, OH: Springfield, 1913–18), hereafter abbreviated as *Report of the Public Utilities Commission of Ohio*, [year(s)].

11. Lee and Martin, *Express and Parcel Post Services*, 96–97; Hilton and Due, *Electric Interurban Railways*, 121; William D. Middleton, "Electric Railway Freight," *Railroad History* 151 (Autumn 1984): 22; A. Eastman, "Express Business on Interurban Lines," *Annals of the American Academy of Political and Social Science* 37 (1911): 79; Frank S. Cummins, "Possibilities of Freight Traffic on Interurban Lines," *Annals of the American Academy of Political and Social Science* 37 (1911): 68–70.

12. Lee and Martin, *Express and Parcel Post Services*, 95–97.

13. Middleton, "Electric Railway Freight," 22–23; Hilton and Due, *Electric Interurban Railways*, 121–23; Harry Christiansen and Liz Christiansen, *New Northern Ohio's Interurbans and Rapid Transit Railways* (Euclid, OH: Trolley Lore, 1983), 823; "Electric Package Agency: Correspondence with Stark Electric Railroad," June 1920, Ohio Edison Collection, Bierce Library, The University of Akron Archives, Akron, Ohio, box 151; James M. Blower and Robert S. Korach, *The NOT&L Story* (Chicago: Central Electric Railfans' Association, 1966), 94–99.

14. Blower and Korach, 94–99.

15. "Transportation of Freight," *Electric Railway Journal* 42, no. 14 (October 4, 1913): 599.

16. A. B. Cole, "Electric Railways Are in a Position to Haul More Freight," *Electric Railway Journal* 51, no. 19 (May 11, 1918): 893–95, reporting on research conducted in cooperation with the War Board of the Electric Railway Association.

17. Cole.

18. Cole.

19. W. C. McAdoo, director general of railroads, "Report to the President of the Work of the United States Railroad Administration for the First Seven Months of Its Existence, Ending July 31, 1918" (Washington, DC: Government Printing Office, 1918), 277, 289.

20. Charles J. Lancey, "Obstacles to Electric Express: Slow Running Time and Many Interchanges Are Cited as Difficulties to a Comprehensive System," *Electric Railway Journal* 54, no. 21 (December 29, 1919): 996.

21. Lancey, 997.

22. Middleton, "Electric Railway Freight,"17–69.

23. Christiansen and Christiansen, *New Northern Ohio's Interurbans*, 823.

CHAPTER 3

1. "Include City in Airline Service," *Mansfield News Journal*, May 25, 1928, 28.

2. Roelif Loveland, "Last Car Passes on Southwestern," *Cleveland Plain Dealer*, March 1, 1931, 9; Max E. Wilcox, *The Cleveland Southwestern & Columbus Railway Story* (Chippewa Lake, OH: Northern Ohio Railway Museum, 1960 reprint); Cleveland, Elyria & Western Railway 1901 timetable (author's collection); Harry Christiansen and Liz Christiansen, *New Northern Ohio's Interurbans and Rapid Transit Railways* (Euclid, OH: Trolley Lore, 1983), 768.

3. W. F. Holzworth, *Men of Grit and Greatness* (n.p.: By the Author, 1970); Henry Howe, *Historical Collections of Ohio*, vol. 1 (Norwalk: State of Ohio, 1888), 525–26; Lury Gould Baldwin, "A Century's History of Berea," *Berea Enterprise*, December 6, 1935 (microfilm reproduction); "Early History of Berea: Story of German Wallace College from Founding until Union in 1913," *Berea Enterprise*, February 12, 1937 (microfilm reproduction).

4. "Passing of Southwestern Brings to Mind Faces and Scenes of Its Bygone Years," *Berea Enterprise*, February 6, 1931; *Poor's Manual of Steam Railroads, 1890*, s.v. "Berea Street Railroad Company."

5. Holzworth, *Men of Grit*, 55, 184–86; Jeffrey R. Brashares, *The Southwestern Lines: The Story of the Cleveland, Southwestern & Columbus Railway between Cleveland, Elyria-Oberlin-Norwalk, Wellington-Lorain-Amherst, Berea-Medina-Wooster, Ashland-Mansfield-Crestline, Galion-Bucyrus* (Cleveland: Ohio Interurban Memories, 1982), 6; Max E. Wilcox, *The Cleveland Southwestern & Columbus Railway Story*, reprint (Chippewa Lake, OH: Northern Ohio Railway Museum, 1960), n.p.

6. Holzworth, *Men of Grit*, 55; *Berea Enterprise*, February 6, 1931; "Company Is to Be Reorganized," *Wayne County Democrat*, December 26, 1906; Harry Christiansen and Liz Christiansen, *New Northern Ohio's Interurbans and Rapid Transit Railways* (Euclid, OH: Trolley Lore, 1983), 5, 795.

7. C. B. Fairchild, "The Cross-Country Roads at Cleveland, Ohio," *Electrical Engineer* 26, no. 540 (September 8, 1898): 222; Holzworth, *Men of Grit*, 55, 184–86; Brashares, *Southwestern Lines*, 6; *Berea Enterprise*, February 6, 1931; *Poor's Manual of Railroads* (1896); Plain Dealer Publishing Company, *Progressive Men of Northern Ohio* (Cleveland: Plain Dealer, 1906), s.v. "Albert Akins"; "Death Calls Traction Man," *Cleveland Plain Dealer*, February 18, 1913, 13.

8. James M. Blower, *Northern Ohio Revisited* (Akron, OH: published by author, 1968), 92; Brashares, *Southwestern Lines*, 6; *Berea Enterprise*, February 6, 1931.

9. *Poor's Manual of Railroads, 1892 to 1898*; Blower, *Northern Ohio Revisited*, 92; Brashares, *Southwestern Lines*, 6; *Berea Enterprise*, February 6, 1931; Fairchild, "Cross-Country Roads at Cleveland, Ohio," 222–25; "A Beautiful Diamond Ring: Presented Manager Pomeroy by the Employees of the Cleveland, Elyria & Western Ry," *Elyria Reporter*, April 17, 1901, 1.

10. Frank R. Ford, "Valuation of Intangible Street Railway Property," *Annals of the American Academy of Political and Social Science* 37 (1911): 122–26; Wallace McCook Cunningham, "Stocks and the Stock Market: Electric Railway Stocks," *Annals of the American Academy of Political and Social Science* 35 (May 1910): 657–73.

11. David Van Tassel and John J. Grabowski, eds., *The Encyclopedia of Cleveland History* (Indianapolis: Indiana University Press, 1987), s.v. "Maurice J. Mandelbaum."

12. George W. Hilton and John F. Due, *The Electric Interurban Railways in America* (Stanford, CA: Stanford University Press, 1960), 13, 268.

13. Brashares, *Southwestern Lines*, 9; *Poor's Manual of Railroads, 1896 to 1898*; Van Tassel and Grabowski, *Encyclopedia of Cleveland History*, s.v. "Maurice J. Mandelbaum."

14. *Poor's Manual of Railroads, 1896 to 1898*; "Both Say So," *Medina County Gazette*, October 4, 1900, 1, 8; "Brighter, the Prospects for the Medina Electric Railway," *Medina County Gazette*, December 6, 1900, 1; *Medina County Gazette*, December 27, 1900, 1; Brashares, *Southwestern Lines*, 10–12.

15. *Poor's Manual of Railroads, 1901 to 1904*; *Wayne County Democrat*, September 30, 1903, 3.

16. Hilton and Due, *Electric Interurban Railways*, 3; Wilcox, *Cleveland Southwestern & Columbus Railway Story*, n.p.; *Poor's Manual of Railroads, 1901 to 1904*.

17. Wilcox, *Cleveland Southwestern*, n.p.; Brashares, *Southwestern Lines*, 18; *Wayne County Democrat*, December 14, 1904; *Wayne County Democrat*, March 14, 1906.

18. Cunningham, "Stocks," 189; Brashares, *Southwestern Lines*, 24.

19. "Trolley versus Steam," *Street Railway Journal* 23, no. 26 (June 25, 1904): 978.

20. George S. Davis, "The Interurban Electric Railways of Ohio," *Street Railway Journal* 18, no. 5 (August 3, 1901): 146.

21. Wilcox, *Cleveland Southwestern*, n.p.

22. Ruth Cavin, *Trolleys: Riding and Remembering the Electric Interurban Railways* (New York: Hawthorne Books, 1976), 24; William A. Duff, *History of North Central Ohio*, vol. 3 (Indianapolis, IN: Historical, 1931), 1096–99, 1120–23.

23. Cavin, *Trolleys*, 24; Brashares, *Southwestern Lines*, 31–35.

24. *Poor's Manual of Railroads, 1907 to 1910*; Brashares, *Southwestern Lines*, 34–35.

25. *Poor's*, Brashares, *Cincinnati Enquirer*, April 3, 1909; *Mansfield News-Journal*, April 1, 1909; *Elyria Republican*, July 4, 1907.

26. *Moody's Analyses of Public Utility Investments, 1920, 1921, 1925, 1930, 1931 and 1932* (New York: Moody's Investors Service), passim; Wilcox, *Cleveland Southwestern*, n.p.

27. Wilcox, *Cleveland Southwestern*, n.p.; *Poor's Manual of Railroads, 1907 to 1912*; Christiansen and Christiansen, *New Northern Ohio's Interurbans*, 798; "Will Sell R.R. at Auction," *Berea Enterprise*, February 14, 1924.

28. J. N. Shannahan, "Creating Trolley Business," *AERA* 1 (August 1912): 37–39.

29. Shannahan, 37–39.

30. Christiansen and Christiansen, *New Northern Ohio's Interurbans*, 72–75; *Berea Enterprise*, March 13, 1914.

31. *Berea Enterprise*, March 13, 1914.

32. *Berea Enterprise*, December 20, 1921; *Berea Enterprise*, January 31, 1913; "Limited Cars for Cleveland, Southwestern & Columbus," *Electric Traction* 9, no. 9 (November 1913): 698; *Moody's Analyses of Public Utility Investments 1920, 1921, 1925, 1930, 1931 and 1932*, passim.

33. "Limited Cars," 698.

34. "Improvements in the Power Equipment of the Cleveland & Southwestern System," *Street Railway Journal* 23, no. 5 (January 30, 1904): 162–72; "Electric Power: Elyria Power House Will Furnish All of the Power," *Bucyrus Evening Telegraph*, January 21, 1910, 3; "Decree of Foreclosure," District Court of the United States, for the Northern District of Ohio, Eastern Division, General Electric Company, et al., vs. The Cleveland, Southwestern and Columbus Railway Company, et al., *In Equity No. 690*, entered February 9, 1924, D. C. Westenhaver, Judge, Letter from G. H. Kelsay, Superintendent of Power & Equipment, CS&C Railway Company, "Exhibit D, Power Supply for the CS&C Railway Company," December 12, 1922, 2.

35. "Decree of Foreclosure," "Exhibit A" by W. E. Davis, Consulting Engineer, dated November 22, 1922.

36. "Application of Receiver for Authority to Enter into Power Contract and for Issuance of Receivers' Certificate Therefor," *In Equity No. 690*, entered February 9, 1924, D. C. Westenhaver, Judge, filed December 16, 1922.

37. "Big Company Back of Electric Line," *Wayne Country Democrat*, December 10, 1912, 4; *Mansfield News-Journal,* December 5, 1916; "Norwalk and Utility Foe in 'Death Grapple' for 'Rights' before United States Court in Toledo," *Sandusky Star Journal*, December 23, 1930, 2; "Hahn Rules that O.E.P. Co. May Stay Till Bonds Paid," *Norwalk Reflector Herald*, February 9, 1931, 1.

38. John H. Pardee, "The Holding Company in Public Utilities: Its Advantages and Dangers," *Proceedings of the Academy of Political Science in the City of New York* 11, no. 4, Trade Associations and Business Combinations (January 1926): 155.

39. Pardee, 147–55; Leonard S. Hyman, *America's Electric Utilities: Past, Present and Future*, 3rd ed. (Arlington, VA: Public Utilities Reports, 1988), 71–83.

Notes 221

40. "Local Plant Is Purchased," *Medina County Gazette*, June 12, 1925, 1, 4; "Power Company Orders Pay Slash," *Akron Beacon Journal*, July 10, 1925, 17; "Power Plant Sales OK'D," *Massillon Evening Independent*, October 6, 1931, 2; "Electric Companies Ask Property Trade," *Marion Star*, October 1, 1931, 1; "Company Promises Improved Service," *Medina Sentinel*, October 1, 1925, 1; "Cleveland, Southwestern Railway & Light Company," *Moody's Manual of Investments, 1931*, 2222–23.

41. *In Equity No. 690*, F. H. Wilson, "Preliminary Report of Receiver," filed January 13, 1922, 7–8.

42. *In Equity No. 690*, F. H. Wilson, "Preliminary Report of Receiver," filed January 13, 1922, 8; Brashares, *Southwestern Lines*, 72.

43. "Big Things Coming," *Medina County Gazette*, November 18, 1924, 1.

44. *Annual Report of the Cleveland Southwestern Railway and Light Company, Cleveland, Ohio to the Interstate Commerce Commission*, December 31, 1928; *Moody's Analyses of Public Utility Investments, 1930, 1931 and 1932*, passim; *Report of the Public Utilities Commission of Ohio*, 1929).

45. *The Book of Clevelanders: A Biographical Directory of Living Men of the City of Cleveland* (Cleveland: Burrows Brothers, 1914), 233; "Organizer of Electric Line Dies at 63," *Cleveland Plain Dealer*, April 2, 1926, 2; "Traction Man's Wife Is Dead: Mrs. Pomeroy Was Active as Club Woman," *Cleveland Plain Dealer*, August 2, 1923, 3; "Death Record: Schneider Funeral," *Elyria Chronicle Telegram*, April 2, 1926, 12.

46. E. F. Schneider, "The Prevention of Accidents," *Electric Traction Weekly* 6, no. 13 (March 26, 1910): 357; Brashares, *Southwestern Lines*, 36.

47. Schneider, "Prevention of Accidents," 355.

48. "Railroad Man Solves Problem of Preventable Accidents," *Troy Free Press*, August 29, 1913, 2.

49. "Officials and Employees Meet: Men Connected with the Green Line Indulge in Heart to Heart Talks," *Norwalk Daily Reflector*, October 26, 1911, 1.

50. "Officials and Employees Meet," 1.

51. Schneider, "Prevention of Accidents," 358; "Blotters for School Distribution," *Electric Traction*, November 1912, 1080; "Steps Taken to Prevent Accident among School Children," *Electric Railway Journal* 37, no. 3 (January 21, 1911): 138.

52. 155 "Accident Instruction for School Children," *Electric Railway Journal* 36, no. 2 (July 9, 1910): 65; "Accident Prevention Campaign of Lehigh Valley Traction Company," *Electric Railway Journal* 37, no. 8 (February 25, 1911): 351–52; "Work for the Prevention of Accidents," *Electric Railway Journal* 37, no. 9 (March 4, 1911): 361; "Talks on Accident to Employees of the Cleveland, Southwestern & Columbus Railway," *Electric Railway Journal* 37, no. 9 (March 4, 1911): 379–80; "Prevention of Accidents," *Electric Railway Journal* 23, no. 9 (June 4, 1910): 975–77.

53. "Will Talk to Farmers along Greenline," *Norwalk Evening Herald*, December 22, 1911, 6.

54. "Four Lives Snuffed Out," *Mansfield News*, January 29, 1917, 2; "Loss of Memory Caused the Death of Four and Injuries to a Score," *Medina County Gazette*, February 2, 1917, 1, 6; "Another Wreck," *Medina County Gazette*, February 2, 1917, 1.

55. "Grade Crossings Deaths in Lead: 27 County To Toll," *Elyria Chronicle Telegram*, December 31, 1924, 1, 2; "Makes Survey to Get Causes of Accidents," *Newark Advocate*, January 21, 1927, 16.

56. "Statement of Mr. Charles L. Henry," *Federal Electric Railways Commission, Proceedings of the Federal Electric Railways Commission: Held in Washington, D.C. during the months of July, August, September, and October, 1919*, vol. 1 (Washington, DC: Government Printing Office, 1920), 712; *Poor's Manual of Railroads, 1907 and 1908*; Wilcox, *Cleveland Southwestern*, n.p.; *Report of the Railroad Commission of Ohio*, 1907–9, 1911, passim.

57. "Coming at Last," *Medina County Gazette*, May 19, 1916, 10.

58. Hilton and Due, *Electric Interurban Railways*, 121–23; Wilcox, *Cleveland Southwestern*, n.p.; Christiansen and Christiansen, *New Northern Ohio's Interurbans*, 823.

59. Brashares, *Southwestern Lines*, 64; *Moody's Analyses of Public Utility Investments 1927*, 189–91.

60. William Franklin Willoughby, *Government Organization in War Time and After: A Survey of the Federal Civil Agencies Created for the Prosecution of the War* (New York: D. Appleton, 1919), 169–71; H. W. Schotter, *The Growth and Development of the Pennsylvania Railroad Company* (Philadelphia: Allen, Lane and Scott, 1927), 347.

61. Willoughby, *Government Organization*, 172–75.

62. Taylor Hampton, *The Nickel Plate Road: The History of a Great Railroad* (Cleveland: World, 1947), 219–22; Ian S. Haberman, *The Van Swerigens of Cleveland: The Biography of an Empire* (Cleveland: Western Reserve Historical Society, 1979), 26–29, 56–57, 59.

63. *Report of the Public Utilities Commission of Ohio*, 1914–32, passim; "Shippers Alarmed by Prospect of Crippled Freight Service," *Mansfield News-Journal*, December 4, 1923, 2.

64. E. B. Atchley, "Possibilities in the Freight Business for Electric Railways," *Electric Traction*, February 1923, 61–63.

65. Atchley, 63.

66. *Report of the Public Utilities Commission of Ohio*, 1914–32, passim.

67. *Moody's Analyses of Public Utility Investments 1930, 1931 and 1932*, passim; "Stark Electric Railroad: Operating Reports, 1919 to 1924," Ohio Edison Collection, University of Akron Archives, box 154.

68. "The Southwestern," *Berea Enterprise*, January 27, 1921; "Will Sell Electric R.R. at Auction," *Berea Enterprise*, February 14, 1924; *Moody's Analyses of Public Utility Investments 1914 to 1932*, passim.

69. *Berea Enterprise*, July 12, 1923, April 17, 1924; *Moody's Analyses of Public Utility Investments 1927*, 189–91.

70. Christiansen and Christiansen, *New Northern Ohio's Interurbans*, 800; *Berea Enterprise*, July 12, 1923; *Berea Enterprise*, April 17, 1924; "Southwestern May Suspend," *Crestline Advocate*, February 21, 1924, 10; "Line Will Go Under Hammer," *Marion Star*, February 16, 1924, 10.

71. *Moody's Analyses of Public Utility Investments 1920, 1921, 1925, 1930, 1931 and 1932*, passim.

72. Christiansen and Christiansen, *New Northern Ohio's Interurbans*, 802.

73. Christiansen and Christiansen, 800–802; Wilcox, *Cleveland Southwestern*, n.p.

74. Christiansen and Christiansen, *New Northern Ohio's Interurbans*, 800–802; Hilton and Due, *Electric Interurban Railways*, 49.

75. *Moody's Manual of Investments 1931*, 2222; Christiansen and Christiansen, *New Northern Ohio's Interurbans*, 800; Brashares, *Southwestern Lines*, 76.

76. *Annual Report of the Cleveland Southwestern Railway and Light Company*; *Moody' Analyses of Public Utility Investments 1930, 1931 and 1932*, passim.

77. Wilcox, *Cleveland Southwestern*, n.p.; *Annual Report of the Cleveland Southwestern Railway and Light Company*.

78. Christiansen and Christiansen, *New Northern Ohio's Interurbans*, 800; *Annual Report of the Cleveland Southwestern Railway and Light Company*; *Moody's Analyses of Public Utility Investments 1930, 1931, and 1932*, passim.

CHAPTER 4

1. John M. McKee, "Population Trends," *Annals of the American Academy of Political and Social Science* 142 (March 1929): 44–50.

2. James F. Richardson, "The City in Twentieth-Century Ohio: Crisis in Stability and Services," in *Toward an Urban Ohio*, ed. John Wunder (Columbus: Ohio Historical Society, 1977), 37.

3. Harry Christiansen, *Trolley Trails through Greater Cleveland and Northern Ohio* (Cleveland: Western Reserve Historical Society, 1975), 2:272–74.

4. "Freight Haulage in Ohio," *Street Railway Journal* 18, no. 8 (August 24, 1901): 209.

5. "Freight and Expenses: Milk," *Street Railway Journal* 28, no. 15 (October 13, 1906): 681; Roelif Loveland, "Last Car Passes on Southwestern," *Cleveland Plain Dealer*, March 1, 1931, 9; William D. Middleton, "Electric Railway Freight," *Railroad History* 151 (Autumn 1984): 23; "Statement of Charles L. Henry," *Proceedings of the Federal Electric Railways Commission,...1919*, vol. 1 (Washington, DC: Government Printing Office), 707.

6. "Medina County Creamery Co. advertisement, Medina County: Up to Date," *Medina Sentinel* (Medina, OH: Medina Sentinel, 1912); "Local and Personal," *Medina Sentinel*, December 15, 1905, 5; "Medina County Creamery Advertisement," *Medina County Gazette*, May 25, 1912, 2; "Medina Creamery Co. in a Big Combine," *Medina County Gazette*, December 23, 1920, 1.

7. "Farmers Should Specialize," *Wayne County Democrat*, April 4, 1906; J. Harold Leaman and E. C. Conkling, "Transport Change and Agricultural Specialization," *Annals of the Association of American Geographers* 65 (September 1975): 425–32.

8. *Medina Sentinel*, February 14, 1913, 5; *Medina County Gazette*, March 31, 1916, 1; *Medina Sentinel*, March 13, 1914, 7.

9. *Medina County Gazette*, March 31, 1916, 1; Marion Wolff, *An Outline History of Brunswick: 1815–1965* (Brunswick, OH: Brunswick Sesqui-Centennial Historical Committee, 1965), 34; Sam Boyer, *Brunswick: Our Hometown* (Brunswick, OH: Brunswick Times, 1976), 10–11.

10. "Citizens Hold Opposite Views," *Wayne County Democrat*, March 14, 1906, 1.; "Which Route," *Medina County Gazette*, January 30, 1902, 1.

11. Dale Samuelson and Wendy Yegoiants, *The American Amusement Park* (St. Paul, MN: MBI, 2001), 37.

12. "The National Amusement Park Association," *Street Railway Journal* 31, no. 4 (January 25, 1908): 129.

13. Jeffrey R. Brashares, *The Southwestern Lines: The Story of the Cleveland, Southwestern & Columbus Railway between Cleveland, Elyria-Oberlin-Norwalk, Wellington-Lorain-Amherst, Berea-Medina-Wooster, Ashland-Mansfield-Crestline, Galion-Bucyrus* (Cleveland: Ohio Interurban Memories, 1982), 101; Harry Christiansen, *Trolley Trails through Greater Cleveland and Northern Ohio* (Cleveland: Western Reserve Historical Society, 1975), 2:272; "This Is the Mansfield That Was," *Mansfield News-Journal*, July 18, 1965, 47; "Interurban Centers and Interurban Cars: Cleveland," *Brill Magazine* 9, no. 2 (February 1915): 44.

14. David W. Francis and Diane DeMali Francis, *Luna Park: Cleveland's Fairyland of Pleasure* (Fairview Park, OH: Amusement Park Books, 1996), 21; "Mansfield's Parks and Amusement Resorts," *Mansfield News*, July 1, 1911, 60; "This Is the Mansfield That Was," *Mansfield News Journal*, January 10, 1965, 55.

15. "History of Richland County by A.J. Baughman," *Mansfield News*, August 15, 1903, 15; "Old Grist Mill at Flemings Falls Made Scout Camp Historic Site," *Mansfield News*, June 26, 1927, 6; "Paul Maiwurm Turned Pretty Gorge into a Resort," *Mansfield News-Journal*, August 28, 1994, 13; "Flemings Falls Advertisement," *Mansfield News-Journal*, July 3, 1917, 11.

16. "An Indian Town," *Akron Beacon Journal*, July 23, 1897, 1; "Notes," *Marion Star*, July 29, 1897, 4; "Seccaium Park Is 29 Years Old," *Mansfield News*, August 18, 1928, 5; "Interurban between Bucyrus and Galion, O.," *Street Railway Review* 10, no. 6 (June 15, 1900): 306; "Seccaium Park Changes Hands," *Mansfield News-Journal*, January 26, 1926, 2, "The Electric Railway," *Crawford County News* (Bucyrus, OH), May 23, 1899, 1; "All Parties Pleased," *Crawford County News*, August 4, 1899, 5.

17. "Effort to Revive Seccaium Park," *Mansfield News-Journal*, May 24, 1913, 4; "Seccaium Park Changes Hands," 2.

18. "Seccaium Park Changes Hands," 2; Frederick N. Honneffer, *Jolly Times at Seccaium Park, 1899–1948*, "Seccaium Park Book Premiere" (Bucyrus Historical Society, 2003), https://bucyrushistoricalsociety.org/gallery_articles/Seccaium.htm; "Honoring a Part of the Past," *Bucyrus Telegraph-Forum*, March 4, 2013, 1–2; "A Trip down Memory Lane: Area Residents Reminisce about Seccaium Park," *Bucyrus Telegraph-Forum*, October 2, 2018, A1–A2; "Seccaium Was Once a Grand Park," *Bucyrus Telegraph-Forum*, May 11, 2013, A3; "Seccaium Park Advertisement," *Bucyrus Evening Telegraph*, July 15, 1922, 3; "Seccaium Park Pool Attracts Bathers," *Bucyrus Journal*, July 14, 1922, 7.

Notes

19. Brashares, *Southwestern Lines*, 101; Christiansen, *Trolley Trails*, 2:272; David W. Francis and Diane DeMali Francis, *Cleveland Amusement Park Memories* (Cleveland: Gray, 2004), 77–95; "Big Financial Deal," *Cleveland Plain Dealer*, January 29, 1899, 5; "Legal Notice of Foreclosure of Cleveland, Southwestern and Columbus Railway," *Cleveland Plain Dealer*, February 14, 1924, 18.

20. Francis and Francis, *Cleveland Amusement Park Memories*, 78–95; "Puritas Springs Park Owner Dies," *Cleveland Plain Dealer*, December 11, 1937, 7; "John E. Gooding Dies," *Akron Beacon Journal*, December 11, 1937, 15.

21. Sharon L. D. Kraynek, *Chippewa Lake Park, 1800–1978: Diary of an Amusement Park* (Medina, OH: published by author, 1988), 27; Brashares, *Southwestern Lines*, 101.

22. "Chippewa Lake Club: Advertisement," *Medina Sentinel*, May 30, 1919, 3.

23. "Chippewa Lake Advertisement," *Akron Beacon Journal*, May 27, 1929, 25; "Chippewa Lake Park Is 100 Years Old," *Akron Beacon Journal*, January 9, 1978, A-7; "Closed Amusement Park Holds Many Memories," *Sandusky Register*, April 4, 2009, 10.

24. Eric Gouldsberry and Ed Attanasio, "The 1900s: Birth of the Modern Age," *This Great Game: The Online Book of Baseball*, https://thisgreatgame.com/1900s-baseball-history/, accessed January 14, 2022.

25. "Many Ball Leagues," *Elyria Chronicle-Telegram*, May 16, 1907, 4.

26. "Many Ball Leagues," 4; Gouldsberry and Attanasio, "1900s: Birth of the Modern Age."

27. "The Pennant Races Revive 'Frenzied Baseball'," *Mansfield News-Journal*, September 26, 1908, 11; "Elyria Team Gets Two New Players," *Elyria Reporter*, May 18, 1905, 8.

28. "Trolley League: The Standing," *Elyria Chronicle-Telegram*, June 9, 1904, 1; "Wellington Lost by Errors," *Elyria Chronicle-Telegram*, June 24, 1904, 1; "Trolley League," *Elyria Chronicle-Telegram*, July 9, 1904, 1; "New Schedule," *Elyria Chronicle-Telegram*, July 24, 1904, 9; "Elyria Won," *Elyria Reporter*, August 11, 1904, 8; "Clash to Come between Rivals," *Elyria Reporter*, September 9, 1904, 1; "Elyria Won," *Elyria Reporter*, September 29, 1904, 8; "Trolley League Champions Defeated," *Elyria Reporter*, September 7, 1905, 1, 4; "Elyria Team Receives Championship Trophy," *Elyria Reporter*, September 7, 1905, 1; "Trolley League Declared Dead," *Medina Sentinel*, April 27, 1906, 5; "Trolley League Down to Four Clubs," *Elyria Reporter*, April 20, 1905, 8; "Talk of New Ball League," *Elyria Republican*, December 20, 1906, 1; "Sunday Games Save the Day," *Elyria Republican*, December 20, 1906, 1.

29. "Elyria Team Receives Championship Trophy," *Elyria Reporter*, September 7, 1905, 1; "Elyria Club Gets Beautiful Cup," *Elyria Chronicle-Telegram*, October 31, 1906, 1.

30. "Charles Follis," *Mansfield News-Journal*, March 26, 2006, 21; "First but Not Forgotten," *Mansfield News-Journal*, August 24, 1997, 1D, 3D.

31. "Colored Athlete Dies Suddenly," *Crestline Advocate*, April 14, 1910, 3; "Short News Notes: Colored Athlete Dies Suddenly," *Mansfield News-Journal*, April 6, 1010, 4; "Noted Baseball and Football Player Dies Charley Follis," *Cleveland Plain Dealer*, April 7, 1910, 8; "Starlight Champs Shut Out," *Cleveland Plain Dealer*, August 20, 1906, 6; "Starlights Wants Games," *Cleveland Plain Dealer*, May 7, 1908, 9.

32. Ohio House of Representatives, State and Local Government Committee, June 7, 2017, Jim Stoner Testimony on HB 229; "First but Not Forgotten."

33. "Handsome Funeral Car Visits City," *Norwalk Evening Herald*, March 11, 1911, 5.

34. "New Funeral Car 'Dolores' of Ohio Interurban," *Electric Traction Weekly* 7, no. 11 (March 18, 1911): 291–92; "Handsome Funeral Car Visits City," 5; "Detail of Movable Equipment, as of February 1, 1924: The Cleveland, Southwestern & Columbus Railway Company," scanned foreclosure documents provided by Brett Dunbar; "Some By-Products of Electric Railroading: Funeral Cars," *Electric Traction Weekly* 7, no. 4 (November 4, 1911,) 1382–85; Wilcox, *Cleveland Southwestern & Columbus Railway Story*, 26.

35. Wilcox, *Cleveland Southwestern*, 26; "Some By-Products of Electric Railroading: Funeral Cars"; "Funeral Care Rate Reduced," *Elyria Chronicle Telegram*, August 8, 1921, 7.

36. "Which Route," *Medina County Gazette*, January 30, 1902, 1.

37. "Which Route," 1; Ernest L. Bogart, "Economic and Social Effects of the Interurban Electric Railway of Ohio," *Journal of Political Economy* 14 (December 1906): 597.

38. "Their Side of It: The South Court Street Men's Statement to the Public," *Medina County Gazette*, April 3, 1902, 1; "Hot to the Last: And the North-Siders Won the Street Ry Contest," *Medina County Gazette*, April 10, 1902, 1.

39. *Berea Enterprise*, February 4, 1916; *Cleveland Plain Dealer*, January 31, 1916, 5.

40. Tom L. Johnson, "Mayor's Message," *Annual Reports, Cleveland, 1905* (Cleveland, 1906), n.p., cited by Thomas H. Smith, ed., *An Ohio Reader: Reconstruction to the Present* (Grand Rapids, MI: William B. Eerdmans, 1975), 189–94.

41. *Berea Enterprise*, May 12, 1916; May 19, 1916; July 11, 28, 1916; May 18, 1917.

42. Christiansen and Christiansen, *New Northern Ohio's Interurbans*, 800; Wilcox, *Cleveland Southwestern*, n.p.; *Berea Enterprise*, July 28, 1916.

43. *Berea Enterprise*, July 28, 1916; July 27, 1917; August 31, 1917; Christiansen and Christiansen, *New Northern Ohio's Interurbans*, 800; Wilcox, *Cleveland Southwestern*, n.p.

44. H. E. Hoagland, "The Movement of Rural Population in Illinois," *Journal of Political Economy* 20 (1912): 914–15.

45. Bogart, "Economic and Social Effects," 600.

46. Richardson, "City in Twentieth-Century Ohio," 41.

CHAPTER 5

1. Department of Commerce, Bureau of the Census, *Central Electric Light and Power Stations and Street and Electric Railways, 1912* (Washington, DC: Government Printing Office, 1915), 208.

2. Department of Commerce, Bureau of the Census, *Street and Electric Railways, 1902* (Washington, DC: Government Printing Office, 1905), 102.

3. George W. Hilton and John F. Due, *The Electric Interurban Railways in America* (Stanford, CA: Stanford University Press, 1960), 9, 42.

4. Wallace McCook Cunningham, "Stocks and the Stock Market: Electric Railway Stocks," *Annals of the American Academy of Political and Social Science* 35 (May 1910): 657–58.

5. Ray Morris, "Trolley Competition with the Railroads," *Atlantic Monthly* 43 (June 1904): 735–36; Frank T. Carlton, "The Electric Interurban Railroad," *Yale Review* (August 1904): 191–92; Hilton and Due, *Electric Interurban Railways*, 208–9.

6. Ernest L. Bogart, "Economic and Social Effects of the Interurban Electric Railway in Ohio," *Journal of Political Economy* 14 (December 1906): 601.

7. John Moody, *Moody's Analyses of Investments: Public Utilities* (New York: Moody's Investors Service, 1920), 5; "Canton in the List of Trolley Centers," *The [Canton] Repository*, May 11, 1905.

8. William Z. Ripley, *Railroads: Finance and Organization* (New York: Longmans, Green, 1915), 53–55.

9. Ripley, 54–57.

10. Ripley, 55; Frederick A. Cleveland and Fred Wilbur Powell, *Railroad Finance* (New York: D. Appleton, 1918), 34–39, 322–24.

11. Ripley, *Railroads*, 14–15.

12. Ripley, 14–15.

13. Ripley, 23–29.

14. Ripley, 31–43; Cleveland and Powell, *Railroad Finance*, 59–61.

15. Ripley, 248–52; Cleveland and Powell, 290–91.

16. Ripley, 248–70; 270–80.

17. Ripley, 252–54.

18. Frank R. Ford, "Valuation of Intangible Street Railway Property," *Annals of the American Academy of Political and Social Science* 37 (1911): 122–26.

19. Ford, 119–41.

20. Cunningham, "Stocks and the Stock Market," 657–73.

21. Carlton, "Electric Interurban Railroad," 189.

22. Bureau of the Census, *Central Electric Light and Power Stations and Street and Electric Railways, 1912*, 180.

23. Martin G. Glaeser, *Outlines of Public Utility Economics* (New York: Macmillan, 1927), 149–53; Eugene F. Brigham, *Fundamentals of Financial Management* (Hinsdale, IL: Dryden, 1980), 150–52, 179.

24. Glaeser, *Outlines of Public Utility Economics*, 84–85, 149–51.

25. Glaeser, 152–53.

26. Paul J. Miranti Jr., "The Mind's Eye of Reform: The ICC's Bureau of Statistics and Accounts and a Vision of Regulation, 1887–1904," *Business History Review* 63 (Autumn 1989): 478–79.

27. James Reed Golden, *Investment Behavior by United States Railroads, 1870–1914* (New York: Arno, 1975), 13, 158–59.

28. *Moody's Analyses of Investments* (1920), 8–10.

29. Bureau of the Census, *Central Electric Light and Power Stations and Street and Electric Railways, 1912,* 214.

30. "Report of the Federal Electric Railways Commission," *Proceedings of the Federal Electric Railways Commission: Held in Washington, D.C. during the months of July, August, September, and October, 1919,* vol. 3 (Washington, DC: Government Printing Office, 1920), 2264, 2286–87.

31. City of Cleveland, Office of the City Street Railroad Commissioner, "The Cleveland Street Railway Franchise: Text of Ordinance No. 16283 A; As Amended by Ordinance No. 20890 B passed July 10, 1911" (Cleveland: City of Cleveland, 1911), 18–20, 24–27; "Statement of Mr. John J. Stanley," *Proceedings of the Federal Electric Railways Commission: Held in Washington, D.C. during the months of July, August, September, and October, 1919,* vol. 1 (Washington, DC: Government Printing Office, 1920), 590–91.

32. "Statement of Hon. Newton D. Baker, Secretary of War," *Proceedings of the Federal Electric Railways Commission: Held in Washington, D.C. during the months of July, August, September, and October, 1919,* vol. 2 (Washington, DC: Government Printing Office, 1920), 1003.

33. Cleveland Chamber of Commerce, Committee on Public Utilities, Amendments to the Tayler Grant, July 31, 1925 (Cleveland: Cleveland Chamber of Commerce, 1925), 3.

34. "Statement of Hon. Newton D. Baker," 1003.

35. *Moody's Analyses of Investments* (1927), 188–89; Central Electric Railfans' Association, *Electric Railways of Northeastern Ohio,* Bulletin 108 (Chicago: Central Electric Railfans' Association, 1965), 28.

36. Joseph G. Butler Jr., *History of Youngstown and the Mahoning Valley Ohio,* vol. 1 (New York: American Historical Society, 1921), 371; Central Electric Railfans' Association, *Electric Railways of Northeastern Ohio,* Bulletin 108, 195; "Annual Detailed Departmental Report, 1919: Mahoning and Shenango Railway and Light Company," Ohio Edison Collection, Bierce Library, University of Akron Archives, University of Akron, Akron, box 13.

37. "Statement of Hon. Newton D. Baker," 1003.

38. Bureau of the Census, *Street and Electric Railways, 1902, 1905*; Bureau of the Census, *Street and Electric Railways, 1907* (Washington, DC: Government Printing Office, 1910); Bureau of the Census, *Central Electric Light and Power Stations and Street and Electric Railways, 1912, 1915*; Department of Commerce and Labor, Bureau of the Census, *Census of Electric Railways, 1917* (Washington, DC: Government Printing Office, 1920); Department of Commerce and Labor, Bureau of the Census, *Census of Electrical Industries: Electric Railways, 1922* (Washington, DC: Government Printing Office, 1925); Department of Commerce and Labor, Bureau of the Census, *Census of Electrical Industries: Electric Railways and Affiliated Motor Bus Lines, 1927* (Washington, DC: Government Printing Office, 1931).

39. Stephen D. Hambley, "The Vanguard of a Regional Infrastructure: Electric Railways of Northeast Ohio, 1884–1932" (PhD diss., University of Akron, 1993), chap. 5, 173–83; *Poor's Manual of Railroads, 1901*.

40. *Poor's Manual of Railroads, 1898 to 1912*; Central Electric Railfans' Association, *Electric Railways of Northeastern Ohio*, Bulletin 108, 195.

41. *Poor's Manual of Railroads, 1898 to 1912*; Central Electric Railfans' Association, *Electric Railways of Northeastern Ohio*, Bulletin 108, 131.

42. James M. Blower and Robert S. Korach, *The NOT&L Story* (Chicago: Central Electric Railfans' Association, 1966), 212–52.

43. *Moody's Analyses of Investments, 1914 to 1931*, passim.

44. "Testimony of JW Welsh, AERA," Federal Electric Railways Commission, *Proceedings of the Federal Electric Railways Commission: Held in Washington, D.C. during the months of July, August, September, and October, 1919*, vol. 1 (Washington, DC: Government Printing Office, 1920), 2221.

45. Ripley, *Railroads*, 433–45; Glaeser, *Outlines of Public Utility Economics*, 86–101.

46. Glaeser, 94–95; Ripley, *Railroads*, 434–36.

47. Charles W. Gerstenberg, "Holding Companies in the Public Utility Field: Brief by Stuart G. Gibboney," *Materials of Corporation Finance* (New York: Prentice Hall, 1922), 570–72.

48. *Moody's Analyses of Public Utility Investments* (1920), 7.

49. Federal Electric Railways Commission, *Proceedings of the Federal Electric Railways Commission: Held in Washington, D.C. during the months of July, August, September, and October, 1919*, vol. 3 (Washington, DC: Government Printing Office, 1920), 2269.

CHAPTER 6

1. George W. Hilton, "The Wrong Track," *Invention & Technology* (Spring 1993): 47–54.

2. Roelif Loveland, "Last Car Passes on Southwestern," *Cleveland Plain Dealer*, March 1, 1931, 9.

Index

A
accidents, 62, 111–14, 127
ACI (average capital intensity), 176, 178, 192
Adams Express Company, 70
AERA (American Electric Railway Association), 94
A. I. Root Company, 154
Akins, Albert, 81
Akron, Bedford & Cleveland Railway, 26
Alliance & Mahoning Valley Railway, 205
Alternating Current, sixty cycle, 101, 107
Alvesta, 126–27
American Express, 70
American Railway Express Company, 70
amusement parks, 52, 95, 137–39, 145–46
APU (Atlantic Public Utilities), 130
ARP (average revenue passengers), 192, 194
Ashland & Mansfield Traction Company, 89–90, 194
Ashland & Western Railroad Company, 173
Ashtabula Rapid Transit Company, 177, 190, 192

B
Baker trolley, 17
Baker, Newton D., 184, 185, 186
Baltimore & Ohio Railroad, 89, 117, 145
Bank of Berea Company, 79
Bedford & Cleveland Railway, 26
Bentley-Knight Company, 13, 14
Bentley, Edward M., 13
Berea & Elyria Street Railroad, 82–83
Berea Village Council, franchise dispute, 156–7
Blinn, A. C., 61–62

Bogart, Ernest L., 158
Brunswick Substation, 100–101
Brush Electric Company, 13
Bucyrus, 72, 85, 92, 108, 116, 120, 138–39

C
C&BS (Cleveland & Berea Street Railroad Company), 80
C&EE (Cleveland & Elyria Electric Railway), 81–82
C&SW Trolley League, 148–50
capital intensity ratios, 174, 177, 179
capital intensity, 176–77, 180, 192
capitalization analysis of Northeast Ohio electric railways ranked, 176
Carpenter, Frank D., 81, 87
CEI (Cleveland Electric Illuminating), 102, 108
Charles Follis Day, 150
Chippewa Lake, 84, 101, 104, 134, 138, 143–6
Christy, Will, 81, 87
Cleveland & Berea Line, 80
Cleveland & Eastern Railway, 134
Cleveland Cuban Giants, 150–51
Cleveland Electric Illuminating Company, 101
Cleveland Electric Railway Company, 183, 206
Cleveland Railway Company (CRC), 59, 151, 155, 183–85, 190–92, 196–98
Cleveland Transit System (CTS), 59
Cleveland Trust Company, 46, 82–83, 90, 97, 142
Cleveland's service-at-cost agreement, 183, 185
Commonwealth & Southern Corporation, 61, 200

230

Index

company picnic charters, 145
conduit system, 13, 15
consolidation of railroads, 170
coordinated electric railway freight services in Northeast Ohio, 76
coordinated freight services in Northern Ohio, 119
CP&E (Cleveland, Painesville and Eastern Railway), 72
CRC. *See* Cleveland Railway Company

D

dairy industry, regional, 135
dc (direct current), 15–18, 22, 24–27, 30, 33, 42
debt interest paid. *See* DIP
debt interest payments, 194, 197, 199
Delaware & Marion Electric, 119, 120
DIP (debt interest paid), 186–87, 189–90, 192–94, 198
direct current. *See* dc
Dolores, 151–53
Due, John, 49, 64, 84, 161, 182, 204

E

Edison, Thomas, 19, 145
Electric Package Agency. *See* EPA
Elyria power plant, 101, 107
EOT (Eastern Ohio Traction Company), 81, 134, 177, 204
EPA (Electric Package Agency), 71–72, 74, 76, 115
Everett-Moore syndicate, 12, 79, 81, 171, 187, 198, 203, 205

F

Fairmont Creamery Company of Omaha, 135
Federal Electric Railways Commission (FERC), 60, 134, 183, 186
FERC report, 61
FERC. *See* Federal Electric Railways Commission
Firestone Tire and Rubber Company, 81, 87
First National Bank of Ashland, 89
First National Bank of Berea, 79
Fisher Book Typewriter Company, 82
Fleming(s) Falls, 138–9

Follis, Charles, 149–51
funeral trains, 152

G

German Wallace College, 79, 109
Gibbs, Farnum H., 136–7
Green Line, 78, 134–36, 138, 145, 154, 210
Guarantee Title & Trust Company, 89
Guardian Savings and Trust Company, 46
Guardian Trust Company, 130, 195

H

Hilton, George W., 49, 84, 182, 204, 207
holding companies, 58, 106, 130, 192, 199–203, 205–7

I

ICC (Interstate Commerce Commission), 118, 175–77, 180
Idora Park, 191–92
Interstate Commerce Commission. *See* ICC

J

Johnson, Tom L., 156, 173
Jolly, Ralph A., 141
Journey-To-Work. *See* JTW
JTW (Journey-To-Work), 68, 95

K

Keystone Water Works & Electric Corporation, 107, 130

L

Lake Shore & Michigan Railroad station, 36
Lake Shore & Michigan Southern, 79, 87–88, 173
Lake Shore Electric Railway Company, 59
Lake Shore Electric Railway, 75, 78, 126
Lake Shore Electric. *See* LSE
LCL (less-than-carload), 71, 77
Lefever Franchise Bill, 56
less-than-carload (LCL), 71, 77
LSE (Lake Shore Electric), 6, 59, 61–62, 72, 75–76, 78, 94, 115, 119, 176, 187, 196–99, 205, 207
Luna Park, 138–39, 141

M

Madisonburg, 100, 101, 104, 113

Mahoning & Shenango Railway & Light Company, 190, 192, 193, 198, 201–2, 205
Mahoning Valley Railway, 190–93
Mandelbaum, Maurice J., 82
MCCC (Medina County Creamery Company), 134–35
Medina Stars, 148
Medina Village, election on route, 154
Million Dollar Amusement Park, 145
Moore, Edward W., 118, 173, 199
Morganizations, 32, 34
municipal, 190
Myers & Company, 109
Myers, F. E., 89, 91, 92, 118

N
National Amusement Park Association, 137
National Railway Day, recognition, 23
Northern Ohio Milk Producer's Association, 136
Norwalk Gas & Electric Company, 84, 102

O
Ohio Brass Company, 146
Ohio Central Traction Company, 85
Ohio Consent Law, 66
Ohio Public Service Company, 76, 101
Ohio Public Service Corporation, 109
Ohio's Consent Law, 66
operating expenses / operating revenues, 196–97
operating ratios, 195–96
operations, service-at-cost, 186, 206
overcapitalization, defined, 168
overhead trolley systems, 11–12, 19

P
Painesville & Eastern, 72, 119, 187
Pennsylvania & Ohio, 176, 181
Pennsylvania-Ohio Electric Company, 119
Pomeroy, Fred. T., 79–81, 87, 91, 95, 109, 123
Pomeroy-Mandelbaum syndicate, 1, 78, 82–84, 87–89, 98, 109, 115, 118. 142, 173
power sales, electric, 27, 65, 96–97, 102, 117, 181, 194
prevention of accidents, 112
problems, electrolysis, 16

Public Utilities Commission of Ohio (PUCO), 54, 56, 102, 105, 108, 114, 162, 165
PUCO. *See* Public Utilities Commission of Ohio
Puritas Springs, 134, 138, 142

R
Railroad Commission of Ohio (RCO), 56, 108, 114, 162, 165
Railroad Control Act, 73
RCO. *See* Railroad Commission of Ohio
receivership, 32–33, 121, 123, 130, 195
Republic Railway & Light Company, 193, 200, 202
Richmond, 19, 22–24, 137
Richmond Union Passenger Railway, 23
rights-of-way, private, 3, 15, 55, 64, 84, 114

S
Safety First, 110, 112
Schiffer, Frank C., 149
Schmidt, Bill, 66
Schneider, Edward F., 109–13, 134, 151
Seccaium Park, 134, 138–39, 140, 141, 145, 146
service-at-cost franchises, 55, 185, 206
service-at-cost plans, 183–4, 186
Shaker Heights Rapid Transit system, 60, 62
Shannahan, J. N., 94–95
Sprague Electric Railway, 22–23
Sprague, Frank J., 1, 19, 21–22, 25
Sprague, Milton A., 81
Stanley, John J., 184
Stark Electric Railroad, 122, 176, 190–91, 193–94, 197, 199, 205
Stark Electric, 119
storage batteries, 10, 12, 80
Stouffer, A. E., 135
Stouffer, J. B., 135
Stout Air Services, 128
Sunday games, 149–50
syndicates, underwriting, 39, 170
system building, 5, 33, 63, 91, 93, 205, 206

T
Tayler Grant, 183–84
Thomson-Houston Company, 13, 24–25, 41

Index

three-stage evolution of urban transit, 40
through-coordinated rail-plane service, 128
Trolley League, 147–51
trust companies, 39, 45–47, 166

U

Underwood Elliot Fisher Company, 82
United States Express Company, 70
United States Railroad Administration (USRA), 70, 73, 118
USRA. *See* United States Railroad Administration

V

Van Depoele, Charles J., 16, 19, 24
Van Sweringen, 118
Van Sweringen's Cleveland Interurban Railroad, 62

W

Western Ohio Railway Company, 82–83, 87
Western Reserve Power & Light Company, 107, 130
Westinghouse, 24–27
Westinghouse and General Electric, 25–26
Westinghouse trolley system, 81
Westinghouse turbine generators, 99
Wilson, Frank. H., 101, 107–8, 123, 128, 130, 148
Wolf, Leopold, 82
Wooster Athletic Association, 149
Wooster Electric Company, 108
Wooster Giants, 148–50

Y

YMR. *See* Youngstown Municipal Railway
Youngstown Municipal Railway (YMR), 183, 185–86, 190, 192, 197, 206
Youngstown's service-at-cost franchise, 185

Stephen D. Hambley has been an elected official for over thirty years, serving as a Medina County Commissioner, a Brunswick City Councilman, and as a member of the Ohio House of Representatives. He earned a PhD in history from The University of Akron, where he was twice awarded a Martin Scholarship. For over twenty years, he taught history, political science, and urban studies at Lorain County Community College, The University of Akron, Cleveland State University, and Lakeland Community College. He is the author of *Historic Tales of Medina County, Ohio*.